Asbury Park's Glory Days

Rutgers University Press

NEW BRUNSWICK, NEW JERSEY, AND LONDON

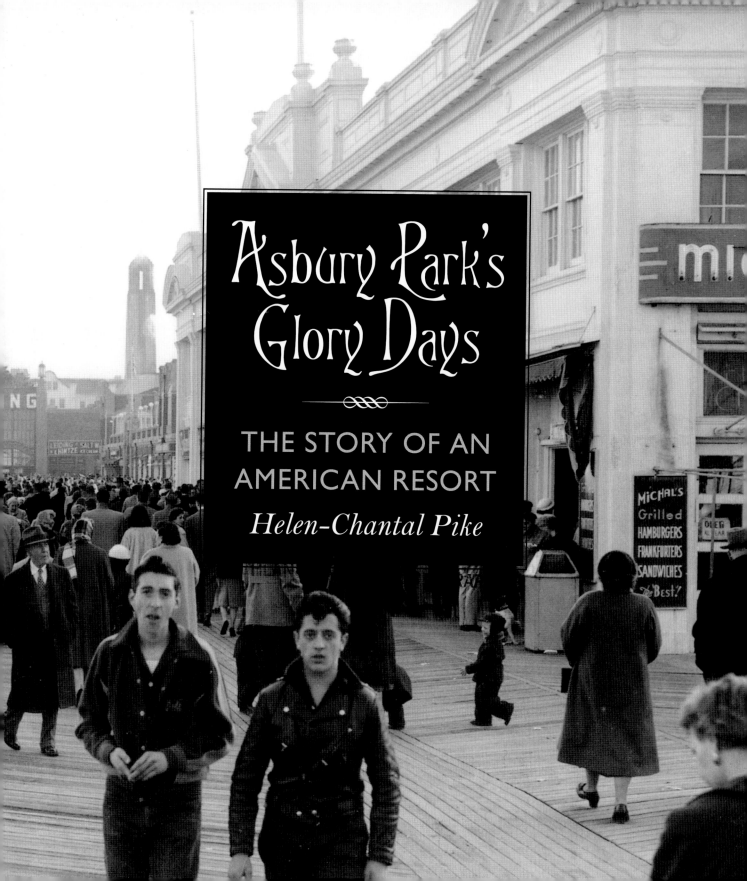

Asbury Park's Glory Days

THE STORY OF AN AMERICAN RESORT

Helen-Chantal Pike

FRONTISPIECE *Vito Petrero, right, and Bill Malick, childhood friends from Long Branch, cruised the Asbury Park Boardwalk as part of their annual Easter Sunday ritual in 1955. "We switched to white sports coats with pink carnations we bought from a store four doors up from Bond on Cookman after the song by Marty Robbins came out," recalled Petrero of the country crossover crooner who scored big with the hit single "A White Sport Coat (and a Pink Carnation)" in 1957. "We were headed to the Paramount to pick up girls. In two years, when we could drive, I had a convertible and we spent summer nights riding the circuit." Classic Photo Collection/Dorn's Photography Unlimited, Red Bank, New Jersey.*

LIBRARY OF CONGRESS CATALOGING-IN-PUBLICATION DATA

Pike, Helen C.

Asbury Park's glory days : the story of an American resort / Helen-Chantal Pike.

p. cm.

Includes bibliographical references and index.

ISBN 0–8135–3547–6 (alk. paper)

1. Asbury Park (N.J.)—History.   2. Asbury Park (N.J.)—Social conditions.

3. Asbury Park (N.J.)—Social life and customs   4. Seaside resorts—

United States—Case studies.   I. Title.

F144.A6P555 2005

974.9'46—dc22   2004008247

A British Cataloging-in-Publication record for this book is

available from the British Library.

Copyright © 2005 by Helen-Chantal Pike

Book designed and composed by Kevin Hanek

Set in Monotype Bell and ITC Bodoni Six

Manufactured in Singapore

In memory of those who opened their homes and their hearts and poured out their memories,
and who passed away too soon, I dedicate this book to Dr. Lorenzo Harris Jr., Assemblyman Thomas Smith,
Philip Rosenbloom, Karen Plunkett-Powell, Georgia Pappyliou Burns, Russell Mirgalia Sr., Pat Moyna,
Elizabeth Smith, Tina Tinois, Henry Van Dyke, Steve Rinaldi, Ronn Magee, Dr. Scuddie and Sarah Magee,
Lou Mecca, Pat Petillo, Jason and Ida Grossman, Pat Vaccaro, Isaac Richardson, Gene Fantini,
Charles H. Maps Jr., Connie Lyons, and Sadie West Greco LeBright.

ALL EXISTENCE IS MEMORY.
— Mark Mathabane, February 6, 2004

Contents

Acknowledgments

THIS BOOK NEVER WOULD HAVE made it to the finish line without the forbearance of Leslie Mitchner, editor in chief of Rutgers University Press, and the support of Barbara Tomlinson and Ellis Gilliam, the most effective outsider and insider sources a writer could hope for when it comes to history—Barbara for her superb perspective on American culture and Ellis for tirelessly reconstructing his hometown. I owe you both a debt of gratitude.

Along the way, Joan McLaughlin Flatley, the retired director of the Greater Asbury Park Chamber of Commerce, provided knowledgeable company, lent a generous hand in the final countdown, and made this an enjoyable journey. Thank you, also, to *Newark Evening News* alumna Liz Clark for invaluable research and insights regarding 1980; *Asbury Park Press* alumna Lorraine Stone; financial writer Marlene Satter; and business author Mary Walton. I want to acknowledge the inspired editing of Willa Speiser. Thanks to Marie Sylvester, Interlaken historian, for suggesting the title for chapter 5. Thank you to Bob Crane of the Save Tillie Campaign for all the introductions you gave me and to Monmouth County historian George Moss for your invigorating debates over the historical merits of Long Branch versus Asbury Park; Maureen Nevin of RestoreRadio, who generously gave me the phone numbers of so many of her guests; and Pete Walton, cyber editor of asburypark.net.

Many thanks to Rainette Bannister Holimon for sharing with me the West Side of her youth and young married life and for introducing me to George Watson. Thank you Betty Ciccolini Petillo for your hospitality and for giving me a unique tour of a bygone Asbury Park.

To Bert Cohen and Stan Flewelling, two extraordinary marbles historians, thanks!

For their company and for their own Asbury Park stories thanks go to Jane Ivins; Art Scott; Mike Frankel; Pam Waterman; the Parreott brothers—Dorian and the Reverend Dave Parreott—and Dave Parreott's son, Derrick, a third-generation police officer in the city; Angelo Petillo; Cathy DeGennaro Cohen; Bob Speck; Mary Fowler; Elizabeth Brown; Nancy Gibson Harvey; Julie Gannon of GoGannon Designs; Thomas and Joan Appleby; and Robert and Doris Carroll.

Thank you Peter Lucia and Raffaie Nahir for the photographic drive-bys we undertook in all kinds of weather; Kelly Erving and Chris Flynn for unique tours of the Palace; Glenn Vogel and Keith Critchlow for our respective Casino romps; Evelyn Lewis, who maintained the best municipally owned museum on the north Jersey Shore; Cheryl Stoeber-Goff for maintaining the Pike Archives; Otis Love because you believed in this project and introduced me to many West Siders; Inez Drumgoole Brown, David Collier, Virginia Rosenthal, and Liz and Sal Caliendo; Sy Getchburg, who shared a rare-book enthusiast's perspective of a sliver of Asbury Park that I remember; and Madonna Carter Jackson for her thoughtful and invaluable insights. Thanks to Catherine Barry and Mike Barry for their generosity.

Thank you also to James Carton; Traci Evans; Sara Eyestone; Elizabeth Stout Henderson; Elizabeth Rodousakis Mattheos; Kate Mellina and Dave Christopher; Stan Tokec; and Stella Young.

I am grateful for interviews with members of the Aeriel Club; Nicholas Baldino; Dolly Reade Borgia; Helen Elliot; Phil Parratt; Suzanne Reade Gage; Vince Gargiulo; Mrs. Sheldon Gunsburg; Millie Green Harris and her brother, Captain Edward Green; John and Jane Bearmore Haulenbeck; Jerry Kamber; Phil Konvitz; Donna Gunsburg Lerner; Mary Vaccaro Martin, her brother Martin Vaccaro, and their nephew, Henry Vaccaro; Russell Miraglia Sr. and Rose Miraglia Fitzgerald; George Michals; Arnold Morris; Hunt Parry; Holly Patel; Ronnie Reade; Hazel Samuels; Domenic Santana; Willie Squalls, Harry Roman, and his son, Paul; Judy Hurley Stanley and James Coleman; and Ruby Strickland wherever you are.

A special thanks the Ranney School community, whose ties to Asbury Park are richly interwoven: Diana Alikas; Toni Vaccaro Bahary; Liz McCumsey Buckley, the Reverend Carl Hunter II; Laura Sanders; James (Rosenbloom) Shepherd; Nancy Weiner; and a special thank you to Allison Rotolo, for her help with the Boardwalk survey.

Public acknowledgment also goes to Wendy Norris, production supervisor, Theatre on Film and Tape Archive, the Billy Rose Theatre Collection, New York Public Library for the Performing Arts; Joanne Koch of the Film Society of Lincoln Center; Michael Roudette, reference librarian, Schomburg Center for Research in Black Culture, New York Public Library; Janet Parks, Drawings and Archival Department, Avery Architectural and Fine Arts Library, Columbia University; Robert Santelli, director, Experience Music Project, Seattle; Jeff Miller, who maintains the History of American Broadcasting Web site; Mariam Touba, reference librarian, New-York Historical Society, New York City; Ford, Farewell, Mills and Gatch, preservation architects, Princeton; Jan Athey, librarian for the Train Collections Association, Strasburg, Pennsylvania, with a special tip of the hat to collector Joe L. Mania for the Lionel train station model numbers; Susan Buss, librarian, Vancouver Maritime Museum, Vancouver, British Columbia; Joe Taylor at the Tile Heritage Foundation, Healdsburg, California; Tom Gardner of the Asbury Park Elks Lodge No. 128; Stan Jacobs, whose documentary *The Pitch People* was a valuable source of history; Frank D'Alessandro, curator of the Stephen Crane House, Asbury Park; Christopher Gray of the *New York Times*; and Peter Filichia of the *Newark Star-Ledger*; Kathy Dorn Severini and Classic Photo Collection/Dorn's Photography Unlimited, Red Bank; Unique Images of New Jersey by Ruth Bennett, Asbury Park; and Andrew Bartlett, president of Murray's Army & Navy, Bradley Beach.

Prologue, 1982

I LEFT THE NORTH JERSEY SHORE and my newspaper job at the *Asbury Park Press* in 1982 to attend graduate school at Columbia University. By that time, Asbury Park was generating memories mostly for daytrippers and rock band groupies. Old-timers told fabulous stories about men in tuxedos and ladies swathed in evening gowns strolling the nighttime Boardwalk, about thrilling movie premieres at the Mayfair and Paramount theaters, Frank Sinatra's career before and after his break with band leader Tommy Dorsey, and shopping for bargains or going to the clubs along the vibrant, ethnically and racially mixed Springwood Avenue, likening it to 125th Street in New York City's Harlem.

But as the 1980s progressed, Asbury Park's status as a popular resort began to decline. The mayor was trying desperately to find a buyer for the city's once thriving Boardwalk. The amusement circuit's two vintage carousels were sold and shipped out of state. The jazz and rock clubs were going to seed. Record scouts, once noticeable in the wake of Bruce Springsteen's maiden album, *Greetings from Asbury Park*, were hard to spot. Mysteriously set fires continued to claim vacated build-ings, and all over the city, huge empty blocks sprouted weeds, broken glass, and the detritus of drugs and street sex. The mentally ill, liberated from state institutions without appropriate housing or services, arrived here, as they did elsewhere in the nation, and wound up panhandling on the Boardwalk and on side streets. They checked in to previously comfortable boardinghouses and motels that were struggling to stay financially solvent as the public's travel habits changed. As the twentieth century came to an end, another government policy—the promise of safe, affordable, low-income, high-rise public housing—soured. Plan after plan for a civic revival failed to take hold.

Just when everyone thought the city's decline couldn't get any worse, it did. When I returned in 1991, Asbury Park resembled a ghost town. It was routinely referred to by some as Beirut on the Jersey Shore and by others as Dresden. The terms reflected a generational distinction between those whose reference point was World War II and those whose images of war centered on the Middle East, but the shared implication— bombed beyond recognition—was clear.

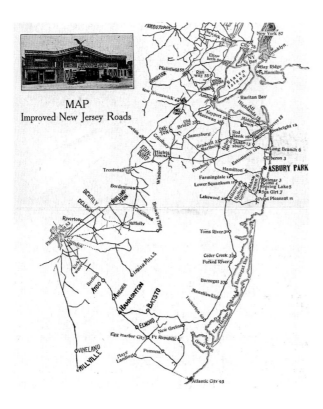

MAP
Improved New Jersey Roads

Garage owner Charles Zacharais printed a map for touring motorists, whether they rented automobiles to drive themselves or chauffeurs to drive for them from his full-service station on Main Street at Sewall Avenue; circa 1911. Pike Archives.

The nearly deserted streets made Asbury Park a convenient commuter drive-through. Highways originally paved to carry vacationers to and from the Shore were now arteries to the newly built Interstate 195. The city's wide streets became shortcuts for employees who lived on the coast but worked in Trenton or elsewhere in burgeoning Mercer County. Meanwhile, schoolchildren, unaccustomed to seeing much traffic, routinely crossed against the flow in what seemed to outsiders a careless disregard for the changing lights. It was not uncommon to see drug deals in broad day-

light. Women, residents and visitors alike, found themselves propositioned by men cruising in cars and trucks even in the more stable residential neighborhoods.

Asbury Park had a police department so wracked by corruption that one enterprising detective ran a private security business from his desk inside the squad room. A mayor was arrested for buying cocaine in a bar across from City Hall after a council meeting. The board of education was ill prepared for implementing more and more state mandates to provide social welfare programs and raise test scores.

Real estate money went elsewhere. After all, there are 127 miles of coastline between Sandy Hook and Cape May and more hospitable, even eager, investment climates. The redevelopment of Atlantic City, with large hotel "showrooms," was finally underway thanks to the special casino account that was part of the state referendum to allow restricted gambling in New Jersey. The boardwalk in North Wildwood maintained its stability largely thanks to two generations of the Morey family, while four generations of Gillians in Ocean City anchored the northern end of the boardwalk in that historically "dry," skillfully promoted, and family-friendly Methodist resort community. The state's oldest seashore resort, Cape May, was firmly established as a bed-and-breakfast destination, capitalizing on reclaimed Victorian splendor, its business and civic leaders working together to find an alternative plan for housing the mentally ill.

I spent the 1990s writing about New Jersey's travel and tourism industry, and noticed that Ocean Grove, Asbury Park's twin city, was experiencing a revival as a result of an aggressive move by business owners to shut down illegal boardinghouses and tighten zoning codes. Even Long Branch, Asbury Park's historic competitor in the local travel and residential markets, was shaking itself out of a decades-long slump with construction of the north Jersey Shore's first significant beach hotel in decades and Miami-style high-rise condominiums.

But Asbury Park remained locked in the embrace of an out-of-state developer whose fortunes were tied to New England banks. Changes made in 1986 to New Jersey's investment tax laws and the country's regional recession of the early 1990s put his grandiose plans for the Boardwalk and the eight blocks of parallel real estate on hold. Meanwhile, the city, grinding into bankruptcy with millions of dollars in unpaid property taxes, was poised to become the fourth urban center—after Camden, Newark, and Jersey City—to be supervised by state officials.

The glamorous, exciting Asbury Park that had drawn wealthy vacationers and celebrities existed only in people's memories. New generations had been born who did not know what it meant to ride the entertainment circuit, buy freshly baked bread on Springwood Avenue, or take pride in a high school academic and athletic program that once dominated state competitions. Even fortuneteller Madame Marie had moved from her Boardwalk booth to a two-story brick building on State Highway 35 in Ocean Township, one of the city's many postwar suburbs.

Driving through the devastation that ravaged both the East and West Sides of the railroad tracks, one couldn't help but wonder what had attracted people to Asbury Park in the first place.

Asbury Park's Glory Days

CHAPTER ONE

Location, Location, Location

WITH TEN YEARS LEFT TO GO before the twentieth century arrived, Asbury Park, New Jersey, was filled with the sounds of construction: pounding hammers, the whirr of saws turning out decorative woodwork, and the clatter of clapboard being delivered to new addresses. The sound of industry was familiar to James A. Bradley, the hardworking proprietor of a highly successful brush factory in New York City. In 1870 Bradley had decided to try his hand at real estate development. Securing the purchase of 500 oceanfront acres just north of Wesley Lake and the Methodist camp meeting of Ocean Grove, Bradley then set about signing contracts with other enterprising men, and a few women, who presumably shared his vision of creating a Christian resort dedicated to improving the holy trinity of mind, spirit, and body.

A convert to Methodism and a Sunday school teacher, Bradley was familiar with the circuit-riding history of the first American Methodist bishop, Francis Asbury, a central figure in the rise of mainstream Protestantism in colonial America. He decided to name his haven for Asbury and the major streets after prominent Methodist ministers. But Bradley also needed to distinguish his nascent city locally. The more established and better-known resort to the north was Long Branch, a name derived from its early development along the lengthy arm of the Shrewsbury River. Its coterie—various U.S. presidents, leading stage actors, wildcat gamblers, and horse-racing enthusiasts—gave it the clubby designation of "The Branch." South of Bradley's utopia was "The Grove," the pastoral sobriquet used by the holy revivalists tenting on the

The Question of Sewage

The increase of permanent and transient population is making the demand for a more thorough and complete sewer system imperative.

– *Asbury Park Journal*,
February 22, 1890

James A. Bradley to Ida A. Maps, lot, Asbury Park, $3500.

– *Asbury Park Journal*,
April 12, 1890

The first popular excursion via the Pennsylvania Railroad from Broad Street, Philadelphia, to Asbury Park, will come today. The fare is $1.50 for the round trip.

– *Asbury Park Journal*,
July 9, 1890

There is a scarcity of small houses to rent in Asbury Park and every day the real estate agents have to refuse applications for such houses.

– *The Shore Press*,
October 24, 1890

Methodist campground. Having witnessed the mid-nineteenth-century landscaped creation of Central Park in Manhattan, Bradley added the word *park* to Asbury.

With its ordered grid of wide avenues and leafy cross streets, and three lakes all located east of the railroad tracks, "The Park" exemplified the ideals of the City Beautiful movement about to be inaugurated in Chicago at the Columbian Exposition of 1893. But Asbury Park also was ideally positioned as a resort destination on the north Jersey Shore, equally attractive to the aspiring middle classes in both New York and Philadelphia who were eager to participate in the new trend of leisure and recreation. By 1890, Asbury Park's dual identity as a full-time residential community and a resort community was in conflict with itself.

Sanitation, Solitude, and Segregation

With a factory location in lower Manhattan, the overworked Bradley, who suffered from hay fever, not only experienced firsthand how unhealthy the industrialized air was but was also aware of the negative impact disease could have on a resort, as it had several years earlier in Long Branch, when a diphtheria outbreak in 1887 had decimated the Irish immigrant working class. Bradley's near fanaticism about preventing the occurrence of typhoid and other airborne diseases from open refuse pits drove him to pay out of his own pocket for fifteen miles of sewer pipes and water mains, giving Asbury Park the first sanitation system on the north Jersey Shore. Maps show that by 1892 he had installed two cesspools, one at the end of First Avenue and the other at the end of Eighth Avenue. But Bradley's efforts to force his property buyers to hook up to his private system did not fare well: vacation home buyers were reluctant to incur additional expenses for houses they occupied only three months of the year.

In his crusade to sell sanitation, Bradley found his greatest support from the medical profession. Indeed, various nineteenth-century doctors were involved in seashore land deals, from Dr. Jonathan Pitney of Morristown, who had established the health resort of Atlantic City, to Dr. Arthur Conover from the Monmouth County seat of Freehold, who was developing Monmouth Beach. In Asbury Park many physicians were arriving to practice medicine and dabble in real estate. With Bradley's blessing, Dr. Henry Mitchell established Asbury Park's first board of health to monitor sewer hookups and track any outbreaks of disease that might adversely affect the resort's reputation. For himself, Mitchell saw in Asbury Park an opportunity to make a reputation in the nascent field of statewide health policies. In the 1890s he sold his medical practice in order to devote more time to the board of health and to play an increasingly larger role in defining New Jersey's health issues and practices. Rising in influence, he became president of the Medical Society of New Jersey and served as secretary of the state board of health. Mitchell also constructed a handsome corner home for himself on the west side of Grand Avenue at Fourth; on the same block of Grand Avenue, north to the Fifth Avenue corner, he built two additional houses as a real estate investment.

Bradley also was keenly interested in solitude to counter the grinding sounds of industry in the country's newly revitalized cities. Slow to develop large blocks of land, especially on the ocean north of Atlantic Square and along most of the southern bank of Deal and Sunset Lakes, he saw these forested acres as a quiet country hideaway. In lots that he did sell, Bradley put deed restrictions prohibiting noisy enterprises and the sale of alcohol. This wasn't the only form of segregation: Bradley did not permit African Americans on the east side of Main Street unless they were in the employ of a family or business, and the presence of Jews was discouraged.

Promoting the Vision

As the new century approached, founder Bradley held to his vision of a leisurely Christian resort firmly rooted in pro-temperance religions and healthy fresh-air pursuits. Equally tenacious were his critics, who were eager to profit from a year-round community. In 1890 these critics were particularly aggressive in pressuring Bradley to sell lots on Deal Lake. In a bold rebuke, Bradley took a grove of trees west of Main Street and had his work crew clear land and build a one-third-mile track for competitive bicycle races. The men also built a wood stadium with covered seating. It was finished in time for the 1894 national convention of the League of American Wheelmen to be held in Asbury Park. The attendance of male and female bicycling enthusiasts that year set a record for the league.

More importantly, the wheelmen's souvenir program was filled with glowing testimonials and superlative prose about Asbury Park's status as an ideal winter health resort owing to its southern location in the Northeast. With the study of meteorology not yet a full-fledged discipline, mild winters were predicted based on the mere existence of coastal trade winds. Asbury Park's modern sanitation system was also prominently mentioned as a factor to attract health-conscious vacationers.

Stylish Asbury Park

"To be sure, the vast majority are here for a vacation pure and simple. They are here because it's vacation-time, and time to leave the city. They don't know what else to do. Some are here because it's stylish; many are here for health. Some are here because people they know are to come to the same place, perhaps to the same hotel. Some mothers are here because it's a good market for marriageable daughters, and not a few young men are arranging to be here that they may have their choice of such marriageable young women. I see not a few fortune hunters of both sexes already planning for a season's campaign."

– *Seashore Life*, June 27, 1896

The league was influential in another way that actually put Asbury Park on the map. With thousands of bicycling members across the country, the wheelmen convinced the legislature in Trenton to be an early sponsor of an interconnected national road system. In 1894 a state commission of public roads was established. In 1916, with the Federal Aid Road Act passed, New Jersey was well on its way to having macadam roads throughout the state to bring more vacationers to the Shore and to Asbury Park.

Bradley's resort was liberally promoted by news organizations that tapped the growing travel market by opening advertising and editorial bureaus in such destinations as Bethlehem, New Hampshire; Colorado Springs, Colorado; and French Lick, Indiana. Using hotel lobbies and train stations to distribute their weekly publications, the pages breathlessly recorded the arrivals, social gatherings, and new attractions; of course, they also carried the local real estate sales and rentals lists. *Seashore Life* and the *Seaside Torch,* which had offices in the Byram building in downtown Asbury Park, noted summer residencies:

F. Howarth, a cartoonist employed on the staff of the great comic publication Puck, will spend the summer at 523 Munroe avenue. Last year Mr. Howarth spent the season in Ocean Grove, but Asbury Park has the preference this summer. Charles

Gillingham and family, of Philadelphia, have leased a cottage on Fifth avenue. This is the fifth season they have resided on the same avenue.

No resort would be complete without souvenir books. Pennypacker Press, whose principals came from Philadelphia to summer in Asbury Park, printed glossy photo booklets on the twin resorts of Asbury Park and Ocean Grove. The images, using wide-angle lenses and rooftop views, showed an Asbury Park in pristine condition. The shingled hotels were solid structures, their Victorian features equal to those of grand hotels in the Adirondacks of New York or the White Mountains of New Hampshire. The Boardwalk was a wide wooden sidewalk of civilization over the golden sand; women strolled under parasols and well-behaved children amused themselves by looking at the antiquities that founder Bradley placed on display. The canopy of trees that framed the parks provided cool picnic refuges, while the lakes were tranquil pools of water for a romantic canoe ride. Who wouldn't want to come here from the hot, fetid cities?

Bradley wasn't shy about promoting his utopia. He launched the *Asbury Park Journal* with editorial content that expounded on everything from modern sewers to contemplative relaxation, the moral virtues of covered bathing, and, of course, abstinence from alcohol. News coverage was a combination of city commissioners' meetings that emphasized the resort's continual progress and the always favorable reportage about the resort's genteel social scene. Unfortunately, over time, the relentless promotional prose about Asbury Park created expectations that failed to match the reality of living in the strict religious resort. After World War II, the gulf widened between Asbury Park's self-perception of a world-class resort and the civic turmoil that roiled beneath the surface.

Drawing Boundaries

In the 1890s, the boundaries of Bradley's Christian city by the sea weren't yet finalized. West of the railroad tracks, most of the unincorporated real estate was promoted as West Park, its wooded acres stretching into the forests and rolling farm fields of Neptune Township. Buying land from descendants of the original eighteenth-century settlers, Bradley resold parcels in this rural section to families of color who arrived from other parts of Monmouth County to work for him in construction. Bradley also owned woodlots from which the lumber came to build the resort. Families who could not afford to stay in the resort camped in the woodlots in tents in the summer. The local Tilton family had a dairy barn. On a finger of Deal Lake was a boat launch ramp. A separate parcel was under development by a Morristown lawyer.

The twentieth century was barely under way when Long Branch sensed its glamorous status among politicians and the theater crowd was aging to that of a dowager destination. In 1904 Long Branch launched an audacious land grab west into Eatontown Township and south six miles to include Asbury Park. By the time the civic dust settled, new municipal boundaries were drawn for a number of Shore towns, including the unincorporated section of Neptune, which Asbury Park proceeded to annex by referendum in 1906. In the end, Long Branch was a little more than 5 square miles while Asbury Park was a tidy 1.5. Together the local resorts were still smaller than the 11 square miles that made up Atlantic City, but their competition for the nation's growing leisure market was no less fierce. Over time, the western half of Asbury Park would evolve as a dense mix of year-round working-class and middle-class housing, with a scattering of upper-class residences, public housing, schools, and factories, leaving Bradley's original East Side purchase largely the domain of wealthy vacation home owners and some of the city's more successful entrepreneurs and politicians.

East Side Enclaves

Asbury Avenue divided the residential resort neighborhoods between old and new, small and large homes. The original development was south of the avenue in a mix of elaborate gingerbread cottages, mansard-roofed mansions, hotels, and the bustling downtown. The closer one got to the ocean and the farther away from Main Street, the larger the lots became. The numbered streets that began north of Asbury Avenue were divided into larger lots, and their exuberant late Victorian-style houses were interspersed with modest hotels and boardinghouses that architecturally fit in with the neighborhood, enhancing its residential character rather than making it look commercial. At Sunset Lake, the property sizes increased slightly again, and the north side of the lake, where the houses basked in the warming rays of the sun as it rose in the east and set in the west, became among the most desirable in Asbury Park. This side of the lake was devoted to single-family residences, with no overnight accommodations until Webb Street. Sunset Lake also marked

TOP *The electric utilities backed the successful presidential candidacy of Ohio Republican Warren G. Harding. About the time of his inauguration, his supporters found this modest cottage on Bond Street just off Fifth Avenue in which to install his pregnant mistress, Nan Britton, and a lady chaperone. Asbury Park physician and "society doctor" James F. Ackerman delivered Elizabeth Ann Britton Harding in 1919. Pike Archives.*

BOTTOM *The nineteenth-century Stick-style cottage of Mr. and Mrs. A. C. Leunggren, 514 Fourth Avenue at Bond Street. In 1916 it was donated to the Woman's Club for use as the club's first headquarters. Courtesy of the Board of Trustees of the Woman's Club of Asbury Park.*

the start of North Asbury Park. At the western end of Sunset Park was the resort's other train station, named for North Asbury Park and built just for this end of town; at the eastern end was the open ocean vista founder Bradley had envisioned. From Sunset to Deal Lakes the houses were larger. Some were built with glassed-in conservatories. Others had magnificent wraparound porches. Most had separate carriage houses with apartments for the hired help. Nearly all were landscaped and maintained by the resort's immigrant Italian population, who lived across the railroad tracks.

The Park Goes Electric

The homeowners of 1890—whether they lived year-round or were summer residents—were prime customers for the emerging use of gas and electricity. Bradley favored gas. He believed that electric lights overexposed a woman's features. In four years he had a second reason to disapprove of electricity. The upstart Atlantic Coast Electric Company, located across Deal Lake in Allenhurst, not only sold gas and light bulbs but also was actively looking to install a paying trolley service to transport all the travelers arriving in Asbury Park. The ultimate goal was a line connecting to Long Branch. Its more immediate aim was to provide an East Side service to move visitors from the Asbury Park and Ocean Grove station through the downtown and into the hotel circuit all the way to Eighth Avenue before heading west and then south on Emory Street to return to the depot. Bradley abhorred the constant dust from the rail installation, to say nothing of the noise that disrupted his solitude.

Bradley died in 1921. The trolleys lasted until 1923, by which point they were worn out and losing money. By year's end the company had switched to buses. And on December 31, 1923, the Indiana Power Company, managed by A. E. Fitkin, reorganized its New Jersey operations as the Eastern New Jersey Power Company and acquired the remaining assets of what was by then known as the Atlantic Coast Railway and Light Company. Fitkin kept the electric franchise and small gas divisions for the utility company and sold the blue and white buses to the new Coast Cities Railway Company. In May 1924, trolley employees and enthusiasts held a funeral for the last remaining Atlantic trolley car. The thirty-year-old car, which had been in operation since 1894, was hung in black crepe. Professor Musto's band played an up tempo funeral dirge, and at one stop in North Asbury Park, a fan hung a wreath of roses over one of its headlights before the electric car made its final turn onto the trolley bridge across Sunset Lake.

Leisure Starts to Lose Ground

The orderly pace of resort development began changing in 1906. That year, the public auditorium known as Educational Hall was moved from Grand Avenue to Railroad Avenue, where it was turned into a repair garage, signaling not only that its glory days for recreational use were over but also that Grand Avenue real estate had shifted in value. An entire block of open land between Second and Third

Cosy Retreat

I see no reason why [the electric trolley] it should usurp everything. Surely there is rush and noise enough around the Asbury avenue pavilion for those who wish for Coney Island–like crowds and enjoyments. Why not keep that cosy retreat, "Cro's Nest" and its surrounding woods free from the incursion of modern improvements and give the cramped up city people, stifled with the heat and the noise, the pleasure they so much enjoy in just such retired places? The shady walks through the pine woods, the view of lake and surrounding country from "Cro's Nest," especially beautiful at the hour of sunset, or resting on the seats or ground, watching the boats on the lake; just to exist in such a spot is new life to many, escaping from city heat and noise.

N.A.P. [North Asbury Park]

– Asbury Park Journal,
March 8, 1890

Avenues west to Emory Street was primed to go residential. Harvey Jones, treasurer of Buchanon and Smock Lumber Company, built a sumptuous orange-yellow brick mansion in which his family lived in the winter; they summered at the Monmouth Hotel on Kingsley Street, which Jones also built. Next door, on the sunny side of Second Avenue, attorney James Carton built a turreted paean to the Victorian style for his growing family. Third in the impressive lineup was the Federal Revival showplace built by society jeweler August Cornelius.

Eleven years later, an early spring fire spurred an even more dramatic shift from leisure to year-round real estate when lightning from a nor'easter touched the electrical wires in the Natatorium. The Good Friday fire of April 1917 not only destroyed the portion of the Boardwalk between First and Second Avenues where the indoor pool had been but also wiped out forty-eight buildings on four city blocks. The fire also claimed the stone Methodist church on Grand Avenue. In all, an estimated $1 million in property was lost.

The fire came on the heels of the country's entrance into World War I, and when new houses were finally built as replacements they were more modest than their rambling Victorian predecessors. But it was on the block closest to the hotel circuit that new construction pushed the change from recreation to residential use. In a neat tidy row on Second Avenue between Kingsley and Bergh Streets, three different apartment houses were built: the Spanish-inspired Jersey in 1924 and Britwoods Court

Jeweler August Cornelius's Federal Revival–style family mansion on Second Avenue was designed by city architect William Cottrell and his son, Arthur. Today it is the Buckley Funeral Home. Courtesy of Richard and Dennis Buckley.

The morning after the Good Friday fire of 1917. Throughout the next decade former hotel sites went residential with the construction of apartment houses. Pike Archives.

in 1928, and the utilitarian Virginia in 1926. With its brick-and-mortar construction graced by front loggias, the fireproofed Virginia took its name from the previous occupant of Second and Kingsley, the wood-frame Virginia Hotel. Not only did these new buildings indicate the hotel market might be overcrowded, but with more modest bungalows opening in the Asbury Park suburbs of Wanamassa, Shark River Hills, and Asbury Gables in Neptune, these modest high-rise properties were well positioned for the pending real estate downturn that followed the Wall Street crash of 1929.

Residential Hotels

It was the Roaring Twenties and the public's travel habits were changing. A new real estate trend was sweeping across America in the form of residential hotels. Not that living in hotels was a new idea. Even James and Helen Bradley gave up their winter home in Williamsburg, Brooklyn, to move into the St. Denis in Manhattan while taking up summer residence in Asbury Park's Coleman House or Grand Avenue Hotel. They weren't alone. A number of the resort's businessmen opted to live in its year-round hotels. But the new trend in real estate was the hybrid residential hotel: two or three rooms offered more space than a cramped single hotel room, with the bonus of the hospitality services of a hotel; with efficiency kitchens and no outdoor upkeep, they were an ideal hybrid for those who wanted a low-maintenance vacation address. They could be rented by the week or on a month-to-month basis.

Asbury Park had three pushing their way above the treetops as elevators buildings: the Kingsley Arms Apartment Hotel overlooking Deal Lake on the northwest corner of Kingsley Street, and on the same block, the Miramar, diagonally opposite on Webb Street and Eighth Avenue. Both were boxy, solidly built buildings and opened in 1931. The third, which opened in September 1929, was the Santander, a tall, slender tower of a building; with its cream-colored stuccoed walls and red-tiled roof it dramatically commanded the northwest corner of Deal Lake Drive and Park Avenue.

Taking its name from a fashionable resort on Spain's northern Atlantic Coast, the Santander was built around a tiled center courtyard with a fountain. Each exterior corner walls featured gargoyles as downspouts. The ground floor on Deal Lake Drive had a year-round restaurant open to the public. The hotel lobby ceiling was done in gesso in a blue-and-gold pattern that evoked the Alhambra. The tiled floor and center staircase were laid with tiles similar to the Arts and Crafts style of leading California tile designer Ernest Batchelder, with masted ships, griffins, trefoils, and other whimsy set into the patterned layout. Two penthouses decorated in Spanish Mission style crowned the ninth floor and boasted stunning views. The Santander was built by Richard Weslord Stout, whose father was an attorney and real estate investor and whose maternal grandfather, George R. Lord, was a West Park promoter. Sadly, Stout lost his glorious $1 million investment in the early years of the Depression, and his family moved out of one of the penthouses and into a house in Interlaken.

The Santander's towering presence was accentuated by the construction of a series of connected, two-story dwellings across Park Avenue on Deal Lake Drive.

SHARK RIVER HILLS "The New Asbury Park Suburb"

Safe Water for Children

Early in the twentieth century, new developments that sprang up out of the eastern end of Neptune Township promoted themselves in relationship to the Shore's best-known residential resort. Pike Archives.

White with aqua trim, the Deal Lake Court Apartments were notable for three reasons. They replaced Alma White's nineteenth-century boardinghouse, which had originally stood on the corner and had been the only overnight accommodations on Deal Lake from Bradley's era. The Deal Lake Court Apartments were one of the first two art deco apartment buildings to be built in the changing resort; the second was at the corner of Grand and Asbury Avenues, replacing the ornate post-Victorian mansion of druggist Hugh Kinmonth. The apartments initially were intended for sale, a precursor to the condominium ownership that would come into

TOP *By the second decade of the twentieth century, property owners on Deal Lake were assessed a special tax in order to bulkhead the lake and create a flume to the ocean. With advances in construction technology, single-family homes began to be replaced by high-rise residences, including the towering residential hotel called the Santander and the lower apartment house to the right, Lake Drive Court. Pike Archives.*

BOTTOM *The Santander Restaurant and Tea Room was listed in a 1940 dining guide. The menu featured seafood thermidor, roast duckling, and pastries; dinners averaged $1. "Their colored waitresses exhibit the finest training we have ever experienced." The restaurant was eventually converted to medical offices as more year-round residents occupied the Santander. Pike Archives.*

play in the last quarter of the century. But with the onset of the Depression they were used as rental units.

The other building that dramatized the Santander's presence was the large late nineteenth-century summer home of New York realtor and Pomeranian dog breeder Gustave Barnett. This house still stands directly behind the residential hotel and is a constant reminder of Bradley's Asbury Park. In the 1940s this became the third clubhouse for the city's nomadic Benevolent Protective Order of the Elks No. 128, which had had two lodges located in Asbury Park's downtown.

Rise in Residents

The Wall Street stock market crash signaled the end to the glory days of mansion building and living. Many large, rambling circa-1890 Victorians were subdivided—from basement to attic—into apartments as the next generation sought hold on to the family properties they had inherited, becoming landlords instead of summer residents and, more often than not, living outside Asbury Park. Those who could do so subdivided once spacious lots, selling the considerably smaller parcels for bungalows, which had stuccoed walls that were easier than wood to maintain in the salt air. Some were sided with asphalt shingles and later, aluminum.

Comedian Bud Abbott was born on the south side of Munroe Avenue during the summer of 1895. That summer his father was selling orangeade at the Excursion House, a concession stand near the Heck Street bridge to Ocean Grove, about a block from the Abbott family's rented home. When the summer was over, the Abbotts left Asbury Park to work for Ringling Bros. and Barnum & Bailey Circus; Bud Abbott's father was an advance man and his mother was a bareback rider. Pike Archives.

While the 1937 United States Housing Act was passed to create shelter for the country's growing poor, city hall made a conscious decision to put public housing on Asbury Park's West Side and to seek commercial apartment construction for the East Side instead. That process accelerated after World War II when, reeling from properties abandoned on its tax rolls, the city put them up for sale. It wanted nothing less than a new glory era of residential construction. The chateau-style Steinbach mansion on Eighth Avenue, diagonally opposite the Santander, was among the first of the properties to be sold. Arthur Steinbach and his second wife, Grace, were more focused on refurbishing the Berkeley-Carteret Hotel, and they had let the mansion go for taxes. It was sold for $15,000, torn down, and before too long a plain two-story red brick apartment house replaced it. More buildings with multiple units were on the drawing boards. What locals called Metzgar Field at the southeast corner of Sunset and Park Avenues was sold and the Moderne-style Sunset Terrace Apartments with its unusual staggered-front design was built. The year was 1955, a time when the municipal government was facing mounting complaints about the city's antiquated sewer system, which had been consolidated into one location from the two cesspools installed by Bradley in the 1880s.

The sewer department was now located at the northern end of the Boardwalk in a modest brick building that matched the architectural style of the arcades. Three enormous below-ground concrete cisterns were built just off the curve of the Ocean Avenue and Deal Lake Drive intersection to hold treated waste during the summer months before discharging it into the ocean after Labor Day. But complaints of toilets backing up even in the public housing on the West Side would trigger the plant's first significant modern upgrade.

By now residences lined the city streets and there was no more open land for single-family home construction. When the Asbury Park exit on the Garden State Parkway opened in 1956, some six miles away from the city itself, new home buyers found spacious ranch houses waiting for inspection on one-time farms. With cheap electric heat, storm windows, Formica kitchens, attached garages, and backyards big enough to install an above-ground swimming pool, the new homes offered buyers attractive and affordable alternatives to the drafty, two-story, coal- and oil-heated homes of their youth.

Asbury Park's need to find more taxable property resulted in the green-lighting of several apartment projects whose outcome would forever change the residential skyline. In 1963, eight boxy new apartment houses sprouted on former hotel and summer home sites. In another three years, another round of apartment construction began, and five new high-rise apartment houses were built, most visibly the FHA-funded Munroe Tower on Munroe Avenue, the closest high-rise to downtown, and the privately financed $1.5-million Carlton House, at twelve stories the second tallest high-rise on Deal Lake Drive after the Santander. The evidence couldn't be clearer that year-round living had surpassed leisure vacation living in the real estate market.

In 1976 the city council sidestepped the tenant-led issue of rent control by endorsing the up-and-coming real estate trend of condominium conversions. This form of home ownership enabled landlords to pass along their buildings' upgrade costs to newly titled owners. Adeline Schofel of Deal took the first plunge into condominium ownership when she converted the fifty-unit Sunset Terrace Apartments. Its construction material was brick and concrete, and the interior walls were made of plas-

Good-bye, Coal!

When I was in eighth grade we moved to a brand new three-bedroom ranch house with a yard in Oakhurst [in Ocean Township] where our only sister [I was one of three brothers] could have her own bedroom. My father paid $25,000 for the house. It had baseboard hot water heat. No more shoveling coal. In Asbury the houses [on the West Side] were real close together. We played basketball in the dirt. It was very bad. My mother and father just wanted to step up and give us kids something more.

– Phil Villapiano
Rumson, New Jersey

ter, but by 1976 the building had rusted hot water pipes and an expensive oil-based heating system that needed replacement. Eventually to be called The Esplanade, the building's condominium conversion and subsequent modernization was a story repeated with other high-rise properties in Asbury Park.

The Trinity Unravels

By 1980, Bradley's vision for an Asbury Park that could restore the holy trinity of soul, mind, and body was faded beyond recognition. A new-old tug-of-war over the recreational use of liquor versus the solitude of residential life erupted when North Asbury Park homeowners went to city hall to block the request for a liquor license transfer from the shuttered Deck House restaurant overlooking Wesley Lake to a hotel at 300 Sixth Avenue that had been vacant for eight years. Michael Bruno wanted to renovate the building into a small luxury hotel with twenty-eight rooms and a cocktail lounge, but residents were fed up. Most of their ire resulted from long-standing problems with Sunset Lounge patrons who made calamitous exits at 3 a.m. every Friday and Saturday night, slamming car doors and honking the horns as they left the popular local watering hole. Residents didn't want another bar in a neighborhood now given over to year-round living. In the end, they won this conflict.

Since the early 1970s, Asbury Park had been under siege from the steady arrival of former mental patients who were finding their way to the faded resort in a poorly planned government-mandated exit from state-run mental institutions. Trenton was just one of many state capitals that decided to close its state hospitals in a move to trim health and welfare costs. To try to meet the challenges posed by these new residents, who had once led supervised lives, city health officer Martin Chomsky asked for federal aid to construct a two-story facility that would house public health services, an ambulatory care center, and doctors' officers on Main Street and Springwood Avenue. His request was denied. And the mentally ill continued to arrive and find shelter in old boardinghouses.

The tug-of-war between recreational and residential use for properties continued when the Monte Carlo pool site was sold to the Presbyterian Synod of New Jersey, which in 1974 built a high-rise senior apartment house on the coveted waterfront location. Pike Archives.

When new federal and state environmental laws required New Jersey municipalities to upgrade their sewer plants to treatment systems, Bradley's desire for a sanitary resort collided with his vision that the east end of his gridded avenues remain open. Like so much else in the city's public infrastructure, the plant on the Boardwalk at Eighth Avenue was worn out. Residents with Deal Lake views objected to a plan for placing the new plant near the boat launch ramp between the Main Street and railroad bridges, with a pipe running the length of the lake to the ocean. Ocean Township residents objected loudly in a special referendum held after Asbury Park tried to use the backing of state and federal environmental protection agencies to force the township to treat the city's effluent. Ultimately, Asbury Park had to turn to Bradley heir Helen Erskine Gillespie, a Virginia Apartments resident, to get permission to alter her uncle's deed restriction in order to change the configuration of Eighth and Ocean Avenues. The footprint for the new three-level facility claimed the entire block plus both avenues for construction. The result short-circuited Ocean Avenue by rerouting outbound traffic down Seventh Avenue. It also changed forever Founder Bradley's vision for avenues open to unobstructed views of the sea.

CHAPTER TWO

The Avenues

*I*N THE LATE NINETEENTH CENTURY a real estate speculator with more modest expectations than James Bradley was clearing away 135 acres he had bought from Britton White, a descendant of one of Neptune Township's original families. Frederick G. Burnham was a lawyer from Morristown, the well-to-do North Jersey community that had earlier seen Dr. Pitney leave to develop Absecon Island. West of the railroad tracks, Burnham's development was a shoebox-shaped parcel where the streets were notably not laid out in a grid nor named for Methodist crusaders. Located south of his parcel was West Grove, a township neighborhood of non-Methodist merchants across from the main gates to Ocean Grove. To the north was West Park, still more surveyed land Bradley and his investors owned in Neptune Township.

West Park's main traveling corridor was Asbury Avenue, the all-important road to Trenton, its status further blessed by the presence of a missionary Methodist church whose original members came from Ocean Grove. West Park's signature residential boulevard was Sunset Avenue, a continuation of the East Side that passed Bradley's athletic fields and a recreational boat launch ramp before crossing over Deal Lake and into southern Ocean Township. The second most desirable addresses were on Fourth and Fifth Avenues, where the lots and houses were slightly larger than those on the lower numbered avenues south to Asbury Avenue.

Burnham's main economic thoroughfare was Springwood Avenue, a lively, bustling roadway lined with shops, storefront churches, tearooms, and taverns, many

Georgianna Johnson is a colored woman with a very uncivil tongue in her head. She was employed by her aunt, who keeps a boarding house in West Park, to wait around the station and look out for customers as they came in on the trains.

This is contrary to the rules, as even whites are not allowed to hang around to solicit custom.

– Asbury Park Journal,
July 5, 1890

The Jews of Asbury Park and vicinity held a big celebration in Marrow's Hall, in West Park, on Tuesday night.

– The Shore Press,
September 26, 1890

The Italian settlement of West Asbury Park was the scene of an attempted murder on Sunday morning and it was no fault of the would-be assassin that his stiletto stopped short of its deadly work, although it was first thought his victim's wounds were fatal.

– Asbury Park Journal,
December 20, 1890

17

with second- and third-story galleries that overlooked the avenue. The Springwood name stopped at Main Street, where Bradley's Lake Avenue began. Westward, Springwood ran all the way up Richardson Heights, and beyond. Once the sacred land of the Sand Hill Indians of the Lenape Nation, the "Heights"—from which the Atlantic Ocean was visible—was home to some of the earliest carpenters and masons hired to build Asbury Park.

Many of West Park's first-time homebuyers were the married sons and daughters of pioneering families who had grown up on the East Side. Their Queen Anne and Colonial Revival houses were protected by two fire companies, the Enterprise on Third Avenue and Comstock Street and the Goodwill on Summerfield Avenue. For their children, city architect Ernest Arend designed a handsome two-story Gothic Revival school with separate entrances for boys and girls. Erected on Third Avenue, it was named for James A. Bradley.

By contrast, Burnham's neighborhood had one firehouse in a shingled garage on Springwood. It had two schools. The Free Colored School, built of wood on Springwood, was run by the indomitable Frisby women—Louisa and Marcelina. The immigrant children from Europe attended the utilitarian brick Prospect Avenue School.

Segregated by different real estate interests, the entire community living west of the railroad tracks had one goal in common. They all wanted a piece of the American dream that lay on the East Side. In 1906 they got it.

A Call to all the People of
ASBURY PARK
TO HEAR
The Greatest Living Negro Leader and Orator
Hon. MARCUS GARVEY
President General of The Universal Negro Improvement Association and Provisional President of Africa

AT

Roseland Hall
Springwood Avenue, Corner Atkins Avenue

On

THURSDAY NIGHT, NOV. 13th 1924
AT 8:15 O'CLOCK

HE WILL SPEAK ON THE WORLD MOVEMENT OF NEGROES AND THE FUTURE OF THE RACE IN AMERICA

COME AND HEAR THIS LEADING STATESMAN OF THE NEGRO RACE

Come and hear about The BLACK CROSS NAVIGATION STEAMSHIP CO. Organized by Negroes to trade with AFRICA, SOUTH and CENTRAL AMERICA, and the WEST INDIES

BIG MUSICAL PROGRAM

Come and Hear! Come and See! Come and do your Part

EVERYBODY INVITED   BE EARLY TO GET SEATS

ADMISSION.   50 CENTS

While W.E.B. Du Bois was preaching at the Great Auditorium in Ocean Grove, his civil rights rival, Marcus Garvey, was exhorting followers on Springwood Avenue. From The Blacks of Monmouth County *by Lenore Walker MacKay.*

Creation by Annexation

By the dawn of the twentieth century, West Side residents represented a formidable demographic whose support the East Side resort industry needed in order to realize its dream of becoming a world-class destination in the same league as Saratoga Springs, Narragansett, and Atlantic City. The issue was the sale of liquor and the need to create a local excise board that would issue licenses for fees paid to the municipality. The state legislature had paved the way with a law allowing for the creation of these special tax boards. The hotels desperately wanted to legalize the serving of alcohol and deadhead the temperance movement that regularly bloomed in the critical summer season. But most East Side property owners were out-of-towners with no local voting rights. Hotel owners well knew that nearly all of their employees lived on the West Side. Getting them on the voting rolls in anticipation of a special referendum would guarantee creation of the excise board.

For their part, residents, particularly in Burnham's neighborhood, were displeased at Neptune Township's lack of interest in extending to them municipal services such as sewers and police protection. Neptune appeared willing to let all the property west of the railroad tracks go, save for West Grove. When the electioneering was over, Asbury Park had doubled its size through annexation. On the surface, the boundary line appeared tidy enough, split right down the backyards of the resort's Ridge Avenue and the township's Myrtle Avenue property owners. Over time, it would be hard to tell where Asbury Park's social and economic issues ended and those of the eastern end of Neptune Township began.

A Political Star Is Born

From 1906 to 1910, Clarence Eugene Francis Hetrick, an Asbury Park High School graduate and Rutgers University dropout who had sold real estate and insurance with his father, was busy with politics in Freehold, where he served as Monmouth County sheriff. Many of his votes had come from Asbury Park's burgeoning West Side population, Jews and African Americans. He was an ambitious man, married but with no children, he was rumored to have a mistress who worked the front desk at Keystone Laundry on Railroad Avenue. In 1910 Monmouth County Sheriff Hetrick, then thirty-seven years old, was casting his eye at a run for the state senate when one autumn day ten-year-old Marie Smith didn't come home from Bradley School.

Early attempts to find the child ended in failure. To stave off the public relations debacle an unsolved kidnapping could cause in a family-promoted resort while at the same time addressing the fears of West Side parents, Hetrick made a calculated announcement. He would spend his own money to hire the nation's foremost detective agency, Walter J. Burns, to find the little girl. On Sunday, November 13, 1910, Marie's partially clothed body was discovered in an undeveloped stretch of

Unlike the East Side's distinct grid, which was controlled by founder James Bradley, Asbury Park's West Side development was determined by competing real estate visions divided between private development and public policy; circa 1970. Pike Archives.

woods at Fourth and Ridge Avenues. In the initial rush to judgment, the first suspect was African American handyman and Smith family neighbor Thomas "Black Diamond" Williams. The charges garnered so much attention that the newly formed National Association for the Advancement of Colored People made Williams's the third case of discrimination it defended. Raymond Schindler, the Burns detective assigned out of his New York office to help find Marie's murderer, ultimately proved Williams's innocence. With the eventual confession of German émigré and Cookman Avenue florist Frank Heidemann, Hetrick emerged triumphant on both the East and West Sides of Asbury Park. But he lost his 1911 senate bid. Hetrick scaled back his ambition, ran for mayor in 1915, and won. With one very brief hiatus, he remained there until 1934.

Clarence Eugene Francis Hetrick was Asbury Park's longest-serving mayor. He was equally revered and reviled. His greatest popularity came from the West Side, where he lived on Fifth Avenue. Pike Archives.

Trading Neighborhoods

After the 1906 annexation, Burnham's development was cast as the West Side. Without question it was the West Side, perceived to be in service to the East Side. Until 1923, hotel and restaurant chefs and owners of small downtown grocery stores shopped the produce market located on the big block of Railroad Avenue between Springwood and Cookman Avenues. Labor unions representing carpenters, waiters, and other trades established employment offices and meeting halls in the 900 blocks west of Railroad Avenue. In state industrial directories, Asbury Park repeatedly described its West Side neighborhood as "suitable for factories with a ready supply of labor," even going so far as to indicate "building sites are still given free of cost to industries that are of a particularly desirable character."

By 1915 the West Side's racial and ethnic composition began to shift dramatically as the great African American migration from the economically beleaguered South picked up steam. Black Americans readily found work in the Jersey Shore's hotel kitchens, livery stables, and laundries and as domestics; a lucky few who worked the summer circuit were able to balance their seasonal summer jobs with similar menial labor at schools and universities during the school year. The prosperous had earlier established themselves on Springwood Avenue and became the West Side's merchant and professional class.

They lived well in large houses on Sylvan, Union, and Atkins Avenues, the residential side streets off Springwood that connected to Bradley's gridded avenues.

As more African American laborers moved in, however, the second generation
of Italians who made up the resort's largest ethnic group starting moving farther
north. Steadily achieving their own economic success as builders, gardeners, bakers,

tailors, and merchants, they moved their Roman Catholic parish, Our Lady of Mount Carmel, from Springwood Avenue to the intersection of Bangs Avenue and Prospect Avenue, where they also established an elementary school. After World War II, the parish moved north again, this time to a sizable piece of property on Asbury Avenue and Pine Street; there it built a handsome orange brick church and a separate elementary school and living quarters for the nuns who taught there. The lot Mount Carmel bought was the former site of the Methodist church that had been lost to fire in 1945. By the time the new church opened its doors, the resort's Little Italy neighborhood had spread from Bangs Avenue to Asbury Avenue. At the eastern end, a block before Railroad Avenue, was a clubhouse that belonged to the Progressive Italian League; west, just beyond Ridge Avenue, was a Sons of Italy Hall.

Growing Up West Side

I GREW UP ON SPRINGWOOD AVENUE. FROM ATKINS Avenue west to the Neptune border was occupied by mostly Italian families, a few Afro-Americans, and a couple of Jewish families. My father, Joseph Rabin, ran a general store at No. 1407 Springwood. Not far away was Cuba's, where the elite from Deal and Spring Lake came "slumming" on Friday and Saturday nights, and the showgirls were from New York. They stayed at the home of Mrs. White [at the northwest corner of Springwood and Ridge Avenues]. My sister and I would wait patiently to be able to see these tall, beautiful, Afro-American showgirls walk by carrying their costumes.

A week before school [started] the Italian women would recruit all the children to help "push" tomatoes. This is a form of canning and a backyard community project. A large, galvanized washtub was filled with water and placed over an open fire in the backyard. Another tub was filled with fresh crushed tomatoes, some salt, and basil. The children placed empty wine bottles into the tomato tub and, with a wooden stick and a funnel, we filled the bottles. They were then corked and put into the boiling water for processing. Sometimes a bottle would explode, to the children's de-

light. It was fun popping tomatoes into our mouths as we "pushed." This went on for a few days until enough tomatoes were canned to make delicious spaghetti sauce for the entire neighborhood for a year.

During 1932–1941, when I attended elementary school, Bangs Avenue School was segregated. But we shared two teachers: Miss Dora Levine, who taught penmanship, and Miss Hagerman, the music teacher. We also shared the auditorium and gym. I would walk to school with my colored friends and remain on the outside of the playground fence until the bell rang, and then I entered the "North" door. After school my colored friends picked me up at the "North" door. All the "North" teachers were Caucasian and the "South" teachers were colored. I liked Mr. Hyland Moore (the "South" principal) much more than Mr. Edinger (the "North" principal) because he lived in my neighborhood and came into my father's store. This arrangement was accepted, understood, and no one mentioned discrimination.

– Celia Tracy, Asbury Park Post Office, ret.
Shrewsbury, New Jersey

The missionary Methodists were also moving farther north. In 1947 they rebuilt their church on Fourth Avenue between Dunlewy and Prospect and began moving into the houses going up on the Deal Lake border with Ocean Township. These houses were built on the last available open land in postwar Asbury Park and were among the last built in the city.

All That Jazz

With the start of Prohibition in 1919, the West Side found it was not immune from police raids even if it did lack police protection from other criminal offenses. The front-page headline of the September 7, 1926, *Asbury Park Press* trumpeted, "Raiders Close Up Leading Cabarets in Negro District: Hundreds of White Patrons Are Driven into Street as Officers Arrest All Employes of Inns."

Just the year before, the star of Broadway's *Chocolate Dandies*, Josephine Baker, had been looking to redesign her Revue Nègre for the Folies Bergère in Paris. Back stateside, she came to the Smile-A-While at 1144 Atlantic Avenue to hear popular swing bandleader Claude Hopkins. Before the night was over, Baker had hired Hopkins and his stage dancers; they left for Paris the next day. Extremely successful with the

The Young Men's Hebrew Association and the Jewish Community Center provided recreational and cultural opportunities for Asbury Park's growing Jewish population, including the aspiring thespians seen in this photo. The center was located on Comstock Street, between Asbury and Sewell Avenues.
Pike Archives.

To this day, mum's the word on the name of this bookie, whose funeral was held at the original Our Lady of Mount Carmel Church. Pike Archives.

Family Ties

My grandparents raised their family of five boys and two girls amidst the difficult days of the early 1900s. My paternal grandmother, Nellie Louisa Rock Burke, owned a bakery on Springwood Avenue next to Hunter Jones's grocery store. He employed my aunt Helen Artis Burke, who lives two blocks from the once-famous Carver Hotel.

My great-grandparents Peter and Lavinia Rock were born in Pinebrook, New Jersey, moving to Asbury Park after their marriage in 1878, and leaving behind Rock family members that included Peter's brother William Elijah Rock, the founder of the first African American newspaper in Red Bank, New Jersey, *The Echo Press.*

– Julian Francis Burke IV,
"Lest We Forget,
A Tribute to My Ancestors"
Palmyra, Virginia

musical talent it booked, the nightclub was filled with a standing-room-only crowd of three hundred patrons during the Labor Day weekend of 1926. Monmouth County detectives staged two midnight raids on Friday night and one on Saturday night. The patrons went free but owners Julius Suarez, age thirty-three, and Albert Mosselle Jr., age thirty-one, were arrested and charged with the illegal sale of liquor. When county detectives returned to the West Side for a third strike on Monday, the Smile-A-While was closed. A block away, at 1155 Springwood Avenue, the Roseland Ballroom was jumping. A raid ensued, but no liquor was found. Nonetheless, the county detectives arrested owner Henry Hart and charged him with maintaining a disorderly house.

Unlike trying to serve hard liquor, betting was a somewhat more secure business during Prohibition. It didn't attract attention with noisy entertainment. It could be done in broad daylight. And just about anyone could take your numbers. In a Springwood Avenue luncheonette, a waitress named Alba carried two different notepads in her apron. If she reached into one pocket, she pulled out the pad to take your food order. If she reached into the other, it meant she would take your numbers. A rabbi selling raffle tickets for his synagogue was picked up on Main Street and Cookman Avenue when police mistook him for a numbers runner. Apologies were made after the cops explained they were watching a second-floor pool hall that doubled as a betting parlor on the same corner where the rabbi had unknowingly been standing. Meanwhile, over on Asbury Avenue a candy store owner ran a numbers racket out of his stock room.

Seemingly harmless on the surface, the illegal activities in Asbury Park triggered a 1934 state probe into how the Monmouth County prosecutor's office was handling the city's criminal cases. An eighty-four-page report detailed payoffs, fixing of grand jury indictments, illegal gambling, whiskey making, and the disappearance of money. It also included charges of gun permits improperly issued to beer baron Irving "Waxey Gordon" Wexler, who had listed his residence as the Berkeley-Carteret Hotel, along with two other hotel residents who later wound up dead in Elizabeth. The report ultimately resulted in the ouster of county prosecutor Jonas Tumen.

But as the post-Prohibition 1930s melted into the 1940s era of Mafia expansion at the Jersey Shore, numbers running and other

BELOW LEFT *Cookman Avenue electrician Henry Van Dyke and his assistant, Sam Genaro, string lights across Springwood Avenue in preparation for the Italian community's annual Columbus Day festival, circa 1905. Pike Archives.*

BELOW RIGHT *After a disastrous fire in 1945 destroyed Ballard Methodist Church on Asbury Avenue, Our Lady of Mount Carmel bought the site and moved its parish from Bangs Avenue and Prospect Avenue. The move indicated just how far north the Italian Catholic parish had relocated since its first church was built a quarter of a mile away on Springwood Avenue. Pike Archives .*

Bangs Avenue

Color was an issue in Asbury Park. It was always an issue. I knew where my people were and we enjoyed our life and had a wonderful life and other people just stuck together. Italians stuck together. The Jews stuck together. The Spanish stuck together. And the sixties came, civil rights came. And everybody started mixing up and everybody didn't like that, and then you saw tensions. Bangs Avenue was where people of mixed race lived.

The day after the riots I was visiting with my parents on their porch on Summerfield Avenue and we saw this wave of people coming down off Ridge and we didn't recognize anybody we knew.

– Madonna Carter Jackson
Atlanta, Georgia

criminal activities didn't disappear; they merely became less visible to the traveling public. Chicago gangster Sam Giancana turned up at the Shore, occasionally frequenting Asbury Park, where he had taken up with a hopeful showgirl from the resort whom he squired around to roadside nightclubs on the Neptune Highway. The betting game got violent only once—ironically, a year after the state investigations commission had begun a new probe into the relationship between the county prosecutor's office and organized crime in Asbury Park. The prosecutor at the time was Vincent Keuper, an attorney and former city councilman. In 1974, a Prospect Avenue candy store owner Michael "Sonny Bopp" Dello, who loved the game of golf, was shot in the back of the head, along with his brother, and found by a Tilton Dairy milkman who was making his usual morning delivery to the store. Tens of thousands of dollars and lists of names were later found in a downtown bank safe listed in his name, but the murders remained unsolved. Meanwhile, a block away, classes continued at Bangs Avenue School across from the Prospect Avenue corner where the execution-style murder had taken place.

If the Smile-A-While's Suarez and Mosselle had any heirs to their successful West Side nightclub formula it was in the post-Prohibition hands of Henry Lopez and Minnie Quatrano. Minnie Quatrano's father, Marcellino, had followed his compatriots from Naples, Italy, and when his daughter became a teenager, he insisted she learn a trade. He put her to work in a factory on Railroad Avenue where she made uniforms for World War I soldiers. When the war was over, the independent-minded daughter told her father that manual labor wasn't for her. In a Springwood Avenue speakeasy, a handsome, dark-skinned foreigner playing cards and speaking with an accent different from that of her father's had caught her attention. Henry Lopez used the nickname "Cuba" to associate himself with the more prosperous Castilian-speaking island in the Caribbean instead of his native but poorer Puerto Rico. Minnie married him, and they opened a restaurant on Springwood Avenue that they called Cuba's Spanish Tavern. With the repeal of Prohibition in 1933,

The African American Travel Market

THE NEGRO MOTORISTS GREEN BOOK WAS A YEARLY travel guide for African Americans published on St. Nicholas Avenue in Harlem in the years immediately following World War II.

In the 1948 edition three West Side hotels paid for entries: The Metropolitan at 1200 Springwood Avenue, Reevy's at 135 DeWitt Avenue, and Whitehead at 25 Atkins Avenue.

Six different women ran tourist homes: Mrs. W. Greenlow at 1317 Summerfield, Mrs. Brown at 135 Ridge Avenue, Mrs. C. Jones at 141 Sylvan Avenue, Mrs. V. Maupin at 25 Atkins Avenue, E. C. Yeager at 1406 Mattison Avenue, and Anna Eaton at 23 Atkins Avenue.

Two Springwood Avenue restaurants paid to be listed: the West Side Dining Room at No. 1136 and Nellie Tutt's at No. 1207.

Cuba's was the only nightclub entry for Springwood, but the taverns on the avenue included Cuba Lopez's Aztex Room at No. 1147, the Capitol at No. 1212, the Hollywood at No. 1318, and 2-Door at No. 1512.

If you needed any repair work done while you were vacationing, garages listed were Arrington's at 153 Ridge and the West Side at 1010 Asbury Avenue. A Mr. Johnson listed his service station at Springwood and DeWitt Place.

For a shave and a haircut on Springwood, black travelers could go to the Consolidated Barbershop at No. 1216 or John Milby at No. 1216. Women on vacation might get their hair done at the Imperial at No. 1107, the Opal at No. 1146, or Marion's at No. 1119.

In its glory days, the Waverly Inn on the east side of DeWitt Avenue just off Springwood was one of the West Side's prosperous small hotels that catered to vacationing black Americans. Pike Archives.

Charles Waters leans on his cane in front of his uncle Joe Waters's variety store on Springwood Avenue. Most African Americans couldn't get credit in the nineteenth and early twentieth centuries, so Joe Waters became the community's bank, loaning money to his neighbors. With a restaurant, a paint and hardware store, and other enterprises to his credit, Waters was among the more successful and respected businessmen on the avenue. Courtesy of Inez Drumgoole Brown.

they received a license that allowed them to add hard liquor to their menu. The enterprising couple also opened a stationery store next door where they sold newspapers, cards, tobacco, and candy. Their glory days came in the 1950s and 1960s when they booked rhythm-and-blues acts such as Ike and Tina Turner, Little Richard, and the Four Tops. Like the Smile-A-While before them, theirs was a nightclub that drew wealthy white patrons from outside Asbury Park. After hours, East Side hotel musicians would come over looking for a chance to sit in and jam.

Better Health and Housing

Founder James Bradley's influence was already surpassed in the public eye by that of Mayor Clarence Hetrick when he died in 1921. Four years later, Hetrick was praising the efforts of the board of health and philanthropic donors whose efforts and donations led to construction of a new masonry child welfare home on Sewall

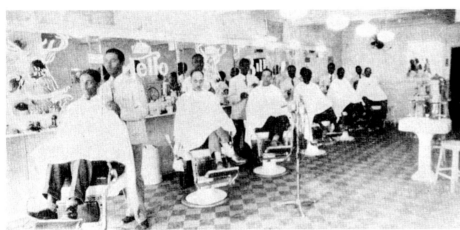

This collection of prosperous businesses was photographed for a political booklet intended to help reelect Mayor Hetrick, whom many African Americans credited with giving them economic opportunities they would not otherwise have had, including positions in city hall. All photos appeared in Asbury Park and Its Colored Citizens, 1911–1931, *written and photographed by Lorenzo Harris Sr. and Aaron A. Mossell. Pike Archives.*

Avenue and Langford Street; it replaced the ramshackle and leaky wooden buildings built in 1913 by Bradley.

"No work has been greater in this city than that of this association," Mayor Hetrick said at the dedication ceremonies June 22, 1925. "I feel that I speak this as one qualified to say so; I feel that I know; I feel that I have been in closer touch with those in need of this organization than the general run of people. You are doing a great work for the city, for its welfare, and for its advancement, and in the final analysis that is the greatest thing."

The new facility had a public physician's office, dining hall, and playroom on the first floor and four bedrooms, a dormitory, baths, and a balcony on the second. By this

Improved Benevolent Protective Order of the Elks of the World

OH THE PARADES! AS A MEMBER OF THE Asbury Elks IBPOE of (that is to say, the Black Elks!), we children and elders marched in many parades, not only in Asbury but also in New York City and Philadelphia.

I loved my uniform! A deep maroon gabardine flared skirt that stopped just at my knees, a satiny gray blouse with full sleeves that ended in buttoned cuffs, and a burgundy sash, lined with silvery gray satin that hung smartly from my waist. Of course we wore boots. White boots with white tassels. A baton and a maroon hat piped with gray were the crowning touches! We were ready to strut our stuff, and strut we did, our banner gliding before us, announcing our presence, proclaiming to the cheering crowds that we knew how to be in a parade.

– Lorraine Stone, performance artist
Eatontown, New Jersey

West Side photographer's daughter Madonna Carter Jackson stands on the car bumper in the photograph her father took in 1956 when the IBPO Elks held their statewide convention in Asbury Park. The convention included a parade down Springwood Avenue. Pike Archives.

ABOVE LEFT *Funded by the proceeds of ticket sales allowing visitors to view the 1934* Morro Castle *burning off the city's Boardwalk, the West Side Mission was located in the 900 block of Springwood on the northwest corner of Prospect Avenue near the Eureka Fire Company. Lillian Waters Drumgoole, seen here, was an examplar of the civic-minded spirit of the West Side. Courtesy of Inez Drumgoole Brown.*

ABOVE RIGHT *The Monmouth County Cotillion was launched in 1950 as a debutante and scholarship event for young college-bound African Americans. The dapper Carl Williams, seen here with Beverly Askew, attended all the social formals and went on to open Mr. Fashion, an upscale men's clothing store on Cookman Avenue across from Steinbach's. Courtesy of Carl Williams.*

LEFT *William Knuckles was Springwood Avenue's most successful African American electrician. He had his own retail operation until looters destroyed his store during the 1970 riot. Courtesy of Hortense Knuckles Reed.*

time, the city's Child Welfare Association already had one hundred members and had been treating children with communicable diseases. There was a neighborhood hospital on Munroe Avenue in the Whitesville section of Neptune just over the 1906 annexation line, plus a city hospital on Asbury Avenue and Comstock Street with an outpatient department on Springwood Avenue. By World War II Dr. Joseph Carter, who later became the avenue's only black pharmacist, was operating a venereal disease clinic on Atkins Avenue. Dr. William J. Parks, on DeWitt, was the leading African American general practitioner. Dr. Sebastian Vaccaro was the leading Italian American doctor, and when he left the West Side and moved his family to Fourth Avenue on the East Side he brought black as well as white patients with him. A number of other doctors, including a mother-daughter homeopathetic team, were also practicing on the East Side. Interestingly, it was the East Side doctors, led by brothers James F. and Joseph Ackerman, who in 1932 established Fitkin Memorial Hospital in Neptune with a huge donation from utilities magnate A. E. Fitkin.

With no end to the Depression in sight, Congress passed the Housing Act of 1937 to solve the problem of insufficient housing for the growing numbers of poor while also providing jobs for the unemployed and much-hoped-for new business opportunities. The act required the construction of new public housing units equal to the removal of substandard, or slum, dwellings. The federal government provided money for housing, but public housing authorities, appointed by local elected officials, were charged with ownership and operation. By 1941 the Asbury Park Housing Authority had two public housing projects on the drawing boards in the city's first federally subsidized urban renewal program. The projects' names included the word "village" in an effort to make the low-rise brick apartment houses seem more hospitable. Wooden shacks, tumbledown houses, and a few commercial buildings along the old border with West Grove were bulldozed to make way for the first in an anticipated series of low-rise brick apartments. The first to be built in 1941 was Asbury Park Village. By that time, population shifts on the West Side had created a nearly all–African American community along Springwood, and the first residents for Asbury Park Village were black.

A second housing project, this one on Washington Avenue, was under construction for poor white residents, notably Italian Americans still living south of Asbury Avenue; in 1943,

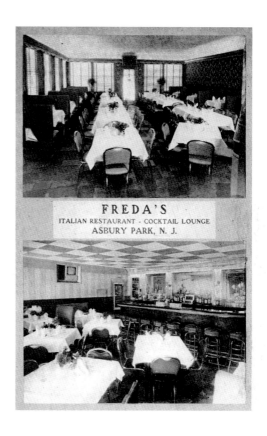

FREDA'S
ITALIAN RESTAURANT - COCKTAIL LOUNGE
ASBURY PARK, N. J.

Medicine

ASBURY PARK WAS CONSIDERED A PRETTY SNAZZY place. Little did I realize what was going to happen in the years to come. When I graduated from Asbury Park High School in 1939, went away to college and medical school, Asbury Park was still doing well. My first office was at 302 Langford Street. In 1961 I moved to Bangs Avenue. Bangs is one of the main thoroughfares in Asbury Park other than Main Street and, of course, Springwood Avenue. Bangs was the same street where the post office is, the same street where the new city complex is. It is highly recognizable.

The population was stable. It was a middle-class town. When I came [back] here, there were only two other doctors on the West Side, Dr. J. F. S. Carter who practiced on Atkins Avenue and Dr. E. A. Robinson who was well along in years. Back in those days, there were no other colored doctors in Asbury Park. We were busy. Even though I trained in internal medicine, a town like Asbury Park was considered a small town and it was not unusual for us to practice general medicine. Women were still having babies, so I delivered a lot of babies. I took care of teenagers and adults. I inoculated post office employees against polio.

– Dr. Lorenzo Harris
Neptune, New Jersey

however, Washington Village was appropriated as housing for "essential war job workers" at Fort Monmouth and Camp Evans. Construction of new housing projects resumed after the war, and by 1960 the housing authority had seven buildings to look after.

From Dream to Nightmare

By 1960, tourism in New Jersey was changing as families were presented with more travel options farther south along the Garden State Parkway and even out of state. Attendance figures, first for overnight visitors and then for day-trippers, started to drop. East Side hotels and boarding houses began closing. Restaurants that had once been filled were struggling to find enough patrons to justify paying their wait and kitchen staffs. Some didn't make it. The East Side, which had provided jobs for two and three generations of West Side residents, was faltering, and the impact across the tracks was a slow, steady erosion of Springwood Avenue's economic underpinnings; in ten years things would turn violent.

The residential corner of Prospect and Mattison Avenues, circa 1920. Pike Archives.

As the 1960s unfolded, the Asbury Park Housing Authority stopped maintaining its properties. So, too, did West Side homeowners and absentee landlords who

TOP LEFT AND RIGHT *Many of the original Burnham houses were small wood-frame houses like this one (left) on Borden Avenue. In the city's earliest attempt at neighborhood renewal many of the originals were re-placed by such houses as the one on Sylvan (right), built of Portland cement. Photo on right appeared in* Asbury Park and Its Colored Citizens 1911–1931, *written and pho-tographed by Lorenzo Har-ris Sr. and Aaron A. Mossell. Photo on left, Pike Archives.*

LEFT *Built in the 1920s, the home of Dr. William J. Parks, a general practitio-ner, was as architecturally sophisticated as any house in the East Side. In 1945 it be-came the West Side Commu-nity Center. Pike Archives.*

RIGHT *City police officer turned nightclub entrepreneur Odyssey Moore, left, and patrons in his newly opened Orchid Lounge. Courtesy Rainette Bannister Holimon.*

BELOW LEFT *The charismatically handsome Puerto Rican émigré and nightclub owner Henry "Cuba" Lopez. Courtesy of Inez Drumgoole Brown.*

BELOW RIGHT *Cuba's wife, Minnie Quatrano Lopez, with noted local singer Betty Johnson. Courtesy of Sheila Solomon.*

rented properties that had been subdivided in the same way East Side mansions had been during the Depression. The problem of alcohol abuse was compounded by the postwar epidemic of drug addiction. Vandalism became a chronic problem. So did unemployment and school truancy. Many community agencies had poorly trained managers and an insufficient number of programs for teenagers. The West Side Community Center was without a director for a year. About halfway through the decade, the housing authority tore down deteriorated houses on the West Side without building any replacement housing.

The civil rights movement was picking up steam throughout the American South and here in New Jersey, and violence was erupting in inner cities around the country. In 1967 the problems hit close to home, with riots in downtown Newark. A year later violence erupted in Trenton, then in the historic African American community in the Monmouth County seat of Freehold, followed by Long Branch and Red Bank. By early July 1970, there were vague rumors about a disturbance planned for Asbury Park. Police officers who arrived for the night shift were told to be prepared. A few hours later, in the early morning hours of July 4, mayhem broke out outside the West Side Community Center. The street fighting spilled off DeWitt onto Springwood. Glass shattered. Flames from Molotov cocktails ignited store merchandise. Police and fire departments from surrounding towns responded with state troopers in tow. Five days later 46 people had been shot, 100 injured, and 170 arrested. When the final figures came in, the West Side had sustained property damage of $5 million. The violence never made it east across the railroad tracks.

The West Side Community Center, once a source of pride, had become a point of conflict between older and younger residents. City hall came under fire for not

Big Bill's Nightclub

IN 1959 THE AVENUE WAS GOOD. OUR PRIME TIME. The place I bought from Phil Konvitz had been the Hampton Inn. I changed the name to Big Bill's. It included a package store and bar across the street from Dr. Ernest Robinson's tennis courts at 1718 Springwood.

I booked a three-piece combo with Sammy Pugh, Ed Jenkins, and Pinkey. No western. No rock. Cole Porter and Tommy Dorsey—the classics. I'd open the club about 9 to 10 p.m. at night. Around midnight the hotel musicians from the East Side of Asbury Park would come in to jam. I'd close around 3 a.m.

Admission was always a dollar. Leo Karp [Turf Club on Springwood and Sylvan] was my biggest competitor. Cuba's was a competitor, but not in the same way. When Martin Luther King and John Kennedy got killed, it was a terrible time for me. It helped that I had about 85 percent white clientele.

But after the riots everything changed. A lot of the stores moved out to the malls. Springwood became a drug circuit. When I couldn't draw people, I put in go-go girls. I handled them like the Rockettes. Built a special room where they could get ready. Had a plane fly a banner over the ocean: Big Bill's Pussycats.

I put Sammy Pugh on a two-year contract. Down the avenue Odyssey Moore changed The Orchid into a jazz club. I bought those tennis courts on Springwood and put up a basketball court. . . . I sponsored a basketball team in a local league. I invited the Knicks over from their summer training at Monmouth College.

– Bill Sanders, Neptune, New Jersey

being "responsive to the political, economic, and social needs of the Negro community." In a few years city hall was under fire again for not doing more to support the avenue's remaining businesses. William Reed, who had bought Leo Karp's Turf Club, asked for more police foot patrols. Of the twenty people loitering in front of his bar, Reed said, fifteen would be drug pushers and five would be buyers. The loitering was giving the city a bad reputation, he added. Tourists were being verbally abused as they waited at traffic lights on the avenue. His request fell on deaf ears.

As they had during the 1940s urban renewal, bulldozers once again arrived on Springwood Avenue. By the time they were finished, the commercial and residential corridor between Railroad and Atkins Avenues and buildings on its side streets was erased from existence. Some streets ceased to exist altogether. Stalled by its own internal politics as well as friction with city hall, the housing authority watched as several West Side churches stepped in to negotiate with the federal government and build low-income garden apartments.

Hearing the News

IT WAS A REGULAR MORNING: UP AT EIGHT TO MAKE my 9 a.m. class. Summertime at Hampton Institute [Hampton, Va.], where I was making up a failed class (oh, cursed chemistry) and having a blast.

Radio's on. Listening to the a.m. jock on WRAP, Norfolk (Calvin "Shakespeare" Perkins, "your black alarm clock"!). R&B tunes flowin'; a little Sly and the Family Stone, a little James Brown.

And then the news. Nothing ever happens in the Tidewater area (tired water, we call it), so I'm only half listening when I hear the newsman say: "... riots in Asbury Park, New Jersey. ... fires ... last night. ..." I'm out of the room in a flash, pounding down the hall to the pay phone.

"Yes, a collect call from Lorraine Stone." Charges accepted. I burst into questions and tears. "Mommy, what's happening? Are you all right? What about Dad?"

She manages to squeeze words into my gushing fears. "I'm fine. You father's O.K., but Springwood Avenue is on fire. Lots of smoke. Smoke everywhere."

I listen, crying, unbelieving. She reassures me. Reminds me I have work to do in summer school. She'll call later in the day to let me know how things are.

O.K., I agree, and I ask her to have my best friend, Jackie Franklin, call me. Jackie calls that night. We cry together. Later she sends me lots of clippings from the *Asbury Park Press*. So much is gone. My side, the West Side of my hometown, smoldering, settling, for the first time, into sadness.

When I come home from school in August, I can't believe my eyes. Thirty years later the disbelief and sadness linger.

– Lorraine Stone
Neptune High School, Class of 1968

Seeing the News as It Happened

IN THE SUMMER OF 1970 I WAS PLANNING MY August 16 wedding at Our Lady of Mount Carmel Church when the riots came to Asbury Park.

I was twenty-two, working at the Fort Monmouth Hexagon, and still living at home. We lived at No. 1416 across from Freddy's [now Jimmy's Restaurant]. My grandparents lived next door and my two aunts lived next door to them.

Seeing armed policemen from neighboring towns marching down my street in riot gear is something I will never forgot. They had on different uniforms and some were carrying shields. There were too many policemen to be all ours.

My sisters and brother and I remember seeing fire trucks came from Port Monmouth and Leonardo [bayshore villages in Middletown Township in northern Monmouth County] and from Monmouth Beach.

I was scared. My father [Arcangelo Petillo] was a city fireman. My mom was very worried about him. He didn't come home for three days. Later he told us police had to escort the firemen to the fires and that people were throwing bottles and rocks at the firemen as they were trying to put out the fires.

We all remember soot and ashes falling down on Asbury Avenue.

– Grace Petillo Vetrano, library clerk
Bradley Beach, New Jersey

The Real Music of Asbury Park

I THOUGHT I CAME TO PARADISE WHEN I CAME TO Asbury Park from Newark. I was eleven. Where I lived, the music was black gospel and R&B mixed in with popular Italian ballads. This was between '55 and '60.

Lenny Welch got his start singing locally with the Vibratones. [Born Leon Welch in Asbury Park in 1938, Welch first got national attention with his R&B-flavored rendition of "You Don't Know Me" in 1960. His hit single "Since I Fell for You" was released in 1964.] Vocal groups were just coming into vogue. Gospel groups like Sam Cooke and the Soul Stirrers, the Dixie Hummingbirds, the Five Blind Boys would come to perform at the Armory. R&B groups like the Heartbeats, the Kodaks, Frankie Lymon and the Teenagers would sing at Convention Hall. The local groups like the Vibratones, the Blenders, and the Juveniles used to sing in the stairways of Boston Way on the third floor. That's where I met some of the guys who used to sing with Lenny.

Every week I would go there, and some black group was singing. Guys from Neptune and Asbury Park. I was in grammar school at Our Lady of Mount Carmel when I first became aware of the music. When I got into high school and found my voice they took me under their wing. Joe Major—now there was a bass singer!—he sang with the Vibratones. Raymond Morris. Bobby Young, Michael Carnegie. Raymond Nolan. Ronnie Coleman. Billy Brown and others would add the leads and harmony.

On Saturday mornings you could hear the R&B rhythm of the Valentines singing "Lily Maybelle," and other songs, coming from the windows of houses on Summerfield and Bangs Avenues. Nobody would complain because almost everybody was playing something that could be heard out of their windows.

In the summer you'd hear the music coming out of storefront churches because there was no air conditioning and the doors and windows were wide open. You'd hear the tambourines and the voices blending together. You'd get to know the kids and the kids would say, "Yeah, my cousin sings with a group and they are going to be famous."

If you could sing, or tone, you were down with it. I remember one of my early experiences with "the music" was in high school listening to some guys who were older singing in the gym. The song was called "When You Dance." Five black guys, maybe juniors in high school. And they were dancing and singing. But you couldn't find this music on the popular radio stations where Patti Page was singing because I later found out it was called race music. Whatever it was called, I knew that I loved it. This was the real music of Asbury Park.

– Nicky Addeo, Asbury Park, New Jersey
Nicky Addeo and the Darchaes recorded for Savoy Records in 1963.

Nicky Addeo, second from left, singing with Sam Siciliano, Barry "Rufus" Edwards, Lou Scalpati, and Patsy Siciliano. Courtesy of Nicky Addeo.

But Saint Stephen A.M.E. Church ran afoul of city hall politics when it asked for a special tax break in order to build a second complex, this one across from its house of worship on Springwood. The plan called for multifamily dwellings, three townhouses, twelve single-family homes, and most important of all, a much-needed commercial plaza for a convenience store, a laundry, and a luncheonette. The mayor and council refused; the developer withdrew his plans, and the land waited for a new plan that turned out to be already on the drawing board.

Cash-strapped city hall also played hardball with the housing authority, which had petitioned to build a new housing project on the avenue. The mayor and council refused to give the authority access to the property until it paid $60,000 in uncollected taxes. In municipal sparring that had become typical, the housing authority counterclaimed that the city had not fulfilled its 1941 promise to provide police protection in its projects, and a stalemate ensued.

Meanwhile, the mayor and council were supporting a proposal approved by the planning board that, when the details were made public, completely ignored the avenue's commercial history and its role as a traffic corridor between Route 35 in Neptune and State Highway 71, which doubled as Main Street in Asbury Park. Al-

Rising Up in the Strength of the Lord

WE LIVED AT 126 ATLANTIC AVENUE, DIRECTLY across the street from Vita Gardens, which my dad built in response to the destruction that happened. [Vita was the first name of the wife of then-Bishop Bright of the First Episcopal District of the African Methodist Episcopal Church.] For my dad, ministry meant more than just church. It meant the reality of the kingdom that people could see. After the riots, that reality became suitable housing for his community.

I can remember the men of Bethel AME. They carried themselves with strength. Not beat. Not hopeless. There was a strong sense of community. As segregated as it might have been, they had ownership of their community. They had a sense of worth. It wasn't hard to find leaders and role mod-

els. They didn't have to be sports figures. They were just guys who went to work every day, who took care of their families.

Today we call it community development instead of urban renewal but we [still] have to do it from the inside out. This time [though] it has to be more than just housing. Subsidized housing, alone, doesn't stimulate the local economy. It has to include an opportunity for homeowner equity. It has to include neighborhood retail. We have to bring the barbershop back. And, we have to look toward the future and plan for fiber optic cable to put the community on the superhighway.

– Rev. Carl Hunter II
S.T.A.R.S. Community Development Corporation
Asbury Park, New Jersey

Thirty-four years after bulldozers leveled nearly five blocks of Springwood Avenue, very little urban renewal had taken place on this commercial artery to downtown Asbury Park, shown in an aerial photograph taken in 1998. Uniform buildings at right are public housing. Courtesy of Daniel Dorn Jr./Classic Photo Collection/Dorn's Photography Unlimited, Red Bank, New Jersey.

ready the city had renamed Springwood Avenue Lake Avenue in a clumsy public relations attempt to put some distance between the present and the past.

Called the Lake Avenue Renewal Project, the real estate development plan proposed by Phil Konvitz, a bail bondsman who also dabbled in construction, called for building thirty-three single-family homes on 10.5 acres. The bilevel, ranch, and two-story townhouses were projected to sell for between $46,000 and $48,000. Through the New Jersey Finance Agency, 10.75 percent mortgages were offered under a Neighborhood Loan Program. But only a handful of the units were ever constructed and sold. The rest of the avenue remained undeveloped into the twenty-first century.

CHAPTER THREE

The Beach, the Boardwalk, and the Palace

*I*N THE NINETEENTH-CENTURY health debate over which provided the better curative atmosphere—seashore or country—James Bradley was determined his resort would triumph with a blend of both. Dutch elms, plane sycamores, and towering pines lined the numbered avenues to the ocean. The roads gently rose from Main Street, crested, and then in a whoosh of expectancy, as houses and hotels receded in their deliberately staggered setbacks from the curbs, the crowded cares of urban life falling away, the final tapered blocks opened two hundred feet wider to embrace the vanishing point created by the azure ocean and the opal blue sky. Beneath the clouds and above the golden white sand lay a delicate line of rustic wooden boards. This was Bradley's vision, with which he was well pleased.

Nothing would intrude on this tranquility. The Boardwalk was for contemplative strolls to restore the mind and body, with the occasional band concert to elevate the spirit. Bathing hours on the beach were limited and bathing was completely banned on Sundays. Jangling amusements were banished to the west side of Ocean Avenue and limited to just three blocks even there. The roller toboggan was at Ocean and Second Avenue, the Old Mill water ride was at Ocean and First Avenue, and Ernest Schnitzler's allegorical Palace merry-go-round was at Lake Avenue

The Season Opens Finely

That the season is upon us no one will doubt after visiting the beach, the places of business and amusement Saturday evening.

The merry go rounds were centres of attraction . . . seats filled with spectators watching the revolving scene or listening to the alternations of music between the steam organ and the *Trenton* band.

But the merriest of all the parties were the hundreds who visited the toboggan chute to look on or to take a car, a lift in the elevator, and then a lightning whirl and then three times around the elongated circular track, and land again at the starting point. The effect is exhilarating, and if the hilarity of many of the passengers in the four seated cars is a criterion, the flying speed was greatly enjoyed.

– *Asbury Park Journal,*
July 5, 1890

Built in 1903 out over the ocean at the foot of Lake and Asbury Avenues, the first Casino featured Atlas holding up the world at the four corners of the roofline. That was just one of the ornate decorations designed by city architect William Cottrell. Pike Archives.

and Kingsley Street. For thirty-three years Bradley successfully enforced this atmosphere. After all, the Asbury Park founder owned the Boardwalk and the land across from it. As he sold those blocks to commercial developers, he prohibited the sale of alcohol and restricted the kinds of businesses that could be built.

Yet Bradley was accommodating. He saw to it that a path for bicyclists was laid parallel between the Boardwalk and Ocean Avenue. He built a $10,000 fishing pier at First Avenue to encourage the newly formed Asbury Park Fishing Club and had it outfitted with a retractable staircase for yachting parties. He spent $10,000 a year to repair his wooden walkway so summer visitors could continue to use it. Bradley even gave his blessing to a special public event—a Baby Parade—because it ideally complemented his vision for a wholesome family resort.

But Bradley's civic patrimony didn't last. Neither did some of his deed restrictions. Commercial pressures in the twentieth century escalated, and before long the Boardwalk and the Ocean Avenue amusements would square off against each other in a competition that would last for eighty years.

From Concessions to Coffers

By 1900 most Jersey Shore resorts discovered that they could increase their municipal treasury with monies generated by beachfront enterprises. In Monmouth Beach, Allenhurst, and Spring Lake that meant pool and bath clubs for which the resorts charged annual membership fees. In Point Pleasant, Seaside Heights, Wildwood, Ocean City, and Cape May it meant rental fees from Boardwalk arcades and concert halls. Even Raritan Bay Shore towns such as Keansburg and Cliffwood Beach in Aberdeen Township added to their municipal coffers by leasing portions of their waterfronts.

With a Boardwalk decorated by founder Bradley with curious antique oddities and an annual municipal budget stretched to its limits, city hall saw opportunity waiting on its beachfront. In 1903, with the persuasive help of druggist-turned-property-investor Dr. Hugh Kinmonth, city hall successfully pressured the seventy-three-year-old Bradley to sell his mile-long Boardwalk and its various pavilions. He received $100,000 for his assets, which included a one-story open-air beach pavilion near Wesley Lake, the fishing pier, an elevated circular band shell, and three bathhouses. City hall immediately started upgrading its mile-long acquisition.

By that summer, a new two-story Casino with windows and a wrap-around porch designed by architect William Cottrell of Asbury Park replaced Bradley's old rustic pavilion. Built for a cost of $60,000, it had a seating capacity of seven thousand, and concessions for rent. Soon a bathhouse and laundry were added. Two years later, a second pavilion was built out over the beach at Fifth Avenue and became the musical summer performance home of Arthur Pryor and his band. Like the Casino, it had space for concessions. For a number of years, the prime space was occupied by the Black Cat Café. For the Seventh Avenue beachfront, budding architect Theodore Brazer drafted plans for a High Victorian pavilion with distinctive rounded ends that earned it the nickname of the Birdcage when it was built.

MR. ARTHUR PRYOR.
ASBURY PARK'S POPULAR BANDMASTER.
"ON JERSEY SHORE"

In 1904 Pryor composed "On Jersey Shore," a march using traditional harmony. Borrowing a technique from his mentor, John Philip Sousa, Pryor would always close his concerts with a rousing march to get the audience up and out. Pike Archives.

One of the Boardwalk's earliest sweets emporiums, Leiding & Hintze had a counter in the Casino that featured Whitman's chocolates, popcorn, Crispettes, saltwater taffy, and chop suey. Leiding & Hintze had a sit-down ice cream parlor in the Natatorium two blocks away on the Boardwalk. Circa 1920. Pike Archives.

City hall's next bold move occurred in 1912 with the opening of the Natatorium. Unlike Allenhurst or Spring Lake, Asbury Park intended this pool club for use in the winter as part of its ongoing efforts to develop into an all-season resort destination. The two-story Greco-Roman pavilion housed a heated indoor saltwater swimming pool with separate hot and cold saltwater baths; concessions faced the Boardwalk. Required by Bradley's deed restrictions to leave the eastern end of each avenue at the Boardwalk open to the Atlantic, the $125,000 swimming pavilion was carefully erected between First and Second Avenues.

This same care was used at the northern end of the Boardwalk, where an outdoor saltwater pool was built across from Brazer's Birdcage. Not coincidentally, the first significant hotel construction in the twentieth century was also going up at this end of Ocean Avenue. The design for both the New Monterey Hotel and the Seventh Avenue pool house reflected the second decade's Spanish Revival movement; both buildings were capped with terra-cotta barrel tile roofs.

SUGGESTIONS

SODAS

With Ice Cream, any flavor	$ .20
Plain, any flavor	.10

SPECIAL DRINKS
Ginger Ale

Cliquot Club	.25
Delatour	.10 and .25
Imported	.25 and .40
"Special"	.20

FRESH FRUIT DRINKS

Orangeade	.20
Lemonade	.20
Grape Juice	.15 and .20
Grape Juice Surprise	.25

PURE MILK DRINKS

Milk Shakes, with Ice Cream	.20
Milk Float	.30
Frosted Chocolate	.20
Frosted Broadway	.35
Malted Milk	.25
Malted Milk with Egg	.30
Milk Shake with Egg	.30

Egg Phosphate	.30
Distilled Water	.10
Mineral Water	.10

CASINO SHOPPE
Edw. Zergiebel
Manager

SUGGESTIONS

ICE CREAM

Chocolate, Vanilla, Strawberry	$ .20
Mixed Flavors	.20
French Vanilla Cream	.25

SUNDAES

Hot Fudge	.25
Mocha Nougat	.25
Chocolate Nut	.25
Maple Nut	.25
Coffee Nut	.25
Marshmallow	.25
Cherry	.25
Pineapple	.25
Strawberry	.25

FRESH FRUIT SUNDAES

Peach	.30
Strawberry	.30
Pineapple	.30

SPECIALS

Peach Melba	.35	Banana Royal	.50
Cantaloupe Frappe	.45	Asbury Park Special	.30
College Ice	.40	Boardwalk Flip	.35
Swiss Chocolate Sundae	.40	Fruit Salad	.30
French Frappe	.35	Chop Suey Sundae	.30
Banana Split	.35	Casino Delight	.35

We Serve French and American Ice Creams

NATATORIUM SHOPPE
M. Bergner
Manager

Leiding & Hintze
Proprietors

Coney Island Comes to Asbury Park

To remain competitive with the Boardwalk, even the Ocean Avenue amusement circuit underwent a transformation, notably at Second Avenue. In 1913, Coney Island amusements impresario George Tilyou inked a deal with George Ameli of Ocean Grove to upgrade Ameli's antiquated nineteenth-century amusements, which he called the Flag. When it came to amusements rides, Tilyou had no equal in the Northeast. Beyond Coney Island, he took his brand to a recreational island off the coast of Bridgeport, Connecticut, and also stamped it on a pier in Atlantic City. With the grinning caricature of his brother as Tilyou's signature marquee, the Steeplechase amusements formula guaranteed financial success. In the aftermath of the Bristol Hotel fire, the Steeplechase corner was extended the full length of the block to Third Avenue. Just as at Coney Island, there was an air hole to balloon women's skirts when they exited on Ocean Avenue. There was a Barrel of Fun, two huge slides, an above-ground roller coaster, a Wedding Ring ride that spun men and women together, and a below-the-street dark ride in boats called the Ghost Ride.

The Second Avenue makeover was well-timed to take advantage of the increased crowds that had come ever since Sunday trains were allowed to stop at the Asbury

---

Sweet Memories

I WAS A TEENAGER WHEN I WENT TO WORK IN THE family business: the Miramar Grill and Diana Sweets on the Boardwalk inside Convention Hall. In the late sixties, everyone seemed to know (or have worked for) my grandfather, Gus Sareotes, who had been running restaurant concessions on the Boardwalk since the early 1920s. He'd tell me endless stories about the "good ole days" when people wore evening coats and gowns to stroll the Boardwalk. There were some not-so-good days—like when his Pier Tea Room met the hurricane of '44 [and] all they found was the storefront façade and the safe, which washed ashore several days later.

My memory of Convention Hall is drawn to the aroma of violently popping corn and caramelized butter, the scent of salt air and damp wood outside. Summer brought a strong bouquet of patchouli, musk, and pot from hundreds of rock 'n' rollers sitting on the patterned marble floor awaiting a concert. A whiff of our famous popcorn ultimately prevailed, and folks would line up for it, for candy apples and my grandpa's homemade pralines and fudge.

My dad, Harry Alikas, starred as the Miramar's chef personality for more than twenty years. His impromptu humor, movie-star good looks (and great cooking!) engrossed an audience of regulars. I still meet people miles from home who remember Dad and smile.

– Diana Alikas, event producer
Santa Monica, California

Park and Ocean Grove station in 1912. But make no mistake: Tilyou and Ameli were also taking aim at their most formidable competitor, who was right there in the resort a mere two blocks away. The men were taking on Ernest Schnitzler.

The Palace

A son of German immigrants who learned the amusement trade in Atlantic City, by 1890 Schnitzler already owned several jewels in the amusements crown. Perhaps the most significant was his carousel, made by famed Coney Island craftsman and German émigré Charles I. D. Looff. The furniture-maker-turned-wood-carver captured in mid-gallop the majestic animals from the African plains; the wild manes, whimsically painted decorations, and colored cabochons of glass garnered the oohs and ahs of young and old alike. Schnitzler built a square carousel house to protect his magnificent purchase; the large barnlike structure had a double hipped roof separated by a row of windows on all four sides. Doors at the street level were fitted with clear glass outlined with small multicolored panes. Oriental rugs graced the floors and tall cachepots containing ferns gave the interior a sophisticated appearance. In good weather, Schnitzler slid the doors back to reveal the richly painted menagerie and let the alluring melody of the steam organ out onto Kingsley Street and Lake Avenue.

The Seventh Avenue pool and pavilion neatly complemented the Mediterranean style of the Monterey Hotel across Ocean Avenue, and hotel guests were given passes to use it. In the background of the photograph is the Asbury Park Auditorium, owned by founder James Bradley. Pike Archives.

Schnitzler's second jewel was the Crystal Maze, which he promoted as the first labyrinth of glass and mirrors in New Jersey. Appropriately enough, the entrance was across the light-reflecting waters of Wesley Lake. Schnitzler lived with his wife and daughter on the second and third floors of the building. Between the two buildings was a narrow opening perfect for his third sparkling attraction.

In 1893 Schnitzler installed a sixty-seven-foot vertical rotating wheel crowned by a twenty-four-foot observation deck. Riders disembarked on one level and then climbed a set of iron stairs to the covered platform to take in a stunning panoramic view of Asbury Park, Ocean Grove, and beyond. Schnitzler's wheel had eighteen coaches, which held up to eight passengers each and were encased with galvanized wire mesh. Each coach was jauntily covered in a striped, peaked canvas roof. Shrewdly, Schnitzler named each car after a prominent city in the United States. The letters were painted in gold against a background of black paint. The observation deck and wheel earned him a patent from the U.S. Patent Office.

Even though rain hampered the wheel's official Fourth of July inauguration, when the skies cleared a few days later an explosion of color in the sky over Wesley Lake beckoned the evening's merrymakers. Festooned with eighty individual lights, the observatory was a beacon piercing the falling twilight. Schnitzler's wheel, studded in a

Tropical Fruit Extracts and Melting Cocoa

LOUIS KARAGIAS, ANGELUS SAKELARIS, AND NICHOLAS Panagiotopoulos came from the land of honeyed nuts and sugared pastries to open candy stores on the Boardwalk before World War II. Before each left the seaside city, all the men had parlayed their considerable cooking skills with chocolate and saltwater taffy into a Jersey Shore tradition.

Karagias opened Criterion Candies in 1929; [he] tried his hand at having a Boardwalk restaurant but switched full-time to candy the day he bought a taffy machine. By the early sixties [it] was all candy all the time, with a choice of brittles, patties, caramel apples, pecan balls, fudge, and taffy.

Sakelaris opened the Caramel Shop, moved to the 500 block of Cookman Avenue across from Steinbach's, and then moved out to Route 35 in Ocean Township in 1957. A 1939 advertisement depicted the Caramel Shop as "the sweetest place in town," and coconut snowflakes sold for 20 cents a pound.

Panagiotopoulos opened the Berkeley Sweet Shoppe in the Warren Whitney–designed arcade opposite the Berkeley-Carteret Hotel in 1925 and eventually opened a kitchen and candy store on the Seaside Heights boardwalk where the family continues to operate the business today.

Another thriving saltwater taffy business was Jonathan's, operated by the Arbes family.

– Adapted from *The Coaster*, February 11, 1999

kaleidoscope of three hundred colored lights whirling at a breathless seven revolutions per minute, spun gaily beneath the lit deck. His invention came none too soon.

Riverside Park opened on nineteen acres along the southern branch of the Shrewsbury River in the Pleasure Bay section of Long Branch. It boasted a hotel, a grove for picnicking plus a more formal dining pavilion, a large outdoor dance floor, fish pond games, and a splendid merry-go-round. Furthermore, there was a spectacular floating theater from which patrons heard the latest Gilbert and Sullivan operettas. As many as ten thousand people attended special events, many coming from Asbury Park via the trolley. It was the ideal, comfortable, middle-class alternative to the boisterous dance halls and gambling parlors that attracted the big city swells to the Branch's oceanfront. Before too long, Long Branch and other seaside resorts struck another competitive blow to Asbury Park. They replicated the wildly successful formula for attracting families that had helped put Asbury Park on the map: a Baby Parade.

Promote, Promote, Promote

To protect its Boardwalk franchise, city hall realized the time had come to reach outside its borders and hire a professional promoter in order to redirect the traveling public's attention to Asbury Park. That promoter was the dapper, mustachioed Harold B. Ayres, who made a number of immediate changes once he signed on. For one, Ayres moved the Baby Parade from July to August to fill in the gap in events between July Fourth celebrations and Labor Day festivities. For another, he found

Baby, Oh, Baby

THE CROWD THAT GATHERED TO WITNESS THIS FIRST parade was the largest Asbury Park had then ever brought together. The wave of enthusiasm that greeted the marchers proved that a pageant had been born that appealed to the heart as well as to the mind. . . . Nearly every country in the world has been represented. Last year long-distance prizes went to contestants from Brazil and London. This Coronation Day is now developing into a revival of the folk-lore stories and revels of those days when the world was younger, of the dreams and fairy tales of childhood and of all the pretty things the memory loves to retain. The Boardwalk, its pavilions, the amphitheater and the larger hotels are gay with a life and laughter that ripples and flows in a ceaseless torrent. All is innocent and joyous.

– Harold Ayres, promotional material, 1910

COMPLIMENTS OF THE
PALACE MERRY-GO-ROUND
ASBURY PARK, N.J.

SOUVENIR CARD

ASBURY PARK

WILBUR WRIGHT

WALTER BROOKINS

The Ocean Grove Auditorium Seats 10,000
Finest in the World
SOUSA AND HIS BAND, Saturday, August 13, at 3 p.m. and 8 p.m.
Children's Festival Concert, Wed. Eve., Aug. 17. Children's Fairyland Festival, Sat. Eve., Aug. 20.
Big Airship Meet here, August 10 to 19 inclusive. Come down and watch the fliers
GET A COPY OF LIPPINCOTT'S MAGAZINE

TOP *Ernest Schnitzler learned the amusement trade in Atlantic City, which he left in 1881 to establish himself in the up-and-coming resort of Asbury Park with a square carousel house overlooking Wesley Lake. Pike Archives.*

BOTTOM *By trading off Asbury Park's reputation as a travel destination, promoters of the Asbury Park Aero and Motor Club lured hundreds to an aviation meet in nearby Interlaken; the meet featured Wilbur Wright. The souvenir postcard also promoted Sousa's band, which was playing at the Ocean Grove Auditorium that same August weekend in 1910. Pike Archives.*

corporate sponsors such as pioneering ready-made baby-food manufacturer and pickle maker H. J. Heinz of Pittsburgh to replace Bradley. Eager to reach as many as ten thousand potential customers in exchange for underwriting the cost of prizes, Heinz signed up. Ayres's flair for florid prose was a bonus.

To increase public participation, Ayres also added a division for young girls and added the category of queen for women. On one notable occasion, the chosen Queen

TOP *Two of the three attractions that existed on Ocean Avenue between the two corner hotels at Second and Third, circa 1900. George Ameli of Ocean Grove owned this modest amusement strip and called it the Flag. Pike Archives.*

BOTTOM *Architect Whitney Warren designed twin Boardwalk pavilions in the mid-1920s. The southern one replaced wooden bathhouses between Asbury and First Avenues; the northern one was attached to the Berkeley-Carteret Hotel via a bridge over Ocean Avenue. Both were destroyed by fires in the early 1960s. Pike Archives.*

Titania was silent-picture actress Mary Pickford, in town to promote a new picture, providing a double bonus of promotion. Ayres even created a men's category named for Puck, the mischievous imp in Shakespeare's *A Midsummer Night's Dream*. Before too long, though, Ayres took his romantic ideas and blowsy bon mots and left to promote the Spanish Trail across America's Southwest.

Convention-al Idea

A new travel trend was taking hold in America. As the Industrial Revolution gave rise to product shows in which manufacturers could display their wares, the sale, distribution, accounting, and retailing of this merchandise in turn gave rise to a new category of employees: office workers, clerical and sales staff, and managers. The rise of trade conventions was paralleled to some extent by the convening of such groups as teachers, lawyers, dentists, doctors, and of course, temperance crusaders. In 1905 Asbury Park hosted the annual convention of the National Education Association, and thirty-five thousand teachers and their families descended on the twin cities of Asbury Park and Ocean Grove for one glorious week that summer.

Working the Boardwalk

ONE SUMMER I WORKED THE PONY TRACK ON FIFTH Avenue, just west of Skokas's hot dog stand. I'd get up at 5 a.m., ride my bike five-plus miles "out back" of Asbury to the stables, comb and saddle the ponies, ride them back through Asbury . . . and spend all day helping young 'uns around the track for maybe a nickel or a dime tip! (I got paid eleven dollars a week.) About 9 p.m. I'd mount up and ride 'em back to the stables, water 'em, and hang up the saddles, and then ride my bike back home.

Grandpa Bacardi, Rum King to this day, came up each summer from Puerto Rico with kids and grandkids to ride on every ride in Asbury. . . . I also worked two summers piloting the swan boat on Wesley Lake, providing kiddies and parents with fun and easy non-purple jokes and answers about the Shore. My boss, Bob Fountain, managed, owned, or leased a lot of such Boardwalk games. [He] always dressed like he came out of a bandbox and I admired his "looks," ethics, and strict rules of behavior.

I also worked for two summers ('36, '37) on Fourth Avenue setting up and taking down a ten-foot-long British telescope with an eight-inch-diameter lens that gave you nonfog visibility up to eighteen miles at sea. Daytime we'd say, "See the ships and people on deck," "Read the ship's name," "Watch local fishing yachts." We couldn't swing it around to watch any girls on the Boardwalk or hotel rooms because Boardwalkers might ram into the barrel!

– Leslie H. Eames
Morris Plains, New Jersey

TOP *Park Steel and Iron Company, Bradley Beach, received the contract to build the Paramount Theater and Convention Hall, seen here under construction in 1928. Courtesy of Catherine and Michael Barry.*

BOTTOM *Convention Hall was built with 60,000 square feet of space that could be used to seat large groups or for displays at trade or sporting exhibitions. It was outfitted with a Kilgen theater organ built in St. Louis. Its first official convention took place on July 5, 1930, when the Friar's Club of New York booked the hall for its annual meeting. Among the celebrities attending were "Gentleman Jim" Corbett, Mitt Gross, Georgie Price, Bobby Clark, and Arthur "Bugs" Baer. Pike Archives.*

The Paramount's interior was done in the classic art deco colors of gold, black, and purple. Wings, which in 1927 had won the first Oscar for best picture, was the first movie shown here, on New Year's Day 1930. Walter Reade Sr. officially marked the theater's opening with a public gala based on a second showing of the movie on July 11. Hollywood luminaries, including Wings leading man Charles "Buddy" Rogers, came, along with the Marx Brothers, Ed Wynn, Fredric March, Carole Lombard, and Ginger Rogers. Courtesy of Unique Images of New Jersey by Ruth R. Bennett, Asbury Park.

Once again, looking for innovative ways to be a year-round resort, city leaders turned to the idea of building a convention center that could attract visitors in the winter as well as summer. They didn't have to look far for a location. Their target was the eyesore occupying the entire block north of Atlantic Square. Used for public meetings, entertainment, and as an indoor winter gymnasium for high school students, the Asbury Park Auditorium was not aging gracefully. Unlike the gleaming new whitewashed pavilions on the Boardwalk, this sagging structure, owned by James Bradley, was unimaginatively dull.

A year into elected office, Mayor Clarence E. F. Hetrick in 1916 hired the nationally recognized architectural firm of McKim, Mead and White to design a convention center for this block. Their plan called for a five-thousand-seat venue that would cost $750,000, plus an additional $50,000 for the land. The only hitch? Founder Bradley refused to sell.

Five years later, to commemorate the city's fiftieth anniversary, a larger-than-life-size statue of James Bradley gazing at the beachfront was placed in the center of Atlantic Square shortly after his death. It was the last open parcel in the Sunset Lake greensward, which spanned seven and a half blocks from the North Asbury Park station to the sea. Bradley's unobstructed view of the Atlantic Ocean wouldn't last.

Arthur C. Steinbach, a buyer for his family's downtown department store, scored a real estate coup when he and his investors bought the Auditorium block from the Bradley estate and proceeded to build the Berkeley-Carteret Hotel. By the time it opened in 1925, the hotel's design included a pedestrian bridge over Ocean Avenue leading to a matching two-story red-brick Boardwalk pavilion similarly designed by the hotel's architect, noted Beaux-Arts stylist Whitney Warren of New York. The hotel's presence forced Mayor Hetrick to find a new site.

Grappling with the Con

SECRECY IN FULL PUBLIC VIEW: I LEARNED IT AT Convention Hall, in 1965, from Dr. Jerry Graham.

He called himself "Dr." Jerry because he had a B.S. in psychology from Arizona State. He was a regular on the pro-wrestling cards promoted by former Asbury mayor Roland J. Hines. (If you wanted tickets, you could buy them at the box office, or just go over to his house. Mrs. Hines kept the choicest ones in a shoebox, amidst living room clutter.)

The rule was, if the bad guy applied an illegal hold, he had until the ref counted to four to break it, on pain of disqualification. In his cunning, Dr. Jerry would choke a downed opponent to the count of three, release his grip momentarily, then grab the throat again. The outrage! The devastation! The exploitation of the rule of law!

I was at ringside, and the crowd was on its feet in anger. Impassively, Dr. Jerry scanned the front row: the elderly lady in the print dress with her stockings rolled at her ankles; the screaming ten-year-old; the guy with the pencil mustache and the cigarillo, with his blonde date; the distraught teen girl, frightened for the stricken hero. All were nearly strangling themselves with moral indignation.

Well—except for me. I remained seated, smiling contentedly. Dr. Jerry's emotionless gaze reached me and stopped a moment. For a golden nanosecond he grinned, then returned to throttling his victim.

No one else saw that grin. They were too enraged to see it. In those days, the wrestlers never let you in on the con.

A lesson well-learned in politic sagacity and the advantages of composure. Dr. Jerry, wherever you may be—right back at you, brother.

– Will Morrisey
Rumson, New Jersey

Now a utilities lobbyist, Hetrick was well aware of the recent opening of Madison Square Garden and its 19,000-seat arena designed for indoor boxing matches, ice hockey games, bicycle meets, and circus events. The mayor also knew of a similar project on the drawing board for Atlantic City. That mammoth hall was to have 140,000 square feet of exhibition space, 40,000 seats, and the capability of holding indoor football games and of flooding the floor for ice shows and hockey games. The initial construction cost was estimated at $5 million. Couldn't Asbury Park approve a mere $2 million for a convention hall and theater to keep the resort competitive?

"While we have hesitated, Atlantic City has added $100,000,000 in valuations," Hetrick fumed in February 1928. "While the Traymores and Breakers and other imposing structures have been built over a period of 25 years, we can show only the Monterey, the Berkeley-Carteret, the Asbury-Carlton, and the Palace," he said in the *Asbury Park Press*.

In 1927, a fire of undetermined origin destroyed much of the Fifth Avenue Arcade, located over the beach, and a month before Hetrick's agitated remarks, a winter fire destroyed the Casino. The two disasters helped deliver the votes Hetrick needed in a special bond referendum to build the theater and hall. Whitney Warren and his lawyer partner, Charles Wetmore, were contracted to design a statement-making civic complex, and they did. Beginning curbside with an arched walkway, followed by a theater sheathed in red brick and purple tile, the compound crossed the Boardwalk in a skylighted arcade and extended 215 feet over the beach and sea on steel-encased concrete pilings. Its placement? Directly in James Bradley's line of vision.

The exuberant architectural and decorative statements the building made were undeniable, and they were enhanced further by its unobstructed location across from Atlantic Square. Not visible, though, were design shortcomings that were to become liabilities in the decades ahead. Unlike Atlantic City's Convention Hall, which backed into Pacific Avenue and was designed with rear and side loading docks, the beachfront

Boxers Jack Dempsey and Max Baer flanked an aspiring pugilist on May 5, 1934. Baer, who had attended Asbury Park High School prior to turning pro in 1929, was training in a makeshift ring near the Boardwalk where paying spectators could watch him work out for his upcoming heavyweight championship match with Primo Carnera on June 14 at the Madison Square Garden Bowl in Long Island City. Baer won in the eleventh round. Pike Archives.

hall had no such access. Furthermore, despite promotional claims that Asbury Park was an ideal winter resort, there was no heating plan for the theater or the hall.

As the city had already contracted with Warren and Wetmore for twin solarium Boardwalk pavilions at Sunset and Asbury Avenues, Mayor Hetrick was running out of space for a heating plant. Although it could have been built three blocks away next to the municipal sewer plant at the Eighth Avenue Boardwalk, Hetrick had something else in mind. He asked Warren and Wetmore for still more buildings, and the municipal burden doubled from the initial $2 million to $4 million of construction debt.

There was the new concrete-and-limestone beach Casino to replace William Cottrell's wood one. Not only did the Warren footprint feature an entertainment arena with a floor that could be used for ice or trade shows, but in a separate wing connected by a covered arcade there was concession space for indoor amusements and food stands. Its anchor was a spectacular three-quarter-circular carousel house decorated with copper, its roofline lined with white lights. It was placed at the Casino's western end at the foot of Lake Avenue. Two blocks away was Schnitzler's Palace merry-go-round.

The new heating plant went up south of the new Casino at the foot of Wesley Lake. Pipes were laid under the Boardwalk to heat the Natatorium, two blocks north of the Casino, and then to the Paramount Theater, another four blocks north. A near duplicate of Warren's blueprint for a library in Louvain, France, the plant was a stylis-

Civil Rights Comes to the Boardwalk

WHEN I THINK ABOUT FIGHTING TO HAVE TEACHERS' pensions funded, my mother's memory comes into my mind. Marie Harris Thomas grew up in Asbury Park in the early 1900s as a member of the only African American family on Heck Street. My family had the only funeral home for ethnic people in Monmouth and Ocean Counties. F. Leon Harris, the son of Fortune Harris, was the first, and only, African American coroner for Monmouth County.

During the civil rights movement in the 1960s, my mother marched on the Boardwalk to [support] justice and human rights for all people. At the time, ethnic minorities were isolated to a certain area of the beach and not allowed to walk the Boardwalk or purchase anything from concessions. The Natatorium was also segregated, and there were no swimming or park facilities on the West Side.

My mother loved telling Bible stories and reading morals to us at the dinner table. The most important thing she told us was to live up to the family's expectations and bring honor to the family name.

– Claire Thomas Garland, president (ret.),
Tinton Falls Education Association
Lincroft, New Jersey

Mayor Hetrick inaugurated an annual tulip festival with the planting of two million bulbs. Local model and movie ingénue Norma Rae Eberhardt was Miss Holland at this May event, which included adventure travel writer Lowell Thomas (with mustache) and Monmouth County clerk and chairman of the county's Republican Party J. Russell Woolley (extreme left). Pike Archives.

tic blend of Beaux-Arts and emerging elements of art moderne, notably in the plant's angular smokestack. The building's Boardwalk frontage featured concessions and a second-floor solarium. Just like the theater and convention hall complex, the sheer mass of the Casino combined with the adjacent heating plant blocked the ocean view while also destroying Bradley's original intent to have a parklike setting on the northern perimeter of Wesley Lake.

This new complex represented more than a heating solution. Looking out for his West Side constituents, Mayor Hetrick staffed the new concession and bathhouse with African Americans and decreed that the beach bordering Ocean Grove was for them; over time the beach earned the racist nickname of the Inkwell. In 1890 Bradley had permitted African Americans some limited beach access at the foot of First Avenue between the hours of four and five o'clock every afternoon, but this new complex created a whites-only beach north of the Casino. The segregation was further heightened by the plant's size, which hid black bathers from the view of white bathers.

The Height of Hubris

Completely unruffled by the troubles of the New York Stock Exchange, Hetrick insisted Boardwalk rents would bring twenty thousand dollars a year to city coffers.

The World's "Largest" Saltwater Pool: The Monte Carlo

- Opening day: June 28, 1942.

- Construction cost: $500,000.

- Dimensions of main pool: 240´ by 175´.

- No. of gallons: 1.3 million.

- Saltwater sources—two 12-inch pipelines from 24 filter pods beneath ocean floor located 1,000 feet off shore; 6,000-gallon-a-minute pumping capacity into the pool's northeast corner.

- Heated to "Gulf Stream" temps.

- Southeast corner: 8´ deep; all other corners: 5´8".

- Diving pool: 60´ by 32´ by 9½´ deep; 4 one-meter boards and 2 three-meter boards; local swimming sensation Dick Steadman was hired for fancy diving shows.

- Children's wading pool: 16" deep; shells decorate the bottom.

- A three-story, 300-foot-long brick colonial structure on the south side of pool housed equipment to care for 7,500 bathers.

- Cabanas with porches lined the first and second floors facing the pool; a four-person cabana with shower rented for $151 for the season while a one-person locker rented for $16.

- A 1,000-seat stadium with sundeck occupied the third floor.

- The facilities for bathers included automatic dryers, and footbaths through which ocean bathers had to pass before entering the pool.

- A second building housed a restaurant and cocktail lounge that featured live music. Tony Pastor and his orchestra opened the 1946 season after the end of World War II.

- Irish junipers and variegated evergreens surrounded the pool on three sides for privacy.

- The U.S. War Production Board granted movie mogul Walter Reade Sr. a fifteen-day extension to finish its construction.

- The Monte Carlo's closest rival at the time was the saltwater pool at Palisades Amusement Park, which measured 400 by 600 feet and held 2.5 million gallons of saltwater.

Walter Reade Sr. built to take advantage of the best of both worlds: a saltwater pool and private cabana club with views of the ocean and Deal Lake, and access to the beach via a tunnel under the Boardwalk. Pike Archives.

As his critics became louder, Hetrick shouted them down with the declaration that the new theater and hall wouldn't have to earn back its investment: their very presence alone would draw awestruck crowds to Asbury Park.

Hetrick further scoffed at protests from theater mogul Walter Reade, who owned four theaters in Asbury Park by this point and was complaining that another stage was a glut on the circuit. "The theater is a necessity," Hetrick retorted, "because if we are to function as a resort we must provide adequate amusement facilities."

Reade did wind up with the city contract to book films, and in a complex film distribution deal he brokered with Paramount–Famous Players–Lasky Corporation, the city theater was christened the Paramount. Reade also wrung from the city the right to book entertainment other than films in order to meet his monthly rent obligation. But city hall limited the entertainment to wholesome family fare, and as the Depression deepened, Reade stopped showing films at the Paramount, and the city closed it in the winter months.

Swimming with Buster Crabbe

IN THOSE DAYS YOU COULD GET WORKING PAPERS at the age of fourteen to work part-time. My summer job (1945–1946) was as a locker girl at the magnificent Monte Carlo pool, which covered the whole block of Ocean Avenue and Kingsley Street. The Olympic-size pool was probably one of the reasons that Buster Crabbe and his troupe were attracted to it.

Word went out that the well-known and very popular Hollywood swim star would be coming to Asbury Park [one-week engagement beginning July 22, 1946] and that they would be in need of some local swimmers to "fill in" for their synchronized swimming act. These were the days of the grand and glorious Esther William films (no one could ever figure out how she could swim underwater forever with a broad smile on her face and not a hair out of place).

There were tryouts and many days of practice. You can imagine how beautiful and sophisticated the Buster Crabbe troupe looked in the eyes of an unsophisticated fourteen-year-old who had hardly left Asbury Park. The costumes, mostly one more beautiful swimsuit after another, the makeup, [the] lighting and sound technicians seemed so worldly having come all the way from Hollywood.

[Crabbe's] troupe arrived several days before the show was to be presented and we began rehearsals. Over and over again, doing leg lifts and shallow dives, turns and twists underwater to the lovely ballads of the day. The high divers and the clowns mostly used the diving pool with the clowns falling off the edge of the diving board, hitting the water in strange positions to draw laughter from the youngsters.

I'm not even sure we were compensated for our efforts. Just the fun and excitement of being part of the show was enough. I think the show ran for three days with two evening performances.

– Mary Arbour Saunders
St. Augustine, Florida

The price tag for the Paramount, the Convention Hall complex, and the Casino complex—intended as monuments to civic grandeur—totaled a staggering $4.5 million. Asbury Park plunged further into debt as the 1930s wore on. The traveling public stayed home, and the city watched its property tax collection drop precipitously.

In an attempt to wring every possible rental opportunity out of its oceanfront, city hall set its sights on the new national craze for miniature golf. The courses didn't interfere with founder Bradley's vision for open-ended vistas at the end of each avenue. Nearly all the landscaped stretches between the Boardwalk pavilions were redone with eighteen-hole courses. Competition soon followed from across Ocean Avenue. On undeveloped tax-paying parcels, entrepreneurs built the largest and most elaborate of all of Asbury Park's miniature golf courses, with two different landscaped courses featuring a total of thirty-six holes. One was located in the middle of the Fifth Avenue block between Ocean Avenue and Kingsley Street. The other was located on the otherwise empty block north of the New Monterey Hotel. For the same price as the Boardwalk courses, patrons could play twice as many holes.

ABOVE *A horse carved by Frank Caretta for the Philadelphia Toboggan Company's carousel No. 87, which was delivered to the Casino in 1932. Pike Archives.*

RIGHT *The Casino, arcade, and African American–owned concession seen from Ocean Grove. Pike Archives.*

But Boardwalk revenue was so meager that the city couldn't afford to advertise, stage, staff, and promote its famed Baby Parade. In 1932 the parade was cancelled, and the department pinned its hopes on a different kind of attraction to bring in families. Something to last the season, not just a special event. What they were hoping for at the foot of First Avenue was that Bob Fountain would lure families to the Boardwalk with a collection of outdoor rides geared toward children.

The city was not alone in its struggles to lure vacationers. On the cusp of the Roaring Twenties, Ernest Schnitzler had retired to Lake Weir, Florida, selling his business to Augustus M. Williams of Brooklyn, New York. Within ten years, Williams switched from coal-powered steam to the cheaper and more efficient electricity supplied by the Atlantic Coast Electric Company to run the Ferris wheel and the carousel. As maintenance costs climbed after the 1929 stock market crash, Williams removed Schnitzler's patented observatory deck. He also added the Palace's first dark ride, a one-level amusement he called the Ghost Train. At the end of Prohibition, Williams bought Schoen's, the German restaurant next door to the Palace on Kingsley Street, and used its footprint to create the Palace's first funhouse.

The Casino arena's interior with the stage set up for a band concert, the floor left open for dancing. Pike Archives.

Commercial Tragedy

As the Depression deepened, the wealthy vacationers that Asbury Park coveted were harder to lure. Airplane travel out of Newark Airport and ocean liners had captured their attention. Adaptations of the designs of World War I transport ships gave rise to the luxury floating hotels that provided those eager to escape Prohibition's restrictions with a chance to do so. One such liner, christened for a fort overlooking the harbor in Havana, Cuba, was the Ward Line's sleek 508-foot *Morro Castle*. It was one of the faster ships to ply the 1,160-mile mail-cargo-and-tourist route to Cuba, where rum was $4 a gallon and shipboard liquor 25 cents a shot.

As long as the Morro Castle *remained marooned off the beach near Convention Hall, the public came and concessionaires stayed open. Georgia Pappyliou Burns, whose parents had a concession, recalled, "Were we ever happy to see all those people." The* Morro Castle *remained until March 1935, when it finally was towed for salvage to New York. Courtesy of Catherine and Michael Barry.*

The liner had a veranda tearoom, a sundeck, and a balcony overlooking the first-class lounge. Public rooms were lavishly trimmed in ornate wood reflecting different styles: Italian Renaissance for the first-class smoking room, Empire for the library and writing room; the ballroom orchestra played in a space designed to resemble a Viking ship. Passengers were older couples, younger singles, sports fishermen looking to angle marlin and tuna, and a steady stream of Cuban and American businessmen. Tickets cost an unbeatable $65, including a two-night stay in Havana.

On September 8, 1934, the six-year-old *Morro Castle* was making its return trip from Cuba when it mysteriously caught fire. It was 3 a.m. The ship was three miles off the Barnegat shore at the northern end of Long Beach Island when the fire first was noticed. Twenty-knot winds from a gathering hurricane fanned the flames. The captain had a fatal heart attack, his second in command was inexperienced, and the radioman later wound up under suspicion for sabotage. Soon the pleasure ship was a floating, burning deathtrap. Fifteen hours after the fire broke out, Coast Guard crews and first aid squads from Point Pleasant to Spring Lake had rescued 414 passengers and crew; 134 individuals were reported dead, including a number of children.

But the ordeal wasn't over. At 6:30 p.m., as tugs attempted to tow the still-burning *Morro Castle* through a nor'easter to New York Harbor, the winds shifted and burned the towlines. In the stormy current, the *Morro Castle* began drifting toward the Asbury Park beach. At 7:34 p.m., WCAP radio announcer Tom Burley was reading

Looky Loos

CRUISE SHIPS DID NOT SAIL FROM PHILADELPHIA in those days, and we didn't have the opportunity to see a real ocean liner up close, only newsreel shots of celebrities and VIPs aboard ships coming or going. So when the *Morro Castle* was beached at Asbury Park my Uncle John decided to drive up to see the stricken vessel. The final portion of the trip we encountered a great traffic jam. My uncle, a Philadelphia policeman, was bold. He pulled over to the road's shoulder and proceeded to pass the long line of cars on the right!

The beached ship showed the signs of distress caused by the fire. Some brave young men were attempting to swim out and board the hulk. One talked of the possible "riches" that might be salvaged. He told of a person who had boarded the ship and returned with an expensive cigarette case. A likely story. Even as a ten-year-old I could see there was no visible means to climb aboard.

We encountered the same traffic jam leaving Asbury Park. By now, other bold drivers were using the road shoulder to bypass the jam coming out of Asbury. We kids were very proud that our uncle had been the first!

– Joe Walker
Philadelphia, Pennsylvania

the headlines from the second-floor studio on the northern promenade of Convention Hall. Burley led with "The *Morro Castle* is adrift and heading for the shore." He paused, looked at the studio clock, then looked out the window. "My God!" he exclaimed into the microphone. "She's coming in right here!"

"Right here" turned out to be on a sandbar within forty yards of Convention Hall. By Sunday morning the storm had passed and crowds started to gather to see

Depression Day-Trippers

HOW WELL WE REMEMBER THE PRUDENTIAL Excursions! They . . . were intended to bolster Asbury Park's economy during the Great Depression, and were also of benefit to the Pennsylvania and New Jersey Central Railroad. . . . The five Branches (none of whom worked for Prudential) and Miss Emily Heath, our aunt who did, had a memorable day, second only to Christmas.

We boarded the train at either the Central Railroad Station on Broad Street or at the new Pennsylvania Station on Market Street. What a train! It must have had fifteen cars and two locomotives and it was packed. The train was just for us: it raced through the stations along the right-of-way as though they weren't there, with its puffing engine headed for ASBURY PARK. We felt very important, looking at the poor people standing by the tracks lost in a cloud of cinders and dust; probably wondering what it was all about. . . . However, we finally arrived at the Asbury Park station, got off the train, and headed down Asbury Avenue toward the ocean. All you could smell was saltwater.

The first order of the day was swims in the [Natatorium] and the ocean. You could rent a swimsuit and bathhouse for the day for fifty cents or so. The suits were made of thick wool, and when they got wet, they weighed a ton and itched like the devil. We changed out [of our] clothes in a little room just big enough to turn around in. They gave you a key with a leather loop on it. If you lost it there was a charge . . . we never lost ours.

How well we remember . . . the booth with the sand sculpture right on the beach, where you could toss in your pennies and make a wish; the five-cent all-you-could-drink sodas; and the miniature golf courses; . . . those fascinating machines that "pulled" globs of taffy. . . . The merry-go-round had rings you grabbed as you flew by, then tossed into the large bin on the opposite side (a free ride if the ring you got was brass); . . . the [Fun] House with the rolling barrel that you could walk through (or could pass around if you were faint at heart). And who could forget the man in the booth who pushed the button for the air to blow up the ladies' skirts.

Last, but not least, there was the Ferris wheel and, during those days, the flagpole sitter. We always wondered just how he got way up there and how he did his thing. . . . On the lake side of the street were the motorboats. How we loved riding in them. . . .

Alas, those days are gone. . . . The Prudential Excursions were a casualty of World War II.

– Frederick W. Branch, Bloomfield, New Jersey,
and James R. Branch, Sarasota, Florida

The full text of this reminiscence can be found in the September 2002 edition of The New Town Crier, *the newsletter of the Historical Society of Bloomfield, New Jersey.*

the ship, which continued to burn, partly because of layers of decorative but highly flammable paint and varnish that coated its interior walls. Residents living near the beach not only sold refreshments but also went so far as to rent rooms, their lawns for tents, and their garages for touring trailers from the curious. City officials and a few opportunity-seeking residents tried to extract 25 cents from every visitor who arrived on the Boardwalk to look at the smoldering ship. In all, $7,750 was reportedly collected by city hall and distributed to various charitable foundations, including the West Side Community Center and West Side Mission. By October, the smell

of charred cowhides intended for leather factories and carried in the cargo hold so thoroughly permeated the air that residents and city hall alike wanted the ship gone. The *Morro Castle* remained offshore throughout the winter, however, before it was towed to Gravesend Bay in New York on March 14. Built for $5 million, it was scrapped for $33,605.

While the *Morro Castle* was a temporary and unplanned economic boon, the railroad companies were deliberately looking for incentives to bring day-trippers to New Jersey beaches. One of the earliest schedules was instituted

The miniature golf craze of the 1930s peaked in Asbury Park with courses on and off the Boardwalk. The largest privately owned course had thirty-six holes. This one was located on the Boardwalk at the foot of Second Avenue. Pike Archives.

June 23, 1930, when the Pennsylvania Railroad announced a new all-parlor car to Shore towns. The special train departed from New York on Fridays and returned on Sunday afternoons. In 1937, the Central Railroad of New Jersey joined with North Jersey corporations to start a new campaign. In one instance, 17,374 day-trippers from Bayonne arrived in Asbury Park on nineteen different train runs, each pulling twelve cars.

But by 1940, those who drove their cars rather than taking the train to Asbury Park found an additional expense waiting for them beachfront parking meters. It was yet another attempt by a hard-pressed city hall to find revenue.

A New Promoter

With seemingly no end in sight to the Depression, the city once again realized it had to go outside the community to hire a professional publicist. In 1935 it signed George Zuckerman, a tall, lanky man with a penchant for the latest in men's fashions and, after he went bald, a stylish hat that was always parked on his pate. He also developed a predilection for inflating weekend attendance figures on the beach and Boardwalk. Zuckerman's first achievement was a 1938 promotional film that could be shown as a "short" in regional movie theaters. Created to beckon travelers to Asbury Park, the camera languidly panned a crowded Boardwalk and beach, the well-manicured public gardens, James Bradley's statue, and the blue waters of Sunset Lake in a continuous loop for close to thirty minutes.

Zuckerman's next coup was arranging for the Mrs. America pageant finals to be staged in Convention Hall after preliminaries were held at Palisades Amusement Park. The rationale was obvious. Asbury Park was the resort that had launched the internationally recognized Baby Parade. While the racier Atlantic City had come up with the Miss America pageant, with its swimsuit competition and patriotic theme, Asbury Park still could pride itself as the North Shore's leading family resort, a wholly appropriate location in which to crown the ultimate housewife, who would

The Steeplechase in winter during the late 1930s. When the boiler blew up in the adjacent Albion Hotel in 1940, both the original wooden hotel and the adjacent amusement building were destroyed. Courtesy of Catherine and Michael Barry.

prove her worth by competing in such categories as speed vacuuming, ironing, baking, crocheting, and turning military corners on bedding. In 1946 Zuckerman also brought back the Baby Parade, placing advertisements for contestants in newspapers from Boston to Washington, D.C., and as far west as Pittsburgh.

Among the more successful promotional events Zuckerman imported to the Boardwalk was the Easter parade. Already popular in Atlantic City, the event held a special significance beyond the Christian observance. Boardwalk concessionaires and the Palace's new owners used the holiday event as a pre-opener for the summer season; they rolled up their shutters from Friday nights through Sunday afternoons until the traditional Memorial Day weekend arrived, all the while hoping for mild early-spring weather to bring the crowds.

Zuckerman, however, had to promote Asbury Park amid still more challenges. World War II rationing of milk, butter, eggs, sugar, meat, and gasoline, along with a recession, triggered a serious decline in overnight travelers. New Jersey's boardwalks were draped in black curtains so patrolling Nazi U-boats couldn't use the lights to site a target at night. Another blow was the devastating hurricane of 1944 and the lack of government aid to undo the estimated $25 million of damage the storm caused on the Boardwalk. Asbury Park was luckier than its rivals of Long Branch and Atlantic City. The Branch completely lost its boardwalk and

The Palace Merry-Go-Round, Ferris wheel, and hall of mirrors along Lake Avenue. To the right is what remained of Shoen's speakeasy restaurant on Kingsley. Courtesy of T. Frank Appleby.

only amusement pier, while the Queen of Resorts lost three of its seven miles of boardwalk. Asbury Park didn't rebuild the Boardwalk north of Deal Lake Drive that once went all the way to Loch Arbor. It didn't rebuild the wooden pavilions that had decorated the east side of the Boardwalk. And it kept the Casino closed until 1950, when there were finally enough funds for its repair despite public calls to tear it down.

After the War

In March 1950, the Central Railroad discontinued six of its Shore trains in response to an Interstate Commerce Commission's order for a 15 percent cut in service. In November 1951 the New Jersey Turnpike opened. It was the first major addition to the state's highway system since the Lincoln Highway in the 1920s. Linked to a growing interstate road network from New England to the mid-Atlantic and southern states, the Turnpike was the first indication that vacationers could traverse the entire Garden State without ever stopping at the seashore.

Up and down the New Jersey coast, the postwar tourism years were punctuated by various morals raids by state inspectors, county detectives, and local police. No

Working the Palace

DURING THE SUMMER OF 1969 I WORKED THE Palace's "Record-Wheel" (where for a dime you could win a 45 r.p.m. single of one of the hits of the day like "Honky-Tonk Woman" or "Pinball Wizard"). We wore pocketed aprons [to] supply change to anyone who wanted to try their luck at one of the myriad pinball machines or games of skill. [There were the days we had to rescue] some poor soul lost in the "Mirror-Maze" or deep inside the "Fun House." [One time] a salesman tested different brands of balloons on the "Water-Pistol" game to see which ones would pop the loudest. Edward Lange, who owned the Palace, was sort of Old World, and he and his son, George, worked very hard [and were] always kind to their employees.

I remember the lunches over at Harry's Diner on Cookman and Heck, taking a walk on the boards during our breaks, checking out Lange's wheel concessions in the Casino, and popping over to the [Stone] Pony after closing time (a few years later, my band, Java, would end up playing there every week). But my fondest memory is the feeling of camaraderie that we all had for each other at the Palace.

– Sandy Berman, feature film sound designer
Hollywood, California

On Easter Sunday 1954, Asbury Park's oceanfront was jammed with pedestrians and automobiles for the traditional start to the summer season. Classic Photo Collection/Dorn's Photography Unlimited, Red Bank, New Jersey.

one was immune, from the hotels and bars that quietly catered to homosexuals to fortunetellers to arcade owners who were locked in a pitched battle with authorities over what constituted illegal gambling—games of skill or games of chance. That controversy dragged on in Asbury Park until 1956, when a Monmouth County Superior Court judge determined that Abe Ruben's electric bingo game, Fascination, was a game of skill and therefore didn't come under jurisdiction of the state's anti-gambling statute.

A lawsuit brought by *Asbury Park Press* editor Wayne D. McMurray brought an end to the decades-long practice of private negotiations with city hall representatives for Boardwalk concessions. For the first time since Mayor Hetrick came into power, city hall had to publish the winning bids in 1956. It also had to list all the bids submitted and by whom. From 1956 through 1960 the city took in more than a half million dollars from twenty-three concessions.

Meanwhile, George Zuckerman faced his largest promotional hurdle when the Asbury Park exit on the Garden State Parkway opened six miles west of the

With preliminary rounds held at Palisades Amusement Park, the final crowning of Mrs. America took place in Asbury Park. Second from left in 1949 was Mrs. Newark, Ruth Cooper. The pageant was discontinued in 1968. Courtesy of Ruth Cooper.

Boardwalk in 1956. As more parkway exits opened, notably to Long Beach Island, the overnight motoring public found destinations other than Asbury Park in which to spend a week's vacation. Even with a steady influx of weekend day-trippers, partly drawn from the newcomers who had moved to Monmouth County, it was clear that the Boardwalk's glory was starting to fade. Its storm-battered bathhouses were in desperate need of modernization, and even the Natatorium was showing wear. After one last attempt to promote its indoor saltwater swimming pool as a shark tank, the city tore it down in 1962. The following year Zuckerman left Asbury Park to become executive director of the New Jersey Conference of Mayors.

From Baby Paraders to Baby Boomers

As city hall tried to figure out how to rejuvenate its Boardwalk, Zimel Resnick and Edward Lange were working on a half-million-dollar overhaul of the Palace, which they had acquired from Gus Williams in 1938. In 1955 they bought the adjacent Newark Hotel on Cookman Avenue and the old Turner's Grill and Ocean Spray Hotel over on Lake Avenue. They had the structures removed, along with the remains of the Kingsley Street funhouse. On Lake they installed overhead electric bumper cars. Farther inside they set up a circular bobsled. A deal with Walter Reade for the abandoned dressing rooms at the Lyric Theater on Cookman Avenue created room for a one-level dark ride that went by assorted names, including To Hell and Back. Moviegoers on the other side of the wall could hear the delighted screams of riders swinging by Boot Hill. The Looff carousel was joined by a fast-food stand shoehorned into the Lake and Kingsley corner, and nearby was a new mechanical circular ride for tots called the Bubble Bounce.

Civil engineer William H. Birtwell of Asbury Park designed a hollow-block concrete building with the kind of vaulted roof usually seen on bowling alleys to complete the new Kingsley and Cookman corner. Lange and Resnick retrofitted the Crystal Maze concept into a new two-story funhouse built against the alley that separated the Palace extension from the Lyric. They gave it a barrel entrance, tilted passageways, moving walkways, and closet-sized rooms where costumed employees hid behind glass to spook visitors walking through the dark maze. On the maze's old site they put in arcade games. Next door to the funhouse was an expanded design for another single-level dark ride, the jungle-themed Tunnel of Love. Under the roof of their new building on Kingsley they erected an intricate two-story, double-pretzel dark ride called the Oriental Express. In front of it they placed a freestanding airplane kiddy ride.

The grinning Coney Island icon used to attract thousands of thrill-seekers to the Palace's old competitor on Ocean Avenue was painted on the outside walls. The

A Different Kind of Revolution

My father ran a hotel in the early 1960s and knew Zimel Resnick because both attended Congregation Sons of Israel [on Asbury Avenue]. As I grew up, my father told me how Resnick had helped arm the Jewish defense in Israel.

Resnick owned a "gun collection" he sometimes kept hidden inside the Palace. Whenever someone approached Resnick about adding to this "collection," he took them on the Ferris wheel to avoid any possibility that the conversation might be overheard. The "collection" grew, and from time to time trucks arrived outside the Palace late at night to take Resnick's collection to the Hoboken docks where they were disassembled, placed in crates marked "sewing equipment," and placed in ships bound for the Holy Land.

– Heshy Rosenwasser, musician
Interlaken, New Jersey

hope was to attract teenagers and young adults whose fondest childhood memories recalled the fun they had at the Steeplechase. With any luck at all, young married adults might bring children of their own in tow.

From Big Bands to Rock Bands

The music scene was changing but hard to predict amid the transition from wartime to peacetime activities. The first postwar booking may also have been the last successful musical engagement for big bands in Asbury Park. Famed trumpeter Harry James, along with his touring orchestra, was brought in to inaugurate the summer

Merry Mibsters

I PRACTICED ON LINOLEUM AND KEPT MY AGATE covered with lard so it wouldn't crack. Those are the secrets to success if you want to be a marbles champ. In 1951 I placed third at the tournament in Asbury Park. I went back the next year and won with a borrowed agate. I was twelve years old.

Whoever played the best eleven games out of twenty-one won. In the finals I shot against James "Monk" Lily, who was fourteen. I won eleven games to six. In marbles lingo that means shooting "sticks" or seven marbles out of the ring in consecutive shots. I got a crown, a trophy, and a free trip to come back next year.

Asbury Park was just a great place. We stayed in a white house with [a] porch. It was a boardinghouse not far from the ocean. . . . I can remember we walked there. I remember playing miniature golf and other games on the Boardwalk.

My crown and trophy are in the National Marbles Hall of Fame in Wildwood, New Jersey. In 2002 I celebrated the fiftieth anniversary of my win. Now I'm training my grandson.

– Russell "Rusty" Gwaltney,
police captain (ret.), Salem, Virginia

Enthusiastically supported by Mayor George Smock II, the nation's annual marbles tournament gave Asbury Park a boost as a family travel destination. In 1952, Rusty Gwaltney and Dorothy Hobbs, both age fourteen, of Augusta, Georgia, were the boy and girl mibster champs. In 1960, the championship matches moved down the coast to Wildwood. Pike Archives.

season with a performance at Convention Hall on June 30, 1946. With midlist studio singers Marion Morgan and Buddy DeVito, James and his band swung through such well-known melodies as "Seems Like Old Times," "Moonglow," "Perdido," and "Who's Sorry Now," a 1923 standard the trumpeter had rewritten for himself and recorded earlier that year. Through an arrangement between WCAP and CBS Radio, the Sunday show was broadcast live on CBS affiliates, giving a nice promotional boost to Asbury Park across the country. But this was also the year when the black vocal harmony group the Ink Spots had two hit singles, "The Gypsy" and "To Each His Own." Anyone listening to the radio in Asbury Park at the time knew change was in the air. In fact, by year end, James retired altogether from performing and turned to raising thoroughbred racehorses.

Ten years later it was falsetto-singing sensation Frankie Lymon and the Teenagers who were booked, along with the Freddie Price Orchestra, a white dance band, to open the summer season at Convention Hall. Just four months earlier Lymon and the Teenagers had released the up tempo dance song "Why Do Fools Fall in Love?" In March budding radio rock DJ Alan Freed booked them for a show at the Brooklyn Paramount alongside the Platters and Bill Haley and His Comets. The next month a second single, "I Want You to Be My Girl," hit the charts, followed by an appearance on CBS-TV's *Shower of Stars.* By the end of April Frankie Lymon and the Teenagers were touring with the "Biggest Rock and Roll Show of 1956."

They arrived in Asbury Park on June 30. Just as they were launching into "Why Do Fools Fall in Love," a fistfight broke out. The 2,700 concertgoers spilled onto the Boardwalk, where an estimated 75,000 people were out enjoying a Saturday night by the sea. Three young men were stabbed, twenty-five people were injured, and city officials blamed visitors from Newark for starting it. They didn't stop there.

Convinced the incident would blight the resort's family image, Acting Mayor Roland J. Hines and the city council discussed a resolution to ban rock-and-roll concerts at Convention Hall. In the end the ban didn't come to pass, but the long-lasting result was an adversarial relationship between successive elected officials and promoters and nightclub owners on Asbury Park's entertainment circuit.

The roller skating craze of the 1940s led to the creation of numerous arenas around the state, including one at the Casino. Barbara Youmans, seated, was the local glamour girl for the 1942 America on Wheels pageant. Courtesy of Gene Grossman.

TOP *Around 1940, Greek émigré James Plasteras signed a lease with the city to turn the Asbury Park Fishing Club house into a restaurant. The Marine Grill was known for its seafood and white-linen service; it was a BYOB establishment. A Long Branch developer tore it down in 1970 but never redeveloped the 1.75-acre lot. Pike Archives.*

BOTTOM *Franchises blossomed in the 1930s, guaranteeing vacationers a certain level of quality and familiarity wherever they traveled. Taylor Pork Roll was native to Trenton. According to Libbie Greenberg, she and her husband were forced by city hall political powers to take the first pork roll license if the Jewish couple wanted the lease renewed on their adjacent gift shop. Classic Photo Collection/Dorn's Photography Unlimited, Red Bank, New Jersey.*

In another ten years it was a new music scene again as the genial Moe Septee, a seasoned theater booker and music promoter from Philadelphia, worked hard to find audiences to fill Convention Hall and the Paramount. His selections included fellow Philadelphian Dick Clark's "Caravan of Stars," an annual summer bus tour filled with a rotating roster of newcomers like Frankie Avalon, Connie Francis, Fabian, and the Supremes. Septee also booked more established acts like the Mel Torme (the "Velvet Fog") and crooner Eddie Fisher. Through contracts signed with national tour companies, Septee was also sent the Beatles, the Who, the Doors, and the Rolling Stones, all rock-and-roll performers he regarded as too extreme to promote effectively at Convention Hall without having to answer to city hall. When he couldn't sell out the house for Peter, Paul and Mary and rhythm-and-blues legend Etta James, Septee knew his run in Asbury Park was nearly over.

But Septee's era—along with that of the northern Jersey Shore's mainstream music scene—was changing for another reason. In 1968 the New Jersey Highway Authority opened the Garden State Arts Center. The futuristic amphitheater designed by innovative architect Edward Durrell Stone could seat 5,085, and the traveling public had only to get to mile marker 117 on the Parkway to hear anyone from New York Philharmonic to James Taylor. No more fighting summer traffic to get to a theater venue. In another blow to the Asbury Park's hospitality industry, talent was put up in the Molly Pitcher Inn, a luxury hotel overlooking the Navesink River in Red Bank.

The only crowds Convention Hall was pulling in with any regularity were those attending the fall and spring trade shows promoted by Jerry and Tom Gasque—

Arias on the Boardwalk

I CAN CLOSE MY EYES AND RECALL SINGING AT THE Paramount Theater, [later] walking onto the Boardwalk and hearing the ocean, the music from the nightclubs, the summer concerts on the roof of the old Howard Johnson's. It was a life-changing experience to work with Madame Era Tognoli, Anton Coppola [conductor], Jerome Hines [bass], and Robert Merrill [baritone; both Hines and Merrill sang with the Metropolitan Opera Company in New York]. It offered local singers a chance to work with professionals and see firsthand what is involved in a musical career. Though the Metro Lyric Opera performed at many venues in Monmouth County, the goal was always to draw people to the perfect opera setting of the Paramount Theater. Rehearsals were anywhere in the old city big enough to house us: the old Lerner's [ladies clothing store], houses of worship, the library, the Berkeley-Carteret. We performed holiday concerts at the hotel and community concerts at the li-

brary, schools, parks, and nursing homes. Some members performed at Posillipo's. The Grand Operas we performed at the Paramount. A few Metro Lyric moments I will always remember include *Aida* when we had live animals on stage, including an adult camel; the rousing, full orchestra edition of "The Star-Spangled Banner" played before every performance; Isidi (Era's sister) backstage, offering us courage, which meant a tot of strong drink! The virtuoso harmonica playing of Stan Harper. Era walking her dogs backstage. Long rehearsals after which we would go to the old Asbury Diner. The cast parties after every performance in the mezzanine lounge where everyone would complain only to find us five minutes later asking; "Which operas are we doing next year?"

– Jim Reese, baritone
Aberdeen, New Jersey

notably a ceramics show and an annual powerboat show they sponsored for nearly thirty years until the boats got too big, the hall too cramped, and a gasoline shortage triggered a national crisis in the early 1970s.

The Boardwalk's Last Burst of Glory

Another devastating hurricane in 1960 forced the city to spend funds it could have used elsewhere to build a protective jetty around Convention Hall. Then, in the summers of 1962 and 1963, two fires of dubious origin wiped out the classic Warren and Wetmore pavilions respectively, creating more unanticipated costs for the Boardwalk. New bathhouses—unimaginative boxes of dull beige brick—replaced them.

In a burst of unexpected civic bravery, though, city hall signed off on what turned out to the last pavilion built on the Boardwalk in the twentieth century. In 1961, Philadelphia architect John Fridy designed a sweeping two-story postmodern pavilion, startling by conservative north Jersey Shore standards. Intended to serve multiple purposes, the deep orange brick structure replaced the tottering remains of the 1905 Fifth Avenue Arcade that were still in use on the Boardwalk as an ice cream parlor and tearoom.

For less than half a million dollars, the new Fifth Avenue pavilion came with a 1,400-seat rooftop band shell. It replaced the previous Arthur Pryor Band Shell, named for the late maestro, at Eighth Avenue. That one sat 400. The new pavilion also came with six concessions and a spectacular two-level, glass-enclosed circular rotunda that by the start of the twenty-first century would house the last remaining Howard Johnson franchise in New Jersey.

The restaurant also represented a clever circumvention of James Bradley's prohibition against the sale of alcohol on the Boardwalk. The liquor license was issued for the Panorama Room, a darkly sophisticated cocktail lounge and restaurant located on the second floor. The traditional bright blues and oranges associated with HoJo's covered the booths and soda fountain that defined the family eatery at the Boardwalk level.

On June 29, 1962, the new Pryor Band Shell was dedicated. Holding the baton was conductor Frank Bryan, who had once played for Pryor. In another sign of the changing times, Bryan had become musical director at Asbury Park High School, and Pryor's heritage of a band that toured nationally evolved into the city's summer municipal band staffed by local musicians.

The Asbury Park Pops

BACK IN THE 1950S, THE ASBURY PARK MUNICIPAL Band played six or seven concerts a week at the Arthur Pryor Band Pavilion. They also broadcast on WJLK every Wednesday night. This was an outstanding concert band whose proud heritage continued the Sousa lineage through Pryor to Frank Bryan, who studied trombone with him. On occasion, Arthur Pryor's widow would be in the audience. At the time, Bryan was the music director at Asbury Park High School, which had a ninety- to one-hundred-member band, as well as being the music director of the Asbury Park American Legion Band. The result of this was that all of the bands had access to a very large selection of music.

Several of the band's first-chair players were from major symphony orchestras. They did not have summer schedules at that time. These players would spend the summer here, and Frank Bryan encouraged many of us to take lessons from these men, some of the best musicians in the world! During the time I was in high school, I took lessons from Gil Johnson, who was the principal trumpet with the Philadelphia Orchestra under Eugene Ormandy. At the same time, friends were taking lessons from Bill Bell, the principal tuba player from the New York Philharmonic. The entire community benefited from opportunities to hear outstanding soloists almost every night during the summer and to take lessons from the world's best.

– Robert D. Edelson
Ocean Grove, New Jersey

Theme Parks Trounce Boardwalks

Around 1970, America's amusement industry began undergoing a dramatic makeover, especially on the East Coast. Walt Disney World opened in October 1971 in Orlando, Florida, launching the first competitive salvo in theme park competition for tourists' year-round vacation dollars. The theme park's opening was made all the more attractive by inexpensive round-trip airlines fares (about $70) from Newark Airport, which brought northern Florida within three hours of New Jersey by air. For almost the same amount of time it took to drive a car to the Jersey Shore, metropolitan New York and Philadelphia families could be enjoying the newest trend in family entertainment in a different part of the country. The same year, across the Delaware River, the sixty-four-year-old Hershey Park in Pennsylvania was relaunched as a national theme park based on the chocolate company's brand name and with a one-price admission, following the Disney lead.

But another threat was developing even closer to home, and Asbury Park's Boardwalk merchants weren't paying attention. West of the Shore in the Pine Barrens, near a community of White Russian expatriates and a key New Jersey Turnpike exit, flamboyant New York restaurateur Warner LeRoy was finishing a radical new concept that combined a themed amusement park with a drive-through zoo.

OPPOSITE *NBC morning TV co-host chimpanzee J. Fred Muggs helped start* The Today Show *in 1953. The chimp's purpose was to attract young viewers, who in turn, brought their parents to early-morning television, thus delivering consumers to the show's advertisers. After allegedly biting comedian Martha Raye in 1954, Mr. Muggs was sent on a nationwide promotional tour. Here he was dressed as Popeye for a stop in Asbury Park. Courtesy of Milton Edelman.*

The Art of the Pitch

"UBER" TV SALESMAN RON POPIEL — KNIVES TO rotisseries—learned the art of the pitch for his own kitchen inventions during the brief period after his mother died when he lived in Asbury Park working for his entrepreneurial uncle, Nathan Morris. Another Morris protégée was a young Ed McMahon, Johnny Carson's announcer and sidekick on NBC's *Tonight Show*, who took Morris's kitchen gadgets and hawked them on the Atlantic City Boardwalk.

One of Morris's more memorable inventions were glass knives, recalled Asbury Park realtor Rose Kapalko, whose first job, when she was still a teenager, was working for Morris and his son, Arnold, who continues to pitch assorted kitchen gadgets. "Boy, those things could sure cut. I wish I had them today."

IN A 1963 INTERVIEW WITH ASSOCIATED PRESS theater writer William Wolf, cartoon satirist Al Capp ["L'il Abner"] recalled spending the summer of 1925 in Asbury Park, working for college money. After having been fired from his job as a Boardwalk artist, the *Tonight Show* regular and BBC commentator said he found work pitching a "monster combination of potato peeler, bottle opener, and just about everything else.

"It was a weapon, but it worked. I chopped off several chunks of finger with it."

An Asbury Park Album

Along 127 miles of New Jersey's Atlantic coastline there was no greater collection of decorative and architectural elements in a resort its size than that found in Asbury Park. The resort's greatest glory days, perhaps, were the Roaring Twenties, when most of its colorful Boardwalk and downtown buildings were built.

Asbury Park's chief amusement and entertainment district overlooked Wesley Lake, which separated the exciting distractions of Asbury Park from the sedate Ocean Grove Camp Meeting Association. Seen here, from left, are the Mayfair Theatre, Corrubia's Restaurant, and the collection of buildings that made up the privately owned Palace Amusements; circa 1950. Pike Archives.

Painter Leslie W. Thomas was hired to decorate the Palace extension when it opened on Cookman Avenue in 1956. The building's most recognizable icon reprised Coney Island impressario George Tilyou's famous "funny face" from his Steeplechase amusements franchise. More than forty years earlier, Tilyou had inked a deal for a Steeplechase arcade on Ocean Avenue. Pike Archives.

ABOVE A block away from Palace Amusements stood the Casino, a complex of buildings commissioned by the city to include a carousel house, an amusement and restaurant arcade, and a 29,000-square-foot exhibition and performance arena built out over the beach. The contract also called for an adjacent heating plant at the foot of Wesley Lake; the heating plant's Boardwalk frontage would be camouflaged by a segregated concession for the resort's African American population and visitors. Pike Archives.

RIGHT Warren and Wetmore, New York, were retained as the lead architectural firm for a new, modern Casino to replace the previous wooden one designed by Asbury Park architect William Cottrell. That one was destroyed in a mysterious fire. His son, Arthur Cottrell, was one of the local designers to be included in the municipal contract for the new Casino, and may have been responsible for some of the fanciful Art Noveau designs—seen here on the carousel house—that graced both the new Casino and the Paramount Theatre and Convention Hall complex. Pike Archives.

The last carousel to be made by the Philadelphia Toboggan Company was No. 87, carved by Frank Caretta with forty-eight horses and two Roman chariots. The new Casino amusements tenant, Cookman Avenue sporting goods storeowner John Seger, bought the merry-go-round and installed it in 1932. Pike Archives.

ABOVE Instead of the ocean, the statue of Asbury Park founder James A. Bradley, right, today looks at the shimmering purple tiles, terra cotta dado, and diamond-patterned red brick front of the Paramount Theater. The New York engineering firm E. G. Woolfolk & Company designed a room below street level north of the theater for an elaborate ice-cooled air conditioning system to bring relief to 2,000 theater patrons. In the winter they were warmed by heat forced from the heating plant six blocks away on Wesley Lake. Pike Archives.

OPPOSITE, CLOCKWISE FROM UPPER LEFT A close-up of one of the themed terra-cotta medallions decorating the Paramount façade. Other terra-cotta details on the theater and hall's façades included seashells, urns, and hanging garlands; French-born painter and interior decorator Arthur Brounet, who had a studio on Broadway in Manhattan, was hired to decorate the panels that flanked the hall's stage. He chose an aquatic fantasy theme with galleons, fish, and other images from the deep; magnificent copper detail of an exotic sea creature topped by a dentil molding of acanthus leaves above a retail bay inside the Paramount-Convention Hall arcade, photographed during a recent restoration initiative. Pike Archives.

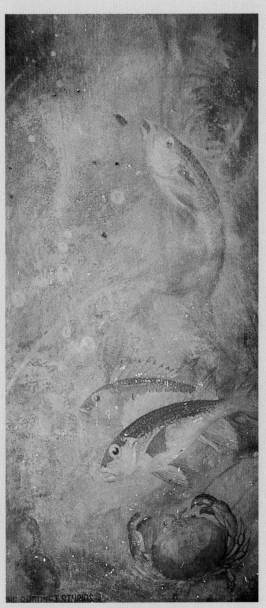

ABOVE Resort resident and artist Theodore Davis was commissioned to design a stained glass window for the western wall of the Asbury Park Public Library. He chose a melodramatic verse from Henry Wadsworth Longfellow's tragic ode to the end of summer "Tegner's Drapa": "They launched the burning ship! / It floated far away / Over the misty sea / Till like the sun it seemed / Sinking beneath the waves." Spectacularly illumined at sunset, the window was made by Louis Comfort Tiffany's studio. *Coaster* photo.

LEFT Trained at the Art Institute of Philadelphia, African American sand sculptor Lorenzo Harris left the crowded beachfront in Atlantic City in the early 1920s for the opportunity that the newer resort of Asbury Park represented. He often chose mythological themes for his sand frescoes, which he built at the foot of First Avenue; he paid rent to city hall for a beach concession. Pike Archives.

ABOVE LEFT The integrated Boardwalk was still at its peak of glory in 1965, with something for all ages. Pike Archives.

ABOVE RIGHT The Fifth Avenue Pavilion designed by John Fridy of Philadelphia was highlighted by art moderne elements, notably the knife-edge style of the roofline of the restaurant at the pavilion's southern end balanced by the open bandshell design

for the northern end. The restaurant opened in 1963 as a Howard Johnson franchise. The Boardwalk's first liquor license ever was issued for the second-floor cocktail lounge. The bandshell was named in memory of famed band leader Arthur Pryor, who played for sixteen consecutive summers in Asbury Park under an arrangement with city hall. The band's previous performance space was in the Seventh Avenue pavilion, which was destroyed in the hurricane of 1944. Pike Archives.

ABOVE Sunset Hall owners built the Ocean Theatre in 1913. Composer Alfred Bryan, who wrote "I Didn't Raise My Boy to Be a Soldier," often played his composition on the theater piano while a hotel guest on vacation in 1917. Walter Reade Jr. renamed the building when he recycled the neon marquee from a Manhattan theater he had just turned into New York's first duplex cinema. SoHo painter and current theater owner Walter Burns commissioned a new Egyptian exterior for the new millennium. Restore By the Shore radio host Maureen Nevin of Asbury Park served as the model. Pike Archives.

OPPOSITE In 1961 Walter Reade Jr. hired Philadelphia illustrator Ida Libby Dengrove, then living in the Asbury Park suburb of West Allenhurst, to paint a Parisian street scene on his Lyric Theater's mezzanine walls. By 1972 Dengrove was working for NBC as the nation's first courtroom TV artist, sketching the likes of David "Son of Sam" Berkowitz, subway vigilante Bernhard Goetz, and diet-doctor murderer Jean Harris. Pike Archives.

ABOVE The interior of Odyssey Moore's Springwood Avenue jazz club was decorated perfectly for its name as the Orchid Lounge. Courtesy of Rainette Bannister Holimon.

RIGHT Thanks to the encouragement and sartorial skills of hairdresser and nightclub owner Margaret Potter, charismatic musician Bruce Springsteen emerged from a slightly menacing, post-1950s greaser/early-1960s hippie look with a more romantically rugged persona that appealed to women and made men want to imitate him; circa 1975. Pike Archives.

Murray Weiner, who married Ida Jacobs's daughter, Jeanette, stands in a suit at the center of Mrs. Jay's Circus Bar, which in 1946 began booking some of the country's pop-rock bands such as the Three Chuckles. Pike Archives.

ABOVE In 1927 the YMCA built a modern brick facility on Main Street and Summerfield Avenue; it was more centrally located than the YMCA's previous addresses just off Grand Avenue. The new building had an indoor swimming pool, basketball courts, and rooms to rent. The Y encountered serious financial difficulties during the Depression years before experiencing a turn-around in the 1950s. The Y's roofline was detailed with a row of terra-cotta seashells and serpents. Pike Archives.

Great Adventure caught all the state's amusement operators unaware when it opened July 1, 1974. Families came in droves to experience the 140-acre site, where a brightly painted main avenue called Dream Street was located deep inside the Enchanted Forest. Another part of the park featured a Wild West experience. The Ferris wheel was 150 feet tall. Most exciting of all was the separate five-and-a-half mile safari that wound its way through an additional 450 acres. In one brilliant package, LeRoy successfully shifted the vacationing public's focus from cramped urban zoos and narrow strips of seashore amusements to a seemingly limitless parklike compound, complete with exotic animals, all-day and all-night entertainment, one general admission price, and perhaps most important of all, unmetered parking. Before long, LeRoy made a deal with Six Flags Over America and Warner Bros. that resulted in Great Adventure's acquiring a well-known icon to compete with Disney's Mickey Mouse: Bugs Bunny.

Boardwalk for Sale

In Asbury Park the glory was fading fast in those final years, especially when nearly all the concession operators from the Casino to Convention Hall chose not to renew their ten-year concession leases, despite some gaming arcades clearing between $60,000 and $70,000 for just three months of work. The Boardwalk was looking increasingly desolate, its outdoor rides worn and rusted, its working arcade games few.

As the 1970s began, the city was earning increasingly less income from its Boardwalk leases. By 1978 city hall had barely broken even from its concessions. Mayor Ray Kramer publicly proposed putting the Boardwalk, assessed at $12.5 million, up for sale in 1979. "History has shown that no government agency can operate a business as efficiently as private enterprise can," Kramer declared.

Carmen and Thomas Ricci, who owned sections of the amusements in Seaside Park, Brigantine, and Atlantic City and had revived the Long Branch Boardwalk, submitted a dramatic proposal: conversion of the Casino into a greenhouse within a shopping mall; construction of an amusement pier next to Convention

Elevation of the Greek Holy Cross

I REMEMBER GOING EACH YEAR TO ASBURY PARK AS a child with my family. We celebrated the Greek Orthodox holiday commemorating the Holy Cross. We dressed in our church clothes as on any other Sunday and drove two hours south to this beloved Shore point.

All Greek Orthodox religious communities from the mid-Atlantic [region]closed their doors for this day, collected their thousands of parishioners in buses and went to Asbury Park for this celebration. A massive divine liturgy was held in the Convention Hall in a makeshift altar with Byzantine icons, religious articles, white slim candles, and burning incense. Sounds of church hymns, friendly greetings, and scraping sandy shoes filled the hall. Outside, finely dressed people wearing mostly the traditional blue crowded the edges of the Boardwalk and the ramps of the Howard Johnson's exchanging pleasantries and competing for a good view of the ocean, the procession, and final moments of the ceremony.

It was customary for the archbishop (in the 1970s, His Eminence Iakovos) to throw a golden cross into the ocean, where small boats filled with boys representing the various communities waited nervously afloat for the signal to dive into the water and retrieve the cross. The boy who reached it first and brought it to shore safely was believed to receive extraordinary blessings that in turn would extend to his family and home and above all his church community. Retrieving the cross placed his church in highest esteem and he as hero forever!

Bishops, priests, deacons, altar boys, choirs, dignitaries, famous Greek American personalities from television, theater, and radio—Ernie Anastos, Telly Savalas, to name

a couple—were led after the ceremony to Howard Johnson, the smell of pancake syrup competing with permeated incense. My family went for pizza usually, my brother and I waiting impatiently for my father to take us later to the all-inviting Palace Funhouse and the Merry-Go-Round. Visions of vaudeville, multicolored puppet faces and golden-robed priests blurring in me as objects do before that mirror we'd stand at as children, distorting reality.

– Irene Polemis,
Double Exposure: Echoes of Two Cultures
Closter, New Jersey

The Reverend Spyridon Coutros served Asbury Park from 1947 to 1977, initiating the Elevation of the Holy Cross in 1948. A daughter, Kelly, married New York TV newscaster Ernie Anastos. Pike Archives.

Hall; erection of a glass-enclosed walkway and shopping emporium plus a five-hundred-unit hotel-condominium complex. The only hitch? The Riccis wanted to own the entire Boardwalk.

Also on the table was a plan by Urban Resorts, a partnership between city engineer Leon Avakian and architects Frank and Joseph Tomaino. Their proposal would have allowed the city to retain ownership of Convention Hall and the Paramount. It called for creation of a civic and cultural center, including a hotel, sports arena, parking garage, skating rink, and outdoor cafes linked by monorail to the downtown train station. Mayor Kramer and his city council couldn't achieve the consensus necessary to pick a buyer.

Meanwhile, city hall began to micromanage its Boardwalk assets, writing bid specifications for amusements it thought entrepreneurs and the public wanted. Tellingly, the water slide bid, for example, received no submissions. To take in some rental income, city hall leased the second floor of its Asbury Avenue pavilion to the Salvation Army for a senior citizens' lunch program. Eventually, the floor above Criterion Chocolates became the Asbury Park Senior Citizens Activities Center and the longest-operating sweet shop on the Boardwalk reduced its retail operations to a bakery in Eatontown.

The deteriorating Paramount became a charity case. In 1979 Richard W. Schwarz Sr., musical director of the First United Methodist Church on Grand Avenue, produced the Cavalcade of Music to raise restoration money for the theater. Proceeds barely made a dent in the deferred maintenance. The following year, when the cash-strapped city looked to cancel financial support of its summer municipal band series, Schwarz offered to underwrite those performance costs as well.

Despite the efforts of former police officer Anthony "Putt Putt" Petillo to revive the Baby Parade by asking family and friends to help, the workload was crushing, and in 1980 Petillo succumbed to a heart attack. With unintended irony, the winner's grand prize that year was travel tickets to Disney World.

Fischer's baker and city resident Frank Fiorentino designed this prize-winning float, which carried his son, Frank Jr., and two friends during one of the earliest Baby Parades after World War II. Pike Archives.

In 1980, just when it was impossible to imagine any more bad news, Asbury Park failed to get listed in the state's annual tourism guide—except as a Parkway exit. The city spent $8,000 on New York City and Philadelphia metropolitan television advertisements and brochures to try to raise Asbury Park's visibility. On the Friday night of the July Fourth weekend, city beach director and third-generation resident Anthony "Jap" Del Pizzo surveyed the crowded Boardwalk and commented it was the best he'd seen since 1968. Said Del Pizzo, "I think people discovered . . . there are good attractions close by."

CHAPTER FOUR

The Entertainment Circuits

ELENTLESS ADMONISHMENTS from Protestant pulpits that leisure
be used for spiritual or intellectual self-improvement could not stop
the traveling public's desire to be entertained in theaters instead of
merely amused on a boardwalk. Neither could ministers curb the cultural preference
of the African American and immigrant working class for vaudeville variety shows
as a release from a week of hard work. The nineteenth century drew to a close in Asbury Park, as it did elsewhere across the country, marked by an increasing desire for
more populist entertainment. The demand coincided with advances in moviemaking technology. Several of the resort's first entertainment entrepreneurs were established businessmen eager to try new ventures that would diversify their bottom
lines. Some briefly succeeded. Others lacked the talent to predict what people would
pay to see live on a stage or flickering across a screen. But as the twentieth century
took hold, a handful of men and women with experience and connections arrived to
shape the resort's entertainment circuits for decades to come.

Neckties to Nickelodeons

Walter Rosenberg and his father left Selma, Alabama, where they had been selling neckties, and headed for New York City, where the youngster began managing
vaudeville theaters for his uncle, Oscar Hammerstein I, a cultured yet profane and
ambitious émigré from Pomerania who, in 1895, had built the first multiple-theater

---

*Around
Town*

"She" is the next production
at the Opera House, on July
10th and 11th.

– Asbury Park Journal,
July 5, 1890

Mr. J. I. Morrison of the Grand
Opera House has done a fine
summer's business, probably
because he has brought such
good attractions here.

– The Shore Press,
September 5, 1890

Mr. Julian M. Morrison has
given up the lease of the Opera House, and it is now in
the hands of Real Estate
Agent Appleby. . . . Mr. Morrison . . . kept the financial
part up with credit, and it
was doubtless to prevent additional loss that he con-
cluded to withdraw.

– Asbury Park Journal,
December 13, 1890

---

complex on Broadway and Forty-fourth Street. Hammerstein owed much of his suc-
cess to his son, William, who was a master of P. T. Barnum public relations tactics.
Rosenberg's apprenticeship included the conversion of Hammerstein's Manhattan
Opera House on West Thirty-fourth Street into a nickelodeon that they called the
Savoy Theatre. He converted another old opera house in Port Chester, New York.
Rosenberg came to Asbury Park and tried to buy the Surf House on the hotel circuit, but his offer was rebuffed because he was Jewish. After founder Bradley sold the
Boardwalk to the city in 1903, Rosenberg returned, winning the competitive bid on
the lease to operate a kinescope in the Casino. He acquired the Rialto, a vaudeville
house on Main Street a couple of doors south of Springwood Avenue. Sometimes
called the "garlic theater," an ethnic slur against the West Side's Italian American
community that patronized it, the Rialto was a storefront theater typical of the period and also featured live performances. A young George Watson, who later became
a technician for the Tuskegee Airmen, performed tap-dancing shows here with his
two brothers. Rosenberg also commissioned architectural plans to convert a bowling alley on the northwest corner of Main Street and Sunset Avenue into another
theater, but he never went through with them.

Bowling for Asbury Park

MY DAD, HAROLD B. EAMES, OPENED THE ASBURY PARK
Recreation Center at 1405–07 Main Street [near Sunset]
as an eight-lane (a divided four and four) bowling alley in
March 1933, the very day after Roosevelt had closed the
banks. Dad had arranged to have the seven-foot-plus-tall
Primo Carnera, heavyweight boxing champ, and new con-
tender Max Baer "roll the first ball down an alley" as a big,
rousing grand opening feature. Each boxer "threw one in
the gutter" to the crowd's hilarious delight, followed by the
past world champ "trick-bowler" who also wowed them.

My dad died early in 1934, and three or four years
later, the eight alleys were each sawed into three parts and
transported toward the ocean and placed into a former
auto/parking storage garage at 207 Fourth Avenue where
eight newly built alleys were freshly constructed, making sixteen lanes across (rather than the four and four).
With a new sandwich and soda counter up front, my mom,
helped by Dad's younger brother, Leslie B. Eames, and her
youngest brother, Steve Green, took over the operation of
the business.

My dad had also bought a rooming house for his mom
to run at 410 Fifth Avenue in the summers while we moved
to Avon. We moved back in the fall to go to school in Asbury.
The name on the small sign that always hung over the porch
was Lakeside Villa.

– Leslie H. Eames
Morris Plains, New Jersey

In those early years, Main Street was an ideal central corridor for the blossoming movie business. The working-class residential neighborhoods were concentrated along the East Side's Bond and Emory Streets, and the West Side was just a block away over the railroad tracks. Rosenberg's strategy virtually guaranteed him movie receipts fifty-two weeks of the year.

In 1910 the budding mogul entered into a partnership with real estate entrepreneur Hugh Kinmonth for a brand-new downtown theater. Kinmonth was investing in a stuccoed office building with hollow-tile walls on Mattison Avenue in the first block off Main Street. It replaced Central Hall, the wooden clubhouse of a local sports club with a baseball team called the Oreos. Rosenberg managed to persuade Kinmonth to build a ground-floor extension off the lobby and into the alley for a 1,500-seat vaudeville theater. In exchange, Rosenberg paid rent for his lobby access, since the doors were part of the street-level retail façade. He sweetened his deal with Kinmonth by giving the developer permanent box seats for all performances. In return, Kinmonth doubled the terms of his lease from twenty to forty years.

Rosenberg named this new theater the Savoy. Casino architect William Cottrell and his son, Arthur, were hired to design the combination office and theater building that housed the Savoy. On March 31, 1912, the Savoy's first official act was to host a nearly frostbitten band and some of the 4,000 members of the public who had gathered ahead of time at the train station to herald the arrival of the first Sunday trains to the resort. By 1945 Rosenberg would own the building.

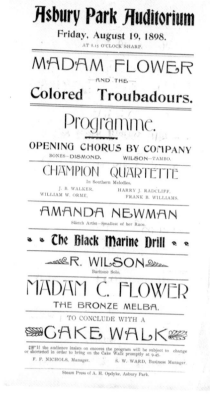

Theater Expansion

Rosenberg didn't restrict his interests to Asbury Park. To achieve the kind of success his uncle had, he needed a circuit of movie houses through which to distribute the new Hollywood flickers, or silent movies. For him, Asbury Park's rivalry with other local resorts was irrelevant. That Long Branch attracted a theater crowd guaranteed customers for other nearby entertainment venues, and he built two movie houses across from each other on Broadway in the vibrant neighborhood closest to the beachfront. Sizing up New Jersey's thriving metropolitan areas, he also built theaters in New Brunswick, Morristown, Perth Amboy, Trenton, and the

Bradley owned the 2,500-seat Auditorium on Sunset and Ocean Avenues and the 1,500-seat Educational Hall on Grand Avenue; both buildings were used for entertainment. More public seating was downtown at the 1,500-seat Opera House on Bangs Avenue and Emory Street; it was privately owned. Pike Archives.

burgeoning riverfront community of Red Bank. In still other communities he entered into partnerships with local businessmen, and his real estate empire of theaters expanded.

In 1914 Rosenberg launched what turned into a twenty-year public campaign to allow Sunday movies to be shown. In 1930 he made headlines by promising to pump $250,000 into renovating his Long Branch theaters if that resort would lift the ban on showing movies on the Christian Sabbath. The state of New Jersey finally rescinded its Sunday restriction in 1934, partly in reaction to the prolonged effects of the Great Depression.

On April 16, 1917, fourteen days after the United States became involved in World War I, Rosenberg broke ground for a brand-new theater in Asbury Park. Closer to the hotel circuit and the Heck Street footbridge from Ocean Grove than his previous

Asbury Park: Ready for Its Closeup

BEGINNING IN 1903, WHEN BANDLEADER AND RESIDENT Arthur Pryor wrote "On Jersey Shore," Asbury Park played a variety of roles in popular song, stage, television, feature films, and even as a home for writers. Pryor's still more popular "Whistler and His Dog" (1905) became the theme song for television's *Leave It to Beaver*. The original ending for Cole Porter's 1934 *Anything Goes*, in which an ocean liner goes up in flames, had to be changed after the *Morro Castle* disaster made international headlines. Howard Lindsay and Russell Crouse were hired to write a new, upbeat ending. Four years later, Porter wrote another musical, *You Never Know*, with a signature song, "At Long Last Love," later made famous by crooner Frank Sinatra. The song included the line "Is it Granada I see, or only Asbury Park?"

That Touch of Mink, a 1959 film about hesitant lovers starring Doris Day and Cary Grant, included a line about those "beaverboard motels in Asbury Park." One of the more memorable episodes of the 1950s TV sitcom *The Honeymooners* featured a get-rich-quick scheme in which Ralph Kramden (Jackie Gleason) and Ed Norton (Art Carney) would sell stock in a uranium mine in Asbury Park. *The Projectionist*, a 1970 film starring Chuck McCann in the title role with Rodney Dangerfield as the miserly theater owner, featured the Paramount Theater. The movie's final chase scene took place in the Mayfair.

Asbury Park was also home to "Sweethearts of the Air" Peter DeRose and his wife, Mary Singhi Breen. DeRose wrote the music, and was best known for singing "Deep Purple" (1933) and "Wagon Wheels" (1934); the lyricists, respectively, were Michael Parish and Billy Hill. Among Asbury Park's writers were Stephen Crane, whose boyhood home is now a museum; poet Margaret Widdemer, who won the 1940 Pulitzer Prize; noted war author John Toland; and adventure travel writer Lowell Thomas, who wrote *With Lawrence in Arabia* while living with his parents in Asbury Park between 1922 and 1923. Investigative journalist and author Fred J. Cook got his start on the *Asbury Park Press* when he covered the *Morro Castle* disaster.

The resort's role in late twentieth-century popular culture was established in 1973 with rock musician and songwriter Bruce Springsteen's debut record album, *Greetings from Asbury Park*. The jacket's design featured a chrome postcard printed by Tichnor Brothers of Boston; the card's balloon letters framed the resort's most popular attractions.

theaters, Rosenberg's new location was on the southwest corner of Cookman Avenue and St. James Place where noted 1890s Baby Parade photographer William Stauffer had had his studio. With demolition underway, Rosenberg hired New York City theater and arena architect Thomas W. Lamb, fresh from his most public successes in Manhattan at that time—Madison Square Garden and Broadway's Strand and Rialto Theaters.

For $200,000 in construction costs, Lamb gave Rosenberg a brown brick theater with soaring pilasters to break up the mass of the building's exterior walls. The 2,300 seats were upholstered in brown plush; the ceiling had working skylights for ventilation. To accompany the silent motion pictures, a theater organ was bought from the M. P. Moller Organ Company of Hagerstown, Maryland. There were men's and women's lounges and a small apartment overlooking Cookman Avenue. But when the St. James opened, its most noteworthy feature was located on the marquee. The name that topped the sign was Reade, and thereafter the father and his only son would be known, respectively, as Walter Reade Sr. and Walter Reade Jr.

West Side lumber baron Charles Lewis was attracted by the money-making potential of the flickers and built seven theaters from Asbury Park to Spring Lake. He hired local vulcanized rubber inventor Daniel D. Dorn (left) to go once a week to New York to pick up the latest offerings. In 1917 Lewis hired Dorn's seven-year-old son Daniel W. Dorn (right) as a movie projectionist for his nickelodeons in Asbury Park and Bradley Beach. Classic Photo Collection/ Dorn's Photography Unlimited, Red Bank, New Jersey.

Movie Palace

As the twentieth century unrolled, the movie industry became increasingly complex as a result of overlapping deals involving cinema construction, film production, and theater distribution. In 1925 Russian émigré Sam Katz, flush with success from building ornately decorated theaters in Chicago, became vice president of Paramount Publix, the construction unit of Paramount–Famous Players–Lasky Corporation, a feature film company whose most famous actress was Mary Pickford. Katz drove the financing and construction of many massive, ornately decorated movie palaces across America, choosing locations where the greatest number of people was likely to congregate. These enormous, atmospheric presentation houses also featured pit orchestras on hydraulic platforms, organists, and stage units for moving scenery around. Not infrequently, a partnership between Paramount and local investors included placing the company name somewhere on the marquee or in newspaper advertisements for promotional purposes.

Such might have been the case in Asbury Park, where property insurance for the tiny Rialto Theatre, which had recently been lost to fire, would never have been enough to finance Reade's next theater project. That project was to cost more than four times what he paid to build the St. James. Given that Reade was active in buying, fixing, and selling a host of theater properties in the New York–New Jersey metropolitan area, though, he may very well have come up with the $1.5 million it was going to take to realize his dream on Wesley Lake.

Talkies had debuted in 1926, and Reade, with his New York connections, saw an unprecedented opportunity to place the latest in Hollywood technology in a glorious presentation house at a popular seaside address. It would be a theater like no other in New Jersey. The public would have to come to Asbury Park for the experience. In 1927 architect Thomas Lamb gave Reade what he wanted.

In contrast to the severe brick of the St. James, the new cream-colored theater had an elaborate exterior of hand-sculpted Spanish stucco, with outside balconies outlined by fantasy arches. It commanded the Lake Avenue and St. James Place corner with a 172-foot campanile tower outfitted with chimes that were controlled by the theater's $40,000 interior organ. With more than a passing nod to one of the ritzier districts in London, Reade named his lavish enterprise the Mayfair.

Heavy grille doors opened into the corner lobby, which was hung with tapestries and adorned with wrought-iron light fixtures and a decorative marble wishing well. Intricate coffers lined the high ceiling. A grand staircase rose from north end of the lobby to the mezzanine, which was decorated with settees and wrought-iron Spanish lamps. The 2,000-seat auditorium was bathed in a sunset illumination that glowed behind the proscenium. The outdoor effect was heightened by the ceiling, which mimicked a sapphire nighttime sky. Looking up, patrons saw clouds drift overhead and caught the occasional glint of a star. The effect was created by two small projectors fixed to the ceilings and fitted with a continuous film loop. Two years would pass before the Mayfair's closest architectural competitor opened—a Spanish Baroque theater built by Reade rival Marcus Loew in Jersey City.

Political Theater: Act I

All was not smooth sailing for Reade's Asbury Park theater plans. The Mayfair had barely opened when Reade became embroiled in a high-profile debate with Mayor Clarence Hetrick about the feasibility of building a Boardwalk theater.

"You don't need any more theaters at Asbury Park and I would hate to see you build one. It would be a financial failure," Reade told Hetrick, "but if you want a high-class amusement pier and Convention Hall for $1.5 million, I will lay out plans and get them drawn for you and it won't cost you a dollar unless you adopt them."

OPPOSITE *The Savoy gave opportunity to many performers, including Mae West touring in* Diamond Lil, *fan dancer Lily St. Cyr, and Vincent Gardenia getting his out-of-town start in* Death of a Salesman *under the aegis of the Asbury Playhouse. Gardenia's director, who was also the Playhouse co-producer, was Philip Dorian, who went on to found the New Jersey Shakespeare Festival. Pike Archives.*

Reades' Theater Empire

WALTER READE SR. AND WALTER READE JR. AMASSED a tidy theater empire during most of the first half of the twentieth century, including one foreign property in London. By 1963, of the eighty-nine [Reade] theaters located from Boston to New Orleans, Chicago to San Francisco, Los Angeles to Seattle, Portland to Washington, D.C., fifty were in New Jersey.

There were ten drive-ins, plus an experimental fly-in at Allaire Airport in Wall Township that Reade took over from Ocean Grove native and Asbury Park businessman Edward Brown. One drive-in was located on the roof of a parking garage at a shopping mall in Dover and featured then-innovative wireless speakers.

Nine were acquired when, in the 1950s, Junior bought the theater chain of Lee Newberry of Interlaken, New Jersey, including the Ocean Theatre in Asbury Park. It brought his theater marquees to six and made Asbury Park the second largest location of theaters after New York City for the

Walter Reade Organization. His properties included a brick warehouse on Railroad Avenue for bags of popped corn and boxed candy for the concession counters.

There were nineteen movie theaters in New York; fourteen were in Manhattan, including the Ziegfeld, which Junior built and opened in 1969 on the exact location of Broadway impresario Florence Ziegfeld's original.

In December 1991, the Film Society of Lincoln Center dedicated a state-of-the-art cinema in memory of Walter Reade Jr. It was built, in part, with a $1.2-million grant from the Reade Foundation and under the guidance of Reade president and founding member of the film society, Sheldon Gunsburg. The first film to be shown was *High Heels* by Spanish director-screenwriter Pedro Almodóvar.

– From an interview with John Balmer, executive vice president, ret., Walter Reade Organization

Hetrick turned Reade down and went ahead with the city's Boardwalk plans. But not too long after the convention and theater center was finished, Reade emerged with the lease to book movies and "polite entertainment." By now, Reade's headline-grabbing declarations, torn from the playbook written by his cousin Willie Hammerstein, were becoming familiar. On May 6, 1930, he declared that the motion picture industry had been stripped of its romance and that he was going to lease all his theaters to Paramount–Famous Players–Lasky for twenty years. Just what the final details may have been will probably never be known, but the immediate result was that the Boardwalk theater received a name, the Paramount.

Beyond the Footlights

Gradually, entertainment neighborhoods emerged around Reade's various theaters. As a measure of Asbury Park's growing status as a year-round community, studios for students whose mothers wanted them to study ballet, piano, drums, or voice began opening up. In 1931 singer-dancer Eddie King arrived from Jersey City and

Moorish arches, swirling columns, heavy moldings, and painted candelabras gave theater patrons the illusion of sitting inside a Spanish courtyard. Courtesy of the Thomas Lamb Collection/Avery Architectural and Fine Arts Library/Columbia University in the City of New York.

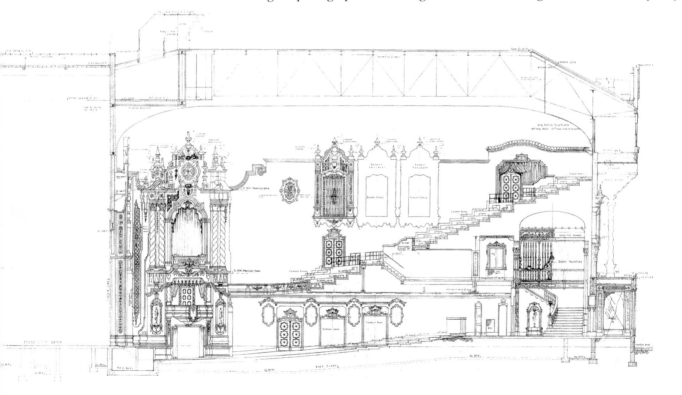

opened a dance studio on the corner of Cookman Avenue and Bond Street. A year later he formed a business partnership with actor Richard Lear, and in another year's time they opened a performance studio for children at 427 Cookman Avenue, one block west of Reade's St. James Theatre. Next door was Ted Kalemba's Shore Grill, a neighborhood hangout with a piano bar where King would later tickle the ivories and sing.

The pair devised a program from the St. James called Radio Kiddies that gave their pupils weekly onstage and on-air experience; the program was broadcast live over WCAP. A regular was teenager June Nicholson from Neptune. The aspiring actress teamed up with King professionally, and together the pair formed a song-and-dance act that was paid to perform at local movie openings and at the ballroom at the Berkeley-Carteret Hotel.

King and Lear's School of Theatrical Arts held a competitive recital at the St. James in 1935. The $250 grand prize came courtesy of sponsors Keystone Laundries and Tilton's Dairy. On June 5, 1936, the Radio Kiddies' Juvenile Follies took place at Convention Hall, where King and Lear's 150 students performed before an audience of 4,500 people. Sadly, it was their last show.

In January 1937, King was seized by police and federal immigration authorities. The public learned that his real name was Eddie Kirschfield. Emigrating from Latvia, he had entered the United States in 1925 as a musician on the SS *Estonia*. Overstaying his visa and ordered deported in 1932, he disappeared from Jersey City and surfaced in Asbury Park, establishing himself as Eddie King. He fought deportation and disappeared from the resort for a while. When King next appeared in Asbury Park, it was as a married saloon singer making the piano bar circuit from the Main Street Tavern between Asbury and First Avenues to the Shore Grill next door to his old studios to the Wonder Bar on Ocean and Sunset Avenues.

Among the businessmen stepping up to buy a liquor license when Prohibition was repealed in 1933 was Fred Fox. Since 1922 Pauline Fox had had a delicatessen

The Mayfair's ornate exterior along Lake Avenue to St. James Place. Corrubia's Restaurant and Motel was located across the street; when this photo was taken (circa 1960) it was featuring Peter Jay and the Jaywalkers from Britain. Courtesy of Milton Edelman.

RIGHT *In the 1930s, Reade resurfaced the St. James's brown brick façade with white stucco and art deco pilasters. Inside the theater he added a proscenium around the movie screen, and reduced the seating to 1,500. Classic Photo Collection/Dorn's Photography Unlimited, Red Bank, New Jersey.*

BELOW *Take your pick: Walter Reade Jr. owned six different theaters in Asbury Park by 1960. The Mayfair and the Paramount were air-conditioned. Pike Archives.*

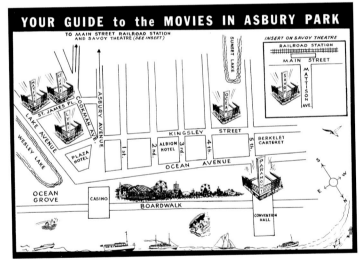

at the point of Cookman and Summerfield Avenues, diagonally across from what would become King's studios. With the license, Fox put in a package store. Eventually, a bar went in, and by the start of World War II Fox's Tavern became a haven for gay British sailors who were billeted at the Berkeley-Carteret and New Monterey Hotels over on the northern end of the oceanfront's hotel circuit.

In the postwar years, Fox had competition for the growing gay clientele in the form of the Hudson Hotel on Heck Street across from the old Elks lodge where the Charms Candy Company had moved in. In 1956, Fox, ready to retire, sold his tavern to Bill Green, the son of a New York City vaudeville theater owner. Before the war Green, who played bass, owned a nightclub and roadhouse in North Brunswick called the Rustic Lodge. After buying Fox's Tavern, the redheaded Irishman put the name of his old club on his new address. He spruced up the smoky dark interior, covered the tables with white linens, and created a separate club entrance on Summerfield Avenue.

This part of his one-story building he called the Plantation Room. The club took off when he invited musicians that used to jam with him in North Brunswick: Duke Ellington, Count Basie, and Lionel Hampton as well as guitarists Tal Farlow and Lou Mecca. The club closed in 1968.

A smaller entertainment circuit developed around Reade's downtown Savoy and fittingly was defined by stores selling pianos, sheet music, Victrolas, records, radios, and, after World War II, televisions. The senior music merchant was Robert A. Tusting, who in 1883 had bought the Main Street instrument business of William Baldwin, the resort's leading piano retailer on Main Street and Mattison Avenue. In 1922 Tusting bought the old Reo Speed Wagon showroom on Bangs Avenue and Bond Street and turned it into a warehouse. For a while maestro Rosario Miraglia, an Italian tenor who had a voice and instrumental music school, lived across Bond. Back on Main Street, popular local bandleader Tommy Tucker expanded his inventory of turntables and radios with appliances and repairs, while at Joe Scott's, the balance was between musical instruments and record players and radios.

Just before Tusting's warehouse on the north side of Bangs, a New York piano crooner with some London gigs to his credit opened a piano bar. Matt Mattlin and his wife, the novelist Norma Keating, who wrote *Giants and Dwarfs*, had came down to the Shore after World War II. Mattlin quickly established a presence and a following at Lou's Cottage Inn on Route 4-N in Sea Girt. Eventually, Mattlin wanted to run his own show, and so a few miles north, just off 4-N in Asbury Park, he found

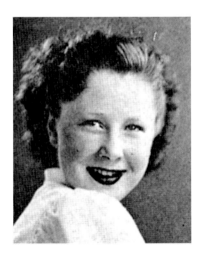

Ethel Nicholson, actor Jack Nicholson's grandmother, was the beautician and hairdresser for Eddie King's 1936 Juvenile Follies; her daughter Lorraine (left) was a performer. Her other daughter, June (Jack's mother), was also a King student. King (right), rumored to be the actor's father, was often seen taking the youngster to Red Petillo's barbershop on Asbury Avenue near the Ridge intersection. Pike Archives.

Many Asbury Hudson guests in the 1950s were patrons of Julius's, the oldest gay bar in Manhattan. Downstairs on Cookman Avenue was the original M & K, the diner-tavern operated by Thomas Mallos and Thomas Karanatos. Across Cookman was Tina's Beauty Salon where the men went to be coiffed for the Hudson's annual Halloween Ball. Pike Archives.

a place to his liking. Hoping that big-name recognition would attract patrons and that his fans would follow him up the highway, Mattlin and Keating called their jazz club the Blue Note after the well-known Manhattan nightclub.

Leisure Lounges

The entertainment circuit around the Reade's Paramount Theatre on Ocean Avenue emerged slowly after repeal of Prohibition and was concentrated at first in the new cocktail lounges in the Kingsley Arms, the Asbury Carlton, the Palace-Ambassador, the Park View, and the Berkeley-Carteret Hotels. The Monterey's Pin-Up Room had the best acoustics, according to jazz guitarist Lou Mecca, who played the hotel lounge circuit in the fifties, because its walls and ceiling were carpeted. That the color was pink didn't seem to give or take away from the sound.

Even with change about to happen as the lounges would switch to the less expensive recorded vinyl entertainment spun by disc jockeys, young adults, some just out of the service, still enjoyed cutting the rug to live music. The place to do it was the Berkeley-Carteret's new Grill Room, where city police officer Anthony Petillo had a combo that played weekend nights. His signature song was an adaptation from the popular musical *Carousel*, where he substituted the verb "dance" for "walk" and sang, "You'll Never Dance Alone."

Restaurants along Ocean Avenue and Kingsley Street also applied for and received liquor licenses after Repeal, and their owners and managers tried their hands at adding entertainment. In the coming decades, the most wildly successful address would be owned by Ida Jacobs who, together with her husband, John, had started out renting a seasonal hot dog stand in 1922 on the southwest corner of Ocean and Second Avenues. Soon they bought the property and expanded the building into a full-scale family restaurant halfway down Second. They named it Mrs. Jay's. During Prohibition they opened a beer garden next door on Ocean and served 2 percent beer. After Repeal they were able to serve hard liquor at their indoor Circus Bar. When their daughter, Jeanette, joined the family business, entertainment was added to the summer offerings. Some nights it was local doo-wop singing sensation Nickey Addeo from the West Side. Other nights they booked national acts like the Three Chuckles, who were popular in the 1940s and early 1950s.

Political Theater: Act II

By 1940, Walter Reade Sr. was publicly threatening to stop showing first-run movies and possibly close his theaters altogether because of the installation of downtown parking meters. Reade charged the meters caused a 50 percent drop in movie attendance and ticket sales. More to the point, Reade was irate with what he saw as conservative machine politics running city hall. In 1945 he put together a party called the Citizens' Victory League. His running mates were Dr. Harry G. Thomas, father of national radio commentator Lowell Thomas, realtor Milan Ross, and two city councilmen up for reelection, lawyer Vincent Keuper and Public Works Director Orville Winterstella.

Reade ran for office, using the St. James Theatre apartment as his city address even though his family lived on Deal Road in Ocean Township on an estate that came to be called the Mayfair House, taking its name from that of the mansion on the large property. Reade's ticket lost but Reade's venom toward Mayor George Smock II did

CLOSE COVER • STRIKE MATCH ON BACK

You are about to meet a sexy stranger...

... at the Colony Baths
500 Summerfield Ave.
Asbury Pk., N.J.

DIAMOND MATCH CO. N.Y., N.Y.

The postwar years were marked by an upswing in morals raids all over the state, and many bars that catered to gays and lesbians had red lights to warn patrons of an impending raid. In 1967, two years before the landmark Stonewall riots in Manhattan, the New Jersey Supreme Court put an end to the raids and ruled that homosexuals could gather in public. Pike Archives

not dissipate. For two years Reade paid a staff to work out of the building originally built to house a branch of the National Bank on Mattison Avenue and Bond Street; the staff's assignment was to report on Asbury Park's municipal failings, and the information was printed in a daily newspaper that Reade called the *Asbury Park Sun*. He shared printing costs, sports coverage, and national columnists with the *Red Bank Daily Standard*. Nothing was off-limits: deteriorating conditions at the Bond Street School; unchecked gambling on the West Side; the secret lease negotiations for Boardwalk concessions; the unlawful practice of fortune-teller Madame Marie Costello; a shady real estate deal for a new City Hall; and delays in Boardwalk repairs after the hurricane of 1944. Reade even took to task *Asbury Park Evening Press* editor Wayne D. McMurray, whose offices were at the opposite end of Mattison Avenue, for the paper's lack of hard-hitting reporting. In 1948, after two years, Reade ran out of steam. When he died in 1952 at sixty-eight, he was venturing into residential real estate development of the former Ross-Fenton Farm nightclub on Deal Lake and building a hotel in Saratoga Springs.

In the 1930s, Greenwich Village bohemian poet Tiny Tim, a friend of Asbury Park poet Margaret Widdemer, briefly opened a gay-friendly tearoom on Bond Street between Bangs and Mattison. By the 1960s, the original nineteenth-century oyster bar was owned by Matty and Pep Bascelici, who had relocated downtown from Kingsley Street, decorating the bar with Morro Castle *artifacts that had washed up on shore. The bar, carved with waves, now sits at Insano's Restaurant on Main Street. Pike Archives.*

Reade: The Next Generation

With his release from the U.S. army at the rank of captain after World War II, Walter Reade Jr. was ready to return to the family business, where he had begun in 1933. While their personalities were dissimilar, both father and son shared a few of the same interests. Both loved the theater industry, were interested in technological advances in moviemaking, and recognized local talent.

Several entertainment figures came from the area. Oakhurst native and B-movie screamer Norma Eberhardt (*Live Fast, Die Young*, and *The Return of Dracula*, both 1958) recalled generous publicity for her movies when they opened in Asbury Park. Princess Jan was Asbury Park High School graduate and Wanamassa schoolteacher Joan Leon, who hosted a children's show for four- to twelve-year-olds on Reade TV, which was broadcast from the Lyric Theatre in the mid-1950s. The Reades relied on another Asbury Park High graduate, photographer Edward Noumair, both to promote movie openings and to film high school football games that aired on Reade TV. Among Noumair's more memorable assignments was promoting the 1939 Greta

Garbo film, *Ninotchka*. Senior hired Noumair to take pictures of women on Cookman Avenue. The come-on? "You have a Ninotchka smile. May I take your picture?" And then he would hand them a free pass to attend the movie.

Besides dabbling in the early UHF television technology, Reade also invested in movie production and distribution deals for theaters and television. *Mediterranean Holiday* was a 1952 travelogue filmed in three different versions, with one intended

On the Aisle

MY GRANDMOTHER, VIRGINIA TUCKER, GREW UP IN Manhattan and was completely captivated by the lifestyle of the Roaring Twenties. She accepted bit parts in small films and even played the piano for silent movies—anything to be part of show business. She married Frank Barry, a man who shared her love for the theater. They moved to Asbury Park in 1927 to raise their family. But my grandmother could not resist the lure of the theater. She would travel to New York often: church groups' theatrical productions or women's clubs were not beneath her. She would do anything and everything to be associated with the theater.

In 1945 she was offered the opportunity of her life when the *Asbury Park Press* hired her to be the drama critic and write "On the Aisle." She was paid to travel to Manhattan, attend the latest Broadway shows, interview some of the stars, and see her critiques published in the Sunday paper.

She was also given her own five-minute weekly radio show on WJLK to report what was happening in New York's theater district. When her column was cancelled, she freelanced for the *Press*, reviewing local community theater pro-

ductions. Her final review, in 1974, was of a folk-rock concert performed by Melanie in Convention Hall; the hook was a senior citizen's impression of a rock concert. She enjoyed the evening until the hall got smoky and someone tried to pass her a cigarette. That was enough for her. An article accompanying her review stated that there was now a smoking ban on all concerts in Convention Hall.

– Michael Barry
Deal, New Jersey

Asbury Park Press *theater critic Virginia Barry founded the Outer Critics Circle for Manhattan's out-of-town and suburban theater critics in October 1950. She is pictured here with lead actor Henry Fonda for the Outer Critics' first best play award, which was given in 1952 to* Point of No Return. *The ceremony took place at the Beef and Bourbon restaurant, New York. Courtesy of Catherine and Michael Barry.*

for the Cinerama curved screen concept promoted by adventure travel writer Lowell Thomas. Cinerama's initial investor was actor-turned-producer Mike Todd, who was looking for ways to produce a 70mm film with a special bug-eye lens intended to give viewers a "you are right here" experience. Todd finally found a property with Jules Verne's classic novel *Around the World in 80 Days*. Reade signed a distribution deal for the right to premiere the film in New Jersey, which he did at the Paramount on July 11, 1957. After the summer season was over and the Paramount closed for the winter, Reade moved the film to the St. James. In all it ran in Asbury Park for six months. While Mike Todd was spotted in the lobby of the Berkeley-Carteret Hotel around this time, his famous wife, Elizabeth Taylor, was in seclusion awaiting the birth of the couple's first child.

Perhaps Reade's biggest promotional bonanza occurred in 1958 when he spent $250,000 on the local premiere of *The Bridge over the River Kwai* starring Alec Guinness. He hired Interlaken architect David Marner to build a replica of the bridge over Cookman Avenue that people could walk across.

In 1962 Reade merged with the Sterling Television Company around the time he began selling over-the-counter stock in his company to raise financing for expansion. In 1966 the company name changed to Walter Reade Organization, Inc. To fill his Manhattan theaters, Reade explored the possibility of broadcasting horse races

Bridge of Courage

THE SUMMER OF 1958 WAS HOT AND SO HUMID YOU could see and feel the misty sea air on your skin. My family was visiting friends in Asbury Park to see *The Bridge on the River Kwai*, which was about to open at the St. James. It would turn out to be quite an adventure for an eight-year-old girl!

That summer, Walter Reade actually had a bridge built over Cookman Avenue. What a sight! The bridge was seventy feet long, fourteen feet high, and four feet wide. Imagine my fright when my older friend, she must have been all of ten, talked me and my baby sister into climbing up the stairs to cross to the other side of Cookman.

Reluctantly I did as she suggested and after much coaxing, stood majestically at the center of the bridge looking out over the entire street, thrilled that I had accomplished this feat! In truth, my motivation was probably the promise from my parents of an ice cream at Kohr's or a chance to win a stuffed animal at one of the arcades.

The wonderment of Asbury Park in the 1950s was not to be replicated by any other experience in my young life. I can only hope that one day children will be able to experience the joy of Asbury Park as it once was.

– Trudi Wolfe-Larkin, teacher
Ocean Township, New Jersey

in order to meet the anticipated demand created by the off-track betting program that New York voters had passed in 1963. Closer to Asbury Park, he entered into negotiations to build his first suburban movie theater in neighboring Ocean Township. Reade also acquired a wood veneer company and a couple of nonrelated theater businesses. By 1970 the organization was in trouble, and to save on winter heating bills, Reade closed the St. James and the Mayfair in Asbury Park. By the time he died in a skiing accident in the Swiss Alps in 1973, his company was operating in the red. It owed the city more than $50,000 in back taxes and another $20,000 to replenish its rent security deposit account on the Paramount.

Night to Rock

By the end of the 1960s, hotel lounge acts were passé. With a slump in his career, even Frank Sinatra was performing outside Asbury Park at Alex Primavera's Shore Motel on Route 35 in Ocean Township. The year? 1966. The postwar babies-turned-teenagers had found a new sound to embrace as their own, one they heard first on live radio broadcasts from New York City theaters and then on television. It was a sound coming up from the South that was rooted in rhythm and blues and turning into rock and roll. Beginning in 1957, teenagers could see what they were listening to when Dick Clark moved his popular *American Bandstand* from radio to television. They also listened and watched *Hullabaloo*, a musical variety program that aired in 1965 and 1966, and finally *Soul Train*, the first African American variety show, which aired in 1971. And so was born a market for musicians who could play, or cover, these new musical standards.

A new entertainment circuit rose up around the old hotel circuit that girded Kingsley Street and Ocean Avenue. Nightclubs like the Student Prince, which opened in a nineteenth-century revival-meeting house on Kingsley Street near First Avenue featured cover bands, letting musicians looking for an original sound to try out their new material later when the evening turned to early morning. Over on Fourth, just west off Kingsley, the Fast Lane opened next door to the bowling alley in an old apartment

house garage that the new owners lined with stadium bleachers. In 1974 the black girl group the Shirelles opened the club.

North Jersey singer, songwriter, and guitarist Bill Chinnock came to the Shore and started looking for other musicians who wanted to create a new sound. Chinnock recalled the 1960s as a period of creative free-for-all in which musicians tried out every style from country rockabilly and blues to jazz and folk, searching in equal measure for self-expression and public respect. For them, covering the standards was merely a way to make sure there would be some pay for them at the end of the night.

In 1968 the rock-and-roll dance parties that hairdressers and hippie bon vivants Tom and Margaret Potter threw became too much for their conservative neighbors in quiet Ocean Grove. The couple moved to the second-floor apartment above Parke Drug Store at 712 Cookman Avenue, but their late-night parties quickly drew too many people to fit into the studio loft. So the Potters made a deal to rent the vacant second and third floors of the building on the southwest corner of Cookman Avenue and Bond Street, and moved the music next door.

Much older than his wife, Potter was already beginning to experience difficulties with his hands, the result of years of handling hair chemicals without wearing protective gloves. Arthritis had also begun to afflict them, and he was looking for ways other than hairdressing to earn a living. Potter's creative talents were undiminished, and, along with his enthusiastic, party-hostess wife, Margaret Romeo, so was his curiosity to try new things.

The second-floor lounge was devoted to folk music and called the Green Mermaid. It opened early in the evening, and food and nonalcoholic beverages were served. The third floor was devoted to rock-and-roll, and was called the Upstage. It opened around midnight or after the Potters had tidied up the Green Mermaid and closed it for the evening. To get the Upstage going, the couple held painting parties and gave patrons brushes and cans of Day-Glo orange, green, yellow, and purple paint to swirl across the black walls. The charge at the door was three dollars, and everyone who came could stay until the sun came up over the ocean.

Unpolished musicians who couldn't get into the rock clubs on the hotel circuit found a haven here where they could play. They also found a willing Mrs. Potter to help groom them and give them confidence about their musical performance. One was a scrawny teenager from Freehold with a long tangle of hair and a slightly menacing look whose musical presence came out once he got on stage. Though booed one

Rock 'n' Roll Rite of Passage

MY PARENTS WERE THE CLASSIC FIFTIES PARENTS, Perry Como fans, didn't know what rock 'n' roll was all about. It was dramatically changing the landscape of America. A lot of music agents who were in their thirties at that time really didn't get it.

Whenever you could be someplace when the kids could be in charge, that defined your passage to adulthood. I was bitten by the process of how to book musical acts when I was my junior prom chair in high school. That was 1968. Two years later I was booking acts for the Sunshine In. It was right in the thick of things. A big old garage set up like a ballroom. There was a chandelier hanging from the ceiling. It had adequate dressing rooms. I booked Leon Russell, Edgar Winters, Miami Steve [Van Zandt].

Next year I moved to the Casino. The Asbury Park City Council at the time didn't get the change in musical tastes. Everything wasn't the Beach Boys. The negotiations to get the contract to book acts in the Casino were contentious. We did two seasons in the old Casino. We had the Band. The coolest show there. And Todd Rundgren.

At the end of the second year Moe Septee called and asked me to lunch. Told me he was going to give me his exclusive at Convention Hall. His heart wasn't into rock 'n' roll. He wanted to go back to concentrating on classical and pop in Philly.

So, we moved our series and made Convention Hall a place where artists wanted to come. We'd have barbecues for the bands before their shows on the veranda overlooking the ocean.

When the acts started to get sophisticated with sound systems and acoustics that dwarfed Convention Hall, we knew the end was coming. Arena shows were the death knell. Convention Hall was never anything more than an adequate building. In ten years arena rock wiped out the theater ballroom experience.

– John Scher, president,
Metropolitan Talent, New York

night at the Green Mermaid by the folk crowd, his original lyrics and melodies struck a chord with the rock-and-roll crowd on the third floor. Together with the sound he was trying to forge, it was clear in those early Upstage sessions that he was different from musicians trying to break into the circuit of clubs on Kingsley Street. His name was Bruce Springsteen. And at the Upstage he was to find his earliest bandmates, drummer Vini Lopez and guitarist Steve Van Zandt.

"They were fun to be with. They always generated a lot of interest in what they were doing. They were good party people," recalled Doug Wilson, Margaret's

Dell'Arte DeVito

"MY MOTHER AND FATHER HAD A VERY VOLATILE kind of relationship," he explains. "They were comic in a commedia dell'arte kind of way. You know, frying pans on the head and shit like that. Kind of a typical Italian American family. Very, very close, very outspoken. They would immediately tell you where to get off, or just speak their mind. And sometimes the comic way was the best way to get your point across without hurting anybody's feelings." . . .

From early on, DeVito wanted to be in pictures. "I used to go to the movies every Saturday and Sunday," he recalls. "The greatest thing was staying home from school sick, curling up in front of the TV and watching a good Tom Mix."

After high school [Oratory Prep, Summit, New Jersey, class of 1962], DeVito went to work at his sister Angela's beauty parlor. There, he decided to become a makeup artist. Street-theater buddy Louie Scalpati remembers DeVito's earliest work. "I was . . . his guinea pig," he explains. "One Halloween . . . he made me up as the Hunchback of Notre Dame. . . . I had a scar, and one of my eyes was hanging out. . . . We went over and visited our priest, Father Edwards. When he came to the door to see who rang, he back-stepped all the way to his room."

That experience under his belt, DeVito decided to go to school for makeup. The only place offering instruction was New York's American Academy of Dramatic Arts, but there was no major in makeup. DeVito would have to enroll as an acting student.

– Robert Seidenberg, "Funny as Hell,"
American Film, September 1989

"Mr. Danny" applied enough hair spray to Judi Wing and Anne Knight's bouffants so they could withstand winds off an oceanfront jetty for a publicity photo for his sister Angela's hair salon; the photo ran in Spotlight *magazine. Courtesy of Peter Lucia.*

brother-in-law, who worked for the couple after returning from his tour of duty in Vietnam. But even this music scene began to change. At the end of 1970, Wilson noted, the drug scene was settling in for the long term, and the Upstage's devotees weren't dancing to the music as much as they were standing in placing nodding to an inner rhythm no one else could hear.

"Tom couldn't stop the drugs," Wilson observed. "He didn't want it in his club, but if people showed up stoned, he couldn't do much to stop them from coming in.

"But the whole aspect of participation changed," continued Wilson. "The music changed. It wasn't nuanced anymore. Just a lot of the driving beat of a bass guitar and drums. The friendly party atmosphere like we were in Tom and Margaret's home disappeared. They couldn't hold on." After two glorious years the club closed.

Disco Fever

Living in Long Branch in 1966, Maggie Hogan came to Asbury Park to open the resort's first women's club in the old Shore Grill at 429 Cookman Avenue. Hogan called the new club Chez L, and attracted a loyal following of lesbians. Before too long the raven-haired Hogan earned the Tennessee Williams–inspired nickname Maggie the

Cat and proceeded to spin her own legend for her Asbury Park habitués: former nun, daughter of a New Brunswick cop, she brazenly used men's room urinals and, as part of the strategy to ensure immortality, had a spectacularly heated rivalry with the new owner of the Rustic Lodge, Ray Palozzi. When it burned to the ground in a mysterious fire, Maggie was seen drinking champagne in the middle of Cookman Avenue before streaking naked all the way to the M&K at Heck Street, where the police finally picked her up.

In the early 1970s, new Asbury Hudson Hotel owner Paul Wisnewski moved the hotel's growing club scene across Heck Street into the abandoned Elks-Charms building. Together with the liquor license of the former street-level M&K Tavern, he opened a gay dance club on the second floor of the old men's social club, using the tavern's old initials. After a fire wiped out his hotel, Wisnewski leveled the remains for a parking lot.

As the disco craze took hold on the shore, Wisnewski approached the Walter Reade Organization about the possibility of buying the shuttered Mayfair Theatre to turn it into a club fashioned after Studio 54 in New York City, the one-time CBS radio studio that had been converted into a cavernous celebrity-driven discothèque. According to Wisnewski, Reade executors offered him both the St. James and the Mayfair for $75,000. He declined; too much money for too many buildings.

"The Mayfair was already in bad shape," recalled Wisnewski about the peeling paint, falling plaster, and moldy seats. By comparison, the simpler art deco construction of the St. James was in better condition. But while Wisnewski turned the Walter Reade Organization down, later he paid $10,000 a year to rent the vacant lots for still more parking for the hugely popular M&K.

Political Theater: Act III

There was to be one more public face-off between the departed Reades and an Asbury Park mayor. Sheldon Gunsberg, who became president of the Walter Reade Organization in New York, had put the company in Chapter 11 bankruptcy proceedings in order to refinance the company's debt and start a schedule of payments to its creditors. As part of his strategy Gunsberg asked city hall for a reduction in property taxes for the hulking movie properties, which were no longer in operation. Gunsberg argued for a reevaluation on the grounds that the last tax rate had been set when the theaters were producing revenue. But city hall wasn't willing to negotiate.

The Pony

THE FIRST DAY THE STONE PONY OFFICIALLY OPENED was February 8, 1974. It snowed six inches and all the deliveries came at once. The heaters didn't work well. The ice machine didn't work at all. Nobody played that weekend. I can remember standing there thinking, "What did you get yourself into now?"

It seemed like everything was sold, taken, or used from Asbury Park, and all that was left was miniature golf courses and parking lots. When I had been six years old my aunts brought me down from Paterson. People used to dress to come to Asbury Park. The restaurants were much better. The shopping downtown was at its peak. Convention Hall had a lot of shows. In 1973 it all seemed to disappear.

In the beginning I used a lot of bands that I knew from working at the Riptide in Point Pleasant. Bands like Colony, Southern Cross. In the beginning we weren't accepted by the local musicians in Asbury. Nobody knew us. The city council didn't want [another] rock-and-roll club. They wanted to close us down. If we received ten write-ups from the police we'd have to go before the council at the time of our license renewal and tell them why we had so many reports on the police blotter.

But our friends came and the bands we booked had a following, and eventually word got out. The first major local band I booked was Blackberry Booze Band. This was also a band local musicians loved to jam with. I booked them for $135 a night because my brother-in-law, Dave Myers, played in it. Over the weeks more and more people came to see them. I can remember Johnny Lyons and Little Steven jamming with the band. A fellow named Bruce Springsteen came in the Pony and everybody got excited. I personally did not know who he was. Someone told me he had an album out, *Greetings from Asbury Park*.

Eventually Southside Johnny [Lyons] and the Asbury Jukes became our house band. The Jukes really pumped the hell out of rhythm and blues. And Sunday nights was the big dance night and people loved to dance to the Jukes. This is what people did. They belonged to a club that's not just a place to go drinking but where they knew everybody. They knew the music. They knew the musicians. They knew what type of music they wanted. I had courtesy cards. Our first courtesy card was called the urine card. U-R-IN—a white card with black lettering. It was for the customers who came six or seven nights a week.

I changed my format to bring in musicians that would want to jam with one another. I always had bands at the Pony that Bruce or Miami Steve or any of the local musicians would jam with. John Eddie. Cats on a Smooth Surface. Beaver Brown. . . . When Jim Messina played down in Convention Hall I had the Jukes here that night. They weren't that big at the time. But Bruce showed up. And then all of a sudden Jim Messina showed up. So, here's everybody on stage. Our closing hour is three. Five o'clock I kept all the regulars in and shut the doors. And they played and played and played. We were open seven nights a week with entertainment. Sometimes I had twenty, thirty bands a week. Sometimes I had five bands a night.

It got hard for a while with disco. But I had my Asbury Jukes Tuesday, Thursday, and Sunday. I might have my Stir Crazy on Monday and my Max on Wednesday. Or, the Nines on Wednesday. Then I put TT Quick, which is a hard-rock band, on Tuesdays. We had a good party atmosphere. Good bands and good people.

– Butch Pielka, manager, co-owner,
the Stone Pony, 1973–1984

"I'd rather see a parking lot there than two empty theaters," said Mayor Ray Kramer, turning down the appeal. Despite a last-stand effort by a group of local movie enthusiasts to find money to buy the Mayfair, the wrecking ball came down. On December 1974 Mayor Kramer got what he asked for, and Thomas Lamb's historic theaters were leveled. The Walter Reade Theatre Organization also got what it asked for: with no buildings on the property, the tax assessment had to be lowered for what was now considered unimproved property. The Lertch Corporation, a Wall Township salvage company hired to clear out the debris, sold the St. James Theatre's seats to the Beach Cinema in Bradley Beach.

The Reades may have gotten the last laugh when the city wound up with the Savoy-Kinmonth-Reade building for back taxes. By 1980 city hall was having no luck putting the aging office-theater building back on the tax rolls. Because Reade had last booked burlesque acts and then X-rated films in the Savoy's last days, the city penned a reverter clause that prohibited the filming or sale of any pornographic material on the property. The city's asking price was $17,000.

Pornography hadn't starred only at the Savoy. The Lyric Theatre changed its name to the Park Cinema and together with the Baronet was showing pornographic films with such names as *Marriage and Other Four Letter Words* and *The Sensuous Detective.*

While visitors weren't going to Asbury Park to see first-run movies on Reade's moribund theater circuits anymore, they had found a new reason to spend time cruising the circuit in the worn-out resort. In January 1973, Bruce Springsteen debuted his maiden album, whose cover was decorated with a colorful postcard emblazoned with the words "Greetings from Asbury Park" (the title of the album); the balloon letters were filled with the Boardwalk buildings that had put Asbury Park on the map nearly fifty years earlier. The salutation made for an ideal album title. In November Springsteen came out with a second album, *The Wild, the Innocent, and the E Street Shuffle* and a song whose haunted lyrics about lost love echoed the title: "Fourth of July, Asbury Park (Sandy)." Throughout 1974 Springsteen toured the country with his collection of rock-and-roll songs that seemed to have walked right off the Boardwalk of his imagination and into mainstream popular culture. The confirmation came in 1975 when both *Time* and *Newsweek* magazines sent journalists to Asbury Park to spend time with the rocker, reporting the influences that shaped the man and his music. That October both publications unveiled October editions with Springsteen on the cover. Asbury Park was reborn as a music destination.

CHAPTER FIVE

Dining Out, Sleeping In

CRENELLATED SKYLINE of rounded turrets, formal square spires, mansard roofs pierced by dormer windows, and the occasional corner cupola with a banner dancing gaily in the ocean breeze defined the hotel circuit up Ocean Avenue and down Kingsley Street. No more than five stories in height, the rambling structures were shingled testaments to the glory days of Victorian resort hotels. Leading accommodations such as the Coleman House, West End, Plaza, Bristol, Brunswick, Fenimore, Lafayette, and Sunset Hall occupied the prime lots, stretching entire blocks from east to west, their wide verandas promising guests they would see and be seen while taking in the healthy sea air. These full-service hotels dominated the leisure market, offering everything from saltwater baths, touring cars, ninepins, *germains*, theater performances, and billiards, despite Sunday sermons from Grand Avenue churches against the sins of wagering.

The appeal of well-dressed tables d'hôtes at the finer hotels was enhanced by a separate meal hour for children and their nannies. Menus for adults featured imported mineral water, Belfast ginger ale, and the domestic Indian Lady Spring water whose brochures carried an endorsement from E. E. Smith, M.D. Despite the constant campaigning of the Women's Christian Temperance Union, liquor was available in 1890; the Plaza, which overlooked the Casino and Wesley Lake, openly advertised free wine

The Season Nearing Its Height

Asbury Park is becoming more and more a resort of the fashionable and gay. . . . [At the] Brunswick Miss Fannie Mills, daughter of Congressman Mills, of Texas, figured in China silk and diamonds; Mrs. Benjamin Butterworth, wife of Congressman Butterworth of Ohio, wore rose colored silk with diamonds. . . . The rule at most hotels is full dress, and no walking costumes on the floor. This adds to the attractiveness of the ballroom. The hops were almost without exception brilliant society affairs.

– Asbury Park Journal,
August 9, 1890

Arrested for Selling Beer

The Asbury Park Law and Order League made another raid Monday on the illicit liquor sellers.

– The Shore Press,
October 3, 1890

with its lunches. Whether champagne served with oysters, a decanter of wine placed next to a rack of lamb, or Washington pudding in port wine sauce, luxury travelers coming to Asbury Park knew they would find the perfect complement to a five-course dinner. If not, they wouldn't have to work hard to obtain it.

Arc Angels

Despite the municipal ban on liquor sales within one mile of the borders of both Asbury Park and Ocean Grove, alcohol came into the more secular Asbury Park in a variety of ways. Drugstore elixirs that promised relief from real or imagined anxieties were filled with raw alcohol masked by tropical flavors. Savvy cottagers knew they could purchase grain alcohol and hard liquor from vegetable or dairy delivery men who smuggled the contraband in pint-size bottles among their produce as they went door-to-door in the late afternoon selling provisions for that night's dinner. Beer makers slipped in after dark, their horse-drawn teams pulling a beer arc from which homemade brews were siphoned, or arc-ed, into waiting pitchers and empty soda bottles.

James Bradley, whose own father had been an alcoholic, was aware of the constant violations to the dry credo for his temperance resort. During the inaugural 1890 Baby Parade two out-of-towners were arrested and charged with drunk and disorderly conduct on the beachfront. Later that fall, a New York wine salesman was discovered soliciting orders door-to-door in broad daylight along Cookman Avenue, gleefully admitting to realtor Thomas Appleby that he had secured a large number of orders. Appleby was part of a special brigade Bradley christened his "arc angels," pro-temperance men and women who turned in violators to the police. While reporting the salesman's presence to the *Asbury Park Journal*, Appleby did not turn him in to police, but merely warned him not to return to fill the orders.

As the twentieth century began, even some of the prominent hotels that James and Helen Bradley stayed in were raided to root the demon alcohol out of the Christian resort. When raids did occur, though, they were usually at season's end. A midweek midnight raid on August 30, 1905, saw the arrest of 158 spirited party-goers

COLEMAN HOUSE
ASBURY PARK,
NEW JERSEY

dressed in masks at a special soiree in the Coleman's downstairs café as they feted the final days of summer. Despite the number of arrests, Frank B. Conover, proprietor of the hotel, was the only one charged, and charged at that with just four counts of illegal liquor sales. Later that same night, two blocks away on Lake Avenue, police arrested Raleigh Hotel owner Mathias Applegate, along with twenty-five of his elbow-bending restaurant patrons. One was a city patrolman. With the advent of Prohibition in 1919, hotel and restaurant owners in Asbury Park, as well as elsewhere around the country, started paying for police protection to head off raids that would inconvenience their guests and adversely affect their ability to do business.

Staying Solvent

After Labor Day each year, nearly all the hotels closed. A handful of smaller properties located near the downtown remained open, catering to business travelers by providing individual heat and hot water, amenities that were more expensive to install in the larger hotels. Some guests were also year-round residents who chose not to own a house, and their regular room rents helped stabilize income for commercial property owners. Asbury Park entrepreneurs who owned the oceanfront hotels as investments had other businesses to occupy their attention during the off-season. But as members of the Board of Trade, they nonetheless spent many winter meetings looking for ways to promote the city as a year-round destination

Billed as "the world's fastest human," bicyclist Arthur Zimmerman was honored by his peers from the League of American Wheelman with a lavish ceremonial dinner at the Coleman House. Pike Archives.

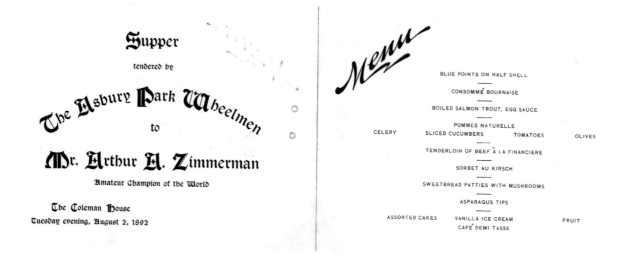

Supper

tendered by

The Asbury Park Wheelmen

to

Mr. Arthur A. Zimmerman

Amateur Champion of the World

The Coleman House
Tuesday evening, August 2, 1892

Menu

BLUE POINTS ON HALF SHELL

CONSOMMÉ BOURNAISE

BOILED SALMON TROUT, EGG SAUCE

POMMES NATURELLE

CELERY   SLICED CUCUMBERS   TOMATOES   OLIVES

TENDERLOIN OF BEEF À LA FINANCIERE

SORBET AU KIRSCH

SWEETBREAD PATTIES WITH MUSHROOMS

ASPARAGUS TIPS

ASSORTED CAKES   VANILLA ICE CREAM   FRUIT
CAFÉ DEMI TASSE

RIGHT *New Jersey's coastal resorts owed much to members of the African American community who toiled behind the scenes at hotels and restaurants. This rare staff photograph was taken by William Stauffer, who was the photographer for Asbury Park's annual Baby Parade. Pike Archives.*

BELOW *Exclusionary ethnic and racial practices, whether advertised or not, existed at hotels as well as on the Boardwalk. Note the caption in the lower-left corner. Pike Archives.*

Hotel Monmouth

On the Ocean Front

SEASON FROM JUNE TO OCTOBER

WE POSITIVELY DO NOT SOLICIT THE PATRONAGE OF HEBREWS

Wm. Applegate, Owner and Proprietor.

Asbury Park, N. J.

despite mounting evidence they might not succeed. Autumn hurricanes frequently ripped the Boardwalk, making repairs necessary and costly. Winter storms glazed the resort in ice, making its avenues and sidewalks treacherous. In the years after World War I, a new vacation season would be inaugurated in the United States with the introduction of downhill skiing.

The nation's railroads also created new competitive challenges for Asbury Park as a sought-after destination. As the companies opened passage to the West Coast, the railroads brought attention to such natural wonders as the Grand Canyon, the Great Salt Lake, and the California redwoods. Status-seeking vacationers had to visit. Concurrently, though, the railroads paid attention to their metropolitan markets and the middle and lower classes, and offered more summer excursions to the seashore on a nearly hourly schedule. In doing so, they created a new class of traveler, the day-tripper. Now, more than ever, Asbury Park's hoteliers wanted the ban on Sunday train service lifted into order to turn these one-day visitors from Philadelphia and New York into overnight guests.

By 1905, many Asbury Park hoteliers were meeting secretly to gather support for a bill winding its way through the state legislature. The bill proposed the creation of local excise boards to issue liquor licenses. Serving alcohol without the fear of a raid would enable hotels and restaurants all over New Jersey to bring in revenue while cash-strapped communities could use the licensing fees to defray such municipal costs as jail construction, road paving, and sewer installation.

To muster the local votes necessary to support this strategy, hotel owners backed a proposal to annex the unincorporated section of Neptune that lay west of the railroad tracks, including Burnham's neighborhood, where most hotel employees lived. Not surprisingly, those against the annexation were the East Side pro-temperance Protestant churches that lined Grand Avenue. The annexation referendum passed, Asbury Park

The Young Women's Christian Association of Philadelphia operated its own recreational hotel for young ladies, the Sea Rest, on the corner of Second Avenue and Heck Street overlooking Library Square. After it was lost in a fire, single-family residences were built on the property. Pike Archives.

Few Asbury Park hotels had managers trained in the hospitality business. The New Monterey was a notable exception. Nearly all the resort's smaller owner-operated hotels and boardinghouses closed down altogether shortly after Labor Day until the following spring. Pike Archives.

doubled in population and size, and shortly thereafter, enough votes were cast in another special election to create an excise board. The city began issuing liquor licenses that permitted the sale of 2.5 percent beer and wine.

The Century's First New Hotel

In 1912, the same year that Sunday trains were first allowed to stop at the Asbury Park and Ocean Grove station, a new hotel opened. Occupying the entire city block north of Bradley's public Auditorium, the hotel set a new construction and style standard in Asbury Park when it opened. Built with Portland cement, one of Thomas Edison's inventions, and fortified by steel, it was the resort's first fireproof hotel. Rising to six stories in height, it was designed with an elevator from the ground up. It was one floor taller and had 102 rooms more than its nearest rival, the wood-shingled New Monmouth Hotel, whose 348 rooms overlooked the Auditorium from its western location on Kingsley Street and Sunset Avenue. Built for $600,000, the new hotel reflected the Spanish Colonial Revival style that had begun sweeping the country from Florida to California in 1910; the style would help influence architecture in Asbury Park for nearly two decades to come.

Appropriately enough, its investors chose a Spanish name for the luxury property: the New Monterey Hotel. As the Asbury Park Hotel and Realty Company, led by Dr. Bruce Keator, was already transforming the old wood-frame Metropolitan Hotel on Asbury Avenue, the board of directors decided the addition of the word "new" to the Monterey property would suffice to clarify the situation for the community.

At 450 rooms, the Monterey's only other competitor was the rambling wood-framed Bristol on Ocean and Fourth Avenues, which had 400 rooms. But a mysterious fire in October 1923 wiped out the Bristol, taking with it the adjacent Garden Theater on Ocean Avenue, as well as the Edgemere, Keswick, and Victoria Hotels west along Fourth Avenue. Closed for the season, the Bristol went up in flames in a mere half hour. Also lost in the fire were a cafeteria and stores with second-floor apartments on Third Avenue. The fire prompted a change in use of the Ocean Avenue property from hotel to restaurant and a small amusement arcade.

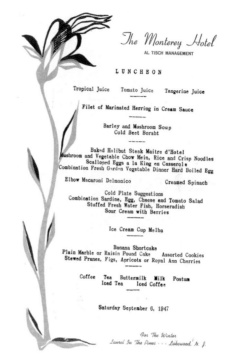

Pike Archives

Hotel Management

IN 1947 WE RAN THE MONTEREY HOTEL. WE ALSO operated Laurel-in-the-Pines in Lakewood. Lakewood was a winter resort and the Monterey seemed to be a natural fit since Asbury was a summer-only resort. The hotel itself wasn't a great hotel, but it was big: 350 rooms. Our family had a management deal with the owners to run the hotel. Actually, the Monterey had been closed down and used by the British during the war. Then a syndicate came along and bought it from the government.

My father, my brother, and I spent some time fixing it up. We thought maybe we could do enough business to make it work, but it was very difficult. I think we charged $100 per week–including food. Kosher menu; Jewish clientele. As it turns out, we were only involved in running the hotel for that one season, three or four months. At the end of the season, the owners said we didn't make as large a profit as they expected. They weren't happy that we made a profit, which was a miracle in itself. We had worked hard to make a profit. And so we said, "Fine. You take *all* the money and let us out of our management deal." They agreed; we left, and the next year they went bankrupt.

My father made a smart business decision; we all knew it was an impossible situation. It was a very difficult town. It was already beginning to slip downhill. See, the "glory days" of Asbury Park ended, really, around 1929. And by the 1930s it was starting to slip. So by the time we got there we were already late in the game.

– Laurence A. Tisch, chairman,
Loews Corporation, New York

War Guests

Just as Asbury Park's second great era of hotel expansion was getting under way, momentum was slowed by the U.S. involvement in World War I. Reservations were off. On Sunday, July 28, 1918, a special excursion train from the Bayway in Elizabeth arrived in Asbury Park, filled with war workers from the Standard Aircraft Corporation.

RIGHT *A boiler fire on April 9, 1940, wiped out the Albion and adjacent Steeplechase. Once the block was cleared, construction of a new fireproof hotel began. It was outfitted with pieces from the 1939 World's Fair in New York City: stair railings from the Florida exhibit; murals from the GM exhibit in its nightclub; and lavatory doors to finish some of the guest rooms with the words Men's and Ladies' faintly visible on some of them. Pike Archives.*

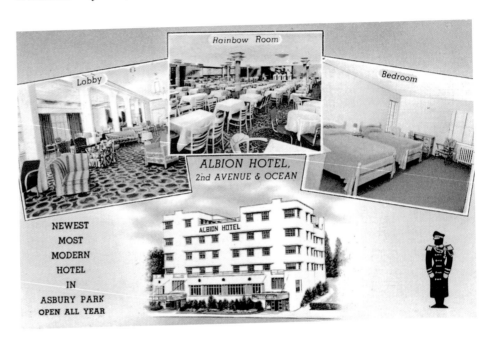

REQUEST CARD

CHARLIE GUEST
At Your Request

WILL PLAY:

_____

_____

_____

_____

Kindly Send or Hand Your Request to Drummer

CHARLIE GUEST
At The Drums

LEFT *Charlie Guest, drummer for the Albion Hotel's Rainbow Room house band, recalled the night a New York agent brought in a young pianist to perform with the band. "Hey, he's pretty good," Guest said to a fellow musician. The entertainer turned out to be Liberace. In the summer of 1963 the house band for the Peppermint Lounge in Manhattan, Joey Dee and the Starliters ("Peppermint Twist"), played a one-night stand at the Rainbow Room. Pike Archives.*

THE ANNESLEY

TELEPHONE

TODD & HALL
OWNERS AND PROPRIETORS

512 FIRST AVENUE

NEAR GRAND AVENUE

CENTRAL LOCATION IN THE
RESIDENTIAL SECTION OF

ASBURY PARK
N. J.

SELECT
FAMILY HOUSE

RATES
$10.00 PER WEEK UP
$2.00 PER DAY UP

CAPACITY, 100

Hotel Saint James, Fred. W. Bock Prop.
Asbury Park, N. J.

SAINT JAMES HOTEL

TOP *The looming issue of whether Asbury Park would move forward into the twentieth century as a seasonal resort or a year-round residential community was neatly defined in this postcard advertisement; circa 1910. Pike Archives.*

BOTTOM *No promotional opportunity was too lurid: The Saint James installed a shark tank display in its corner lobby at Cookman Avenue and Webb Street in the wake of the horrific 1916 shark attacks off the Jersey Shore. Pike Archives.*

There was no housing left in North Jersey, and the company had sent the workers to the Shore to find housing in hotels for themselves and their families.

Already living in the Shore's resort hotels were employees of T. A. Gillespie Company's munitions yard in South Amboy. On Monday, July 29, 1918, a train just for

The Hotel Fenimore was handsome to look at from the outside, but as this early twentieth-century floor plan shows, only a few rooms on the first sleeping floor had private baths. As the traveling American public increasingly sought more privacy while on vacation, hotels faced a cost dilemma over combining rooms and installing additional plumbing in order to remain competitive. Pike Archives.

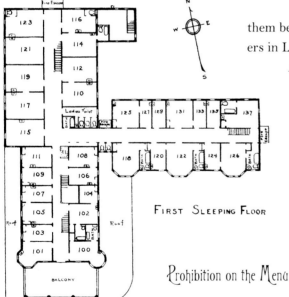

FIRST SLEEPING FLOOR

them began a daily run from Asbury Park, picking up more workers in Long Branch and Red Bank before delivering them to South Amboy. Four weeks later, a dedicated train for Standard Aircraft employees launched its seventy-eight-mile round-trip run from Asbury Park to Elizabeth with a specially subsidized round-trip train ticket of thirty cents for the daily commute. But on November 11, 1918, the Armistice was signed, and on April 30, 1919, the last train of workers and their families left the Shore to return to North Jersey and other parts of the country. The stage was now set for a different kind of war.

Prohibition on the Menu

In 1919 the federal government passed the Volstead Act in an attempt to put an end to the sale and consumption of alcohol. But in New Jersey, where Governor Edward I. Edwards had declared that the state would remain "as wet at the Atlantic," the local municipal excise boards were open for business, selling licenses for 2.5 percent beer. Hard liquor was also available, just much more difficult to come by.

Most of it was delivered from passing freighters in the Atlantic shipping lanes; sailors tossed the illegal cargo overboard so rumrunners in speedboats could retrieve the illicit bounty bobbing in the ocean. Retail outlets were the speakeasies in the basements of private homes and in the rear of restaurants. One was Frederick Shoen's German eatery on Kingsley Street between the Palace Merry-Go-Round and the Newark Hotel. A two-way mirror was installed to protect the identity of those drinking in the clublike back room. When James Bradley died in 1921, he did so regretting what Asbury Park had become. By 1923, Prohibition enforcement in New Jersey was largely left to federal treasury agents. Local enforcement had lapsed, partly thanks to paid protection—except in the cases of hotels and restaurants that wouldn't pay and were raided to appease the Women's Christian Temperance Union and Protestant ministers.

LEFT *Next to a public park that ran along Grand Avenue, Prospect House had one of the coveted locations on Lake Avenue and looked across Wesley Lake to Ocean Grove. Frank W. Woolworth stayed here in 1899 when he was scouting locations for a new five-and-ten-cent store. After World War II, the property began deteriorating and was headed for demolition after its last use as a bar-restaurant known as Corrubia's Deck House before it was restored. In 2002 it became the new location for the restaurant Moonstruck, formerly of Ocean Grove. The original barrel roof graces the restaurant's wine storage room. Pike Archives.*

RIGHT *The turreted Belmont was one of a number of hotels operated by women. By the last quarter of the twentieth century it had become a federally subsidized residential facility. Pike Archives.*

RIGHT *The hotel circuit's most coveted location was occupied by the Berkeley-Carteret Hotel. Its architect, Whitney Warren, also designed a bridge to connect the hotel to his Boardwalk pavilion, which he had designed for the city in a similar style. The cupola in the foreground belongs to the Monterey. Pike Archives.*

BELOW *The original Continental Ballroom was known for its decorative ceiling and for French doors that opened onto Kingsley Street. Pike Archives.*

The Century's Last New Hotel

As the Roaring Twenties picked up steam, so did the public debate about replacing Bradley's dilapidated Auditorium with a convention center. Behind the noise, no one was paying attention to acquisitive department store buyer Arthur C. Steinbach, who had quietly negotiated with the Bradley estate to buy the entire Auditorium block.

It was now Steinbach and his investors who wanted to build the biggest luxury hotel in Asbury Park, one that would best the Monterey and offer ballrooms that could double as convention space. After all, if Mayor Hetrick was correct in his prediction about all the convention business that would come to Asbury Park, shouldn't there be enough accommodations for all the conventioneers?

Steinbach's grandiose name for the hotel project was the Berkeley-Carteret, an oddly obscure historical allusion to the two British lords who had once owned much of colonial New Jersey. Certainly the names carried

ABOVE *The original Oval Lounge today is one of the smaller ballrooms used by the Berkeley-Carteret Oceanfront Resort Hotel and Conference Center. Pike Archives.*

LEFT *In the 1950s the Berkeley-Carteret hosted a regional candy convention; Steinbach department store models represented the five-cent candy bar makers. Candy queen was Nancy Riley, representing P. Margarella. Courtesy of Nancy (Riley) and Irwin Gerechoff.*

a certain cachet and enabled Steinbach to create a coat of arms and motto for his project. To make the architectural statement he wanted, Steinbach turned to Whitney Warren and his lawyer partner Charles Wetmore. Warren was New York's leading Beaux-Arts architect who had designed not only Grand Central Terminal but also the mass of hotel buildings that surrounded it: the Biltmore, the Commodore, and the Roosevelt.

Warren drew a cross-shaped design for the Berkeley-Carteret. Eight stories tall, the hotel eclipsed the Monterey and blocked its southern view. All but the Berkeley's west-facing rooms had ocean views. Built by the Turner Construction Company of Philadelphia, the hotel was made of steel and concrete, and sheathed in red brick. A three-story glassed-in cupola crowned its roof. From the second-floor mezzanine, doors opened to a broad footbridge that spanned Ocean

Avenue, connecting to a brand-new Boardwalk pavilion that Warren just happened to be hired by city hall to design.

On June 30, 1925, the Berkeley-Carteret Hotel Corporation opened its doors to the traveling public with an open-house party. The tiered dining room was the scene of a lavish banquet. The Mandarin Grill was filled with row after row of white-linen-draped tables, laden with chafing dishes. The banquet hall, which converted to a ballroom, was one of the planned convention rooms with seating for 1,400. Iridescent chandeliers with thousands of pendants of finely cut glass sent shimmering rays of light across the ivory-and-gold-decorated room. The carpet was rose-colored, and so were the chair seats. Steinbach arranged for a fashion show, and the cream of greater Asbury Park society filled the beautifully upholstered chairs and settees to see the latest creations from Milady Fashions.

The Berkeley-Carteret had 420 rooms, each with baths and showers that featured fresh *and* salt water running from the faucets. Steinbach furnished the rooms with twin beds, writing desks, lamps, telephone stands, and French chifforobes for hanging clothes. On September 6, 1925, the hotel capped its inaugural season with 485 registered guests. Two thousand meals were served that night. Eight years later, when Congress repealed the Volstead Act in February 1933, the Berkeley-Carteret received the first liquor license in Asbury Park. In May of that same year, the Fifteenth Annual

TOP *By 1950 the Montauk Hotel, located in a residential neighborhood just off Main Street at First Avenue and Bond Street, was an apartment house, no longer catering to travelers. Pike Archives.*

BOTTOM *Destroyed by a mysterious fire, the West End Hotel property changed from leisure to year-round living when the Civil Service Foundation built Philips Seaview, a high-rise dwelling for low-income seniors. It was named for long-time city employee Gabe Philips. Untouched by the fire was Asbury Park's first motel, the Flamingo, built in 1958 on the block's northwest corner. Courtesy of Milton Edelman.*

Spring Hotel Exposition was held in Convention Hall. The giveaways were tasting samples of the new 3.2 percent beer.

New War Guests

With political turmoil churning again in Europe in 1939, the United States was preparing to enter yet another war. In 1941 Congress passed the Lend-Lease Act, which enabled the federal government to rent private property in order to house members of the American and allied armed forces. A mountain retreat near Balti-more, as well as hotels in Miami, Atlantic City, and Asbury Park, were listed. The resort's signature residential hotels on Deal Lake Drive—the Santander and the Kingsley Arms—as well as the Asbury Carlton Hotel on Seventh Avenue, housed the U.S. Signal Corps while its men trained in Convention Hall.

The Berkeley-Carteret and the Monterey were set aside for rest and relaxation for the allied forces. The properties were surrounded by a ten-foot-tall security fence with pointed wooden tips. When 7,500 Royal British Navy personnel arrived, they dubbed the twin hotel compound the HMS *Asbury* to ensure they were paid "aboard ship."

The Monterey housed enlisted men; the Berkeley housed officers, including British actor Alec Guinness, who was so bored by his commission that he successfully

pulled enough strings to get back on stage, albeit in New York, not London. Sixth Avenue between the two hotels served as the parade ground for morning drills. Sailors assigned to HMS *Asbury* while waiting for repairs to their ships or for new assignments arrived at the North Asbury railway station, sometimes in the middle of the night, and marched in formation up Sunset Avenue to the oceanfront. Most nights the Salvation Army canteen came to the main gate at the Berkeley to give out cocoa. A month after the British left in February 1943, the U.S. Navy Pre-Midshipmen's School moved in with 70 officers and about 3,000 enlisted men.

Postwar Fallout

A 1919 fire destroyed the wood-frame Sunset Hall. In 1937 a three-story brick apartment was built on the western end of the empty hotel property. The property went back to leisure use when the apartments were replaced with an art moderne motel called the Orbit. Pike Archives.

The Monterey never recovered from the allied forces' occupation and the devastating effects of the 1944 hurricane. It spent its last year in decline and was demolished in November 1963. Arthur Steinbach spent a year restoring and refurbishing his beloved Berkeley-Carteret, borrowing money from his older brother, Walter. In a last burst of creativity, Arthur built an outdoor swimming pool by enclosing most of the hotel's Sunset Avenue frontage and lining it with cabanas, or what he called lanai rooms, giving them such Hawaiian names as Koui, Kokio, and Paleakala. A honeymooning couple was the first to register when he reopened on April 27, 1946. That year, the

Berkeley-Carteret hosted members of the world and national conventions of the Women's Christian Temperance Union, which convened from June 5 through 13.

But the hotel market was changing, especially after the Garden State Parkway opened in 1956. More middle-class vacationers wanted uncomplicated accommodations where they could just pull the family car up to their motel-room door. In fact, Asbury Park's first motel, the Flamingo, would go up in the shadow the hulking West End Hotel in 1958. In March 1957, Louis Glickman and Julius Mager, both of New York, bought the Berkeley-Carteret from the Arthur C. Steinbach estate for $1.08 million. Five years later it underwent a major facelift; a new indoor pool and heated spa were installed, and the Rib Room, a dining room paneled in hand-stained mahogany and outfitted with stunning red leather chairs, was inaugurated.

While the restaurant looked good, the food received little acclaim. The hotel went back on the auction block, and in 1964 the New Berkeley Corporation, an investment group, bought it for $1.25 million.

By this point, the shift in Asbury Park's hospitality business was clear. Full-service hotels were no longer destinations in and of themselves. In their place, restaurants had assumed the dominant role for attracting visitors. Savvy businessmen realized that an appealing menu with the right prices could attract a steady supply of repeat diners from the growing year-round population, with summer specials for day-trippers who came on organized bus tours. Many restaurants were family owned, touted their ethnic or homemade cooking, and were tightly run by two or three generations of an extended family, determined to move away from the labor-intensive baking, butchering, or even candy-making of their fathers' generation and into the seemingly more prestigious and financially rewarding business of fine dining.

Vegetable Soup and Fruit Pies

MY FATHER STARTED AS A TEENAGER ON THE PIER, working for [William] Couse. In 1932 he opened a lunch counter in a hardware store on Main Street called Nuts and Bolts. In 1961 we bought the building from the Hogarty family, gutted it, built a new kitchen, doubled the size of the luncheonette, and were there until 1989.

My grandmother was a baker. She would bake pies and cakes every day, and that was the kind of thing we were known for. She taught me and taught my two daughters. We used fresh fruit, no commercial fillers. My dad used to go every night to the farmer's market in Neptune City between Steiner and Railroad Avenues. Every night from July Fourth until after Labor Day the farmers came in from Holmdel, Middletown, Neptune, everywhere you can think of because they were all farms then, and backed their pickups into stalls. The lights were bulbs on wires. They would open in late afternoon and would be there until ten, eleven o'clock at night.

It was big. I mean, every kind of produce that you could think of in the summer, from vegetables to all kinds of fruits.

You could smell the peppers. The peaches, you bit into a peach and the juice would just run right down the front of you. It wasn't like the pithy, dry peaches today.

We used to serve strawberry-rhubarb pie. And stewed rhubarb with strawberries. Oh, and we made all kinds of soups from shrimp bisque to every kind of chicken soup to bean soup. A lot of Yankee bean, kidney bean, split pea. Tuesday evenings it would be roast leg of lamb. We'd buy domestic; they run around fourteen pounds. That's a big leg of lamb. And we used one or two of those on Tuesday evenings.

It seated around 120. We used to have two high school girls that would work on the sidewalk [taking names and number of diners]. The line would go from our front door to Fourth Avenue. Prior to July 4, 1970, we had forty people working there. After the riots we never had a standing line again until the day we closed.

– David Taborn, proprietor,
Taborn's Townhouse Restaurant, Asbury Park

Dining Out

Felix Giordano, a Salerno-born émigré who had come to Asbury Park in 1919 and began his trade as a carpenter, was the first to set the new restaurant standard. In 1929 Giordano opened a dining room in a former boarding-house on Main Street and Second Avenue owned by his in-laws, the Candianos. He named his establishment Posillipo in an appeal not only to the local crowd who hailed from that part of Italy in the province of Naples but also to diners who wanted an elegant touch of the Old World. Significantly, Posillipo's location on Main Street was outside the West Side's Italian enclave. By not going to the oceanfront, Giordano's restaurant also stood a better chance of weathering the seasonal impact on annual revenues. It didn't hurt that Main Street was listed on state touring maps as Route 4-N.

In 1969 Giordano retired and sold the prosperous restaurant to Dr. Carl G. Sammarco, the dentist son of a former business partner, Dominic Sammarco, who had been in the local syrup and soda trade. Sammarco, a champion athlete from Asbury Park High School, decorated the ground-floor banquet room with team pictures from his days on the gridiron under revered football coach Gus Bruno.

Mrs. Jay's

After the 1933 repeal of Prohibition, Ida and John Jacobs were among the first restaurant owners on Ocean Avenue to apply for, and receive, a liquor license. Having acquired their rental and seasonal snack stand from Roland Hines, they were busy turning it into what they hoped would be a year-round restaurant. Together with their daughter, Jeanette, and son-in-law Murray Weiner, the Jacobses expanded along Second Avenue, putting in the Circus Bar and a kitchen. On their kitchen staff was a young Tommy Smith, working his way through Howard College; he would one day become Asbury Park's first black police chief and mayor.

In Mrs. Jay's Beer Garden they rented space to Diana, a palm reader who provided entertainment. By the 1960s, Jeanette Weiner was running her mother's establishment.

HOTEL PLAZA GRILL
SPECIAL SHORE DINNER $2.00
Chicken Dinner also a la Carte Service

COFFEE SHOP SPECIAL
Course Dinner 75 cents
Course Dinner 60 cents
(without Soup or Cocktail)
MENU

Tomato Juice Cocktail   Fruit Cocktail

Chicken Okra Creole   Consomme

Fillet of Sole, Tartare Sauce
Lamb Chops
Fried Soft Clams, Tartare Sauce
Pot Roast with Noodles
Roast Spring Lamb, Pan Gravy, Apple Jelly
Breaded Veal Cutlets, Tomato Sauce

Choice of 2 Vegetables
Snow Flake Potatoes   Boiled Potatoes
Green Peas   Buttered Beets

Fruit Jello   Ice Cream   Watermelon
Cocoanut Custard Pie
Apple Pie   Huckleberry Pie

Coffee   Tea   Milk
CLUB BREAKFAST 35 cents up

All Sea Food Served, Caught Daily From
Our Own Boats.

In the heart of the amusement circuit between the Palace and the Casino, the chic Hotel Plaza tried a more casual approach to dining during the Depression with the addition of a coffee shop. Pike Archives.

In 1965 she expanded the beer garden's offerings with go-go dancers: women wearing fringed two-piece bathing suits, shimmying through the frug, the watusi, and the monkey on the bar top. Then one night a dancer wore a see-through blouse and no bra underneath, and before too many nights went by city police held a raid. In the early 1970s the family subdivided the property and sold the restaurant, keeping just the beer garden, which had become a popular bikers' hangout.

The original Mrs. Jay, Ida Jacobs. Her daughter, Jeanette Jacobs Weiner, handily assumed the nickname when she and her husband, Murray, took over the business and brought entertainment to the restaurant and adjacent beer garden. Courtesy of Joan Tepper-Neal.

Recreational versus Residential

In the last quarter of the twentieth century, the Asbury Park's hotel industry was fading fast as the resort's character was slowly and deliberately changing from recreational to residential. Owners of small hotels and boardinghouses had a difficult time paying property taxes. The financial stability that could be guaranteed by year-round residential guests was considerably more attractive than elusive seasonal income. Some operators started taking in senior citizens who had retired to Asbury Park hoping to evoke happy childhood memories. With the 1974 creation of federally subsidized low-income (Section 8) housing, other property owners became landlords. Still others turned to taking in the mentally ill despite not being licensed or trained to care for them as Trenton began closing its psychiatric hospitals as a cost-cutting measure.

A study by the Urban Health Institutes estimated that 3,651 mental patients moved into Asbury Park between 1975 and 1978. Based on its own estimates, the city figured it had between 1,500 and 1,700 formerly institutionalized patients living within its borders. Frustrated by the growing number wandering the wide avenues and residential side streets, Acting City Manager Sam Addeo in 1978 charged the Central Jersey Health Planning Council with deliberately sending deinstitutionalized patients to the state's neglected inner cities where the old and abandoned housing stock was unsuited for group living. Addeo further charged the state with not fairly distributing the mentally ill among all its municipalities. He estimated that hotel owners knew they could take in $215,000 annually as residential landlords, or four times the amount they would have made had their establishments remained as overnight accommodations. Addeo's complaints fell on deaf ears.

In a statewide referendum held in 1976, voters said yes to legalized gambling in moribund Atlantic City. Two years later, on May 26, 1978, Resorts International Hotel and Casino opened, soon followed by more new casino hotels. Besides the seemingly limitless opportunities to gamble, this new wave of hotels featured enormous showrooms for entertainment and, to hold further the public's attention, hired master chefs to create the kind of elaborate food buffets typical of cruise ships.

Despite going to Atlantic City with several restaurant and other business associates to see what could be replicated in Asbury Park, Mayor Ray Kramer returned to city hall and dusted off a strategy from the playbook of former mayor Clarence Hetrick: a modern convention center. Public debate was once again focused on founder Bradley's old Auditorium block, where the Berkeley-Carteret Hotel

Despite the resort's reputation, which rested on the heavily promoted Baby Parade, it was rare to find a children's menu in any restaurant in Asbury Park. Tapping into the postwar television cowboy culture personified by Howdy Doody, this cut-out mask menu is circa 1950. Pike Archives.

Tips for Life

I WAS WAITRESSING AT MRS. JAY'S THE SUMMER OF my freshman year in college when a cocktail waitress wore a see-through blouse minus a bra and the police showed up to arrest her. The next day I heard about it from her husband [Murray Weiner, Mrs. Jay's son-in-law], who was bartending. I [must have been] pretty young and conservative for the times, because I remember being shocked by his attitude.

"That's the way she makes her tips," he said.

That whole summer was an experience: driving around "the circuit," using doctored IDs to get served in bars (the drinking age was twenty-one), having a friend on the way to work point out a girl walking on the sidewalk, saying that she was Bruce Springsteen's girlfriend.

I got my biggest tip ever, twenty dollars, from a nice-looking guy and his friend. Out-of-towners taking in the sights, of course.

At the time, it was hard to find any skirt length except for mini in stores. Not even the waitress uniforms we bought on Cookman Avenue had long hemlines. I think mine was three or four inches above my knee. An older waitress at Mrs. Jay's had been eyeing me for a few minutes and then inquired as to whether she could ask me a question. When I answered yes, she sneered as she asked, "Do ya THINK you could get that any shorter?"

– Pat (Patti) Olsen, writer
Tinton Falls, New Jersey

was no longer paying municipal property taxes. In fact, by this point, the city had had to foreclose on the property for $317,090 in back taxes. A subsequent physical audit revealed a leaking roof, cracks in the structural frame of the Warren-designed hotel, a neglected heating system, and a kitchen stripped of all its appliances and fixtures. Some members of the city council favored converting the old hotel into a senior citizens' home. Kramer lobbied hard for a proposal to use the building as an incentive to a prospective developer to who might want to build a new Boardwalk convention center. As with other municipal issues in Asbury Park, consensus was hard to come by. Some favored tearing down the old hotel. Others wanted a 250-room addition built, plus a parking garage, plus renovation of the even older Convention Hall–Paramount Theatre complex—all packaged into one bid specification. The city council was also mired in the details over what it wanted for the vacant Marine Grill restaurant site beyond the north end of the Boardwalk: a combination hotel and convention center; a motel and convention center; a residential high-rise; or a banquet hall.

Sweet Fast Food

I WORKED A FEW MORNINGS A WEEK AT THE Coffeebreak Donut Shop [northwest corner of Sunset and Main] for seventeen years, starting in 1970, and I loved it! At that time there was no Burger King, WaWa, or 7-11. Our busy hours were between 7 and 11 a.m., and there was always a line of people. The coffee, a private brand, was the best around, and the doughnuts and raisin and apple swirls made by baker Smokey Hertzog of Wanamassa were delicious! Smokey was more than a doughnut maker. He could make chocolate chip cookies (which were better than I made at home), brownies, cheese danish, and napoleons to die for. Walking by and inhaling the mouth-watering smells emanating from the shop just made you stop in. Most of our customers ate the same doughnut all the time; sour cream sticks and old-fashioneds were two of the favorites.

Many of the customers came in every day or several times a week so they got to be friends more than customers. There was Gypsy from the high school; Rudy the ac-countant from Allenhurst; Dave who worked for the board of education; Leon, the city's engineer; kids from the high school who weren't supposed to be there. I remember one morning the truant officer came in. Fortunately the young man saw him coming, and ran into the baker's room so he wasn't caught–at least not that time.

No matter where I go, I see former customers. They ask how they know me and I say, "Think of me in a uniform." Unfortunately many say a doctor's office, so then I have to clue them in.

I was sorry when it was time for me to go on to other things, and, of course, the shop is no longer there, becoming a chicken-pizza-convenience store. But I have many happy memories.

– Doris Carroll
Asbury Park, New Jersey

50¢
Dinners
Also
35¢
DAILY
CAFETERIA
Specials

OPEN
ALL
YEAR

The Main-Central Cafeteria & Restaurant
"OVER A MILLION MEALS SERVED"

SAMPLE MENU
(Served in Asbury Park Restaurant)
CHOICE OF
FRESH FRUIT COCKTAIL
FRESH GRAPE FRUIT COCKTAIL
GRAPE FRUIT JUICE
PINEAPPLE JUICE

CHOICE OF SOUP
Cream of Asparagus or Clam Chowder

RELISH—CELERY AND RADISHES

CHOICE OF BROILED FRESH BLUE FISH
FRIED FILET OF SOLE, TARTAR SAUCE
BROILED HALIBUT, BUTTER SAUCE
FRIED OYSTERS
ROAST LOIN OF PORK, APPLE SAUCE
ROAST PRIME RIBS OF BEEF, AU JUS
ROAST LEG OF LAMB, MINT SAUCE
VEGETABLE PLATE (Choice of 5 Vegetables)

SALAD—LETTUCE AND TOMATO

Rye and Wheat Bread, Home-made Rolls

Choice of Two Vegetables—All Fresh
MASHED OR SWEET POTATOES
CARROTS   SPINACH   SQUASH
FRESH GREEN PEAS   STRING BEANS

LEMON CHIFFON PIE   ICE CREAM
CUSTARD PIE   GREEN APPLE PIE
VANILLA LAYER CAKE   RICE PUDDING
CUP OF COFFEE OR TEA
Menu Changes Daily

Eventually city hall published a legal advertisement requesting proposals for just the Berkeley-Carteret block. Two bids came in. The American Realty Corporation of Englewood, represented by Belmar attorney Joseph J. Hillman Jr., submitted a $40,000 bid that called for partial renovation of the Berkeley-Carteret. The other, for $5,000, came from Israeli entrepreneur Liberman Rafael, who listed his stateside business as Amore Inc. in Point Pleasant Beach. With no public outcry, the city council voted to give the hotel block to Rafael who didn't have the $5,000 on hand to purchase the property. When asked how much he intended to spend renovating the city's last remaining signature hotel, Rafael responded, "The less the better." Told he had received the contract, Rafael directed the mayor and council to submit any further questions in writing to his New York lawyer. By the end of 1980, nothing had been done to the Berkeley-Carteret Hotel, and it remained the property of Asbury Park. The year also closed without the mayor and council making a decision about what to do with vacant Marine Grill site.

Cafeterias were one of the leading restaurant trends during the Depression. By 1936 the original seasonal Cooper's Ice Cream stand on Second Avenue was the Main-Central and cross-promoted its location by showing the wood-frame Albion Hotel next door. Pike Archives.

Déjà Vu

Ninety years after James Bradley believed he had established a seaside health resort where no liquor would ever touch the lips of vacationers and citizens, Asbury Park found itself wrestling with a century-long hangover. Residents and business owners

The southern corner of the worn-out Steeplechase amusement property was made over into an elaborately decorated restaurant called the Actaion, which never opened. Instead, after the hurricane of 1944, Spiros Michals, wanting to get out of the Natatorium and the overcrowded Boardwalk candy business, bought it, renamed it, and promoted the health benefits of seafood. Pike Archives.

FISH is a Health Building Food

EVERY DAY IS SEA FOGD DAY AT THE SEASHORE

Fresh Sea Food is High in Vitamins
and Energy Building
Healthy bodies are laid directly to
Sea Food containing
Iron, Copper, Iodine, and the
necessary elements to aid the
Human Body

TO INSURE GOOD HEALTH

on both the East and West Sides were complaining about lack of police and city hall law and code enforcement. Two of the more serious complaints in 1980 had to do with the renewal of liquor licenses, the third, with a transfer.

From the West Side, one hundred residents of the Ridge Avenue neighborhood jammed a city council meeting to protest the drunk and disorderly crowds who each night congregated outside the overcrowded Horse Shoe Bar on the southwest corner of Ridge and Summerfield Avenues. Bar owner Thomas Dumansky defended his establishment, saying the customers were the dispossessed patrons from a bar down on Prospect Avenue that had closed more than twelve months earlier. In response to the public outcry, the city council delayed renewing Dumansky's liquor license until a solution could be found.

From the neighborhood of the Palace Amusements and old Lyric Theatre on Cookman Avenue came a protest against renewing a liquor license, this one by a businessman. Nick Dalia, who had opened Nick's Clam Bar in the old Villa Penza restaurant, complained about rival Donald Stegler, who owned the Southbound Inn next door, and his disruptive patrons. Dalia's specific complaint was with Southbound habitués who crowded into his bar after the Southbound closed, breaking windows and leaving trash in the streets. In this case, the city council chose to renew Southbound's liquor license with the stipulation that a security guard be posted.

World's Best Corned Beef

I REMEMBER SWIRLING IN A PACK OF GIRLS, THE Karens Resnick, Popok, and Goldberg, some skinny twins, a Lisa or two, on the wide concrete sidewalk outside Temple Beth El where we attended Hebrew school on Monday and Wednesday afternoons. In fact the clarity of my recollection of the sand-colored striated surface of that sidewalk contrasts with my rather vague memories of what went on inside. I can dig up one song in Hebrew—*Doh-veed! Melech Isro-ail! Chai! Ve-chai-yum*!—and the taste of some terrible "treat" called King David's bark.

The real treats were around the block at Harry's [Rubin] Confectionary on Bond Street, the kind of place you might see in a Norman Rockwell painting, complete with a bespectacled shopkeeper and chubby-cheeked young clients. We endured long stories of tribes and deserts and kings until the moment we ourselves were set free. Then it was straight around the corner with our nickels and pennies for a necklace made of sugar beads, a few rows of sugar dots on paper, wax bottles of sugar syrup, chalky sugar cigarettes with daubed-on fuchsia tips. Sugar—my clearest memory of Hebrew school.

On Tuesdays we had a weekly ritual: dinner with my grandparents Papa and Gigi at an old-fashioned deli on Main Street called Grossman's where no one made us sit still and we were allowed to take apart our sandwiches to make what we called num-nums—slice of their delicious roast beef wrapped around their incomparable half-sour dill pickles, lightly salted and peppered and stuffed in the mouth like Jewish corn dogs.

After Grossman's shut down, Papa and Gigi had to take us to Tuesday dinners at a chain restaurant in the Monmouth Shopping Center, a cluster of stores in a parking lot off Route 35 in Eatontown that was the earliest incarnation of the huge mall that is there today. It pains me to say we liked the Lock, Stock and Barrel or Steak and Ale or whatever it was better than the dusty old deli. What I wouldn't give for a num-num at Grossman's now.

– Marion Winik, author, *The Lunch-Box Chronicles*, and National Public Radio commentator

Joseph M. Grossman carving his "world famous corned beef" from a 200-year-old family recipe in the window of his restaurant, the former Moose Lodge at 810 Main Street. Courtesy of Sherri L. Grossman.

RIGHT *Before it met the wrecking ball in 1963, the Monterey's owners tried one last time to promote by association its culinary offerings as seen in this advertisement in the* Beachcomber, *one of the many short-lived summer entertainment guides. Pike Archives.*

BELOW *Croatian native Stan Tokec moved his Main Street Tavern business from what had become State Highway 71 to the old Sunset Lounge on Kingsley Street across from the Berkeley-Carteret Hotel. The move gave him much-needed parking plus the additional prospect of more patrons. He called his new restaurant the Adriatic. Pike Archives.*

In Florida It's
WOLFIE'S—PUMPERNICK'S—DARBY'S
In Asbury It's
THE MIAMIAN
THE ONLY RESTAURANT OF ITS KIND—For the First Time in Asbury Park
WHERE THE CELEBRITIES MEET & GREET—Open Daily 7:30 A.M. Till 4 A.M.
BREAKFAST - LUNCHEON - DINNER - SUPPER - COCKTAIL LOUNGE
"From Our Own Bakery Every Hour — Arthur Godfrey's Famous Pumpernick Bagels"

All Our Baking Done on Premises By MIAMI BAKERS
THE MIAMIAN
RESTAURANT ♦ SANDWICH SHOP
At the MONTEREY

By popular demand, we have opened a take-out counter. Take home some our own baked pastries, pies, cheese cake, rolls and our own famous— PUMPERNICK BAGELS

6th and OCEAN AVENUE   ASBURY PARK, N. J.
DIRECTLY ON THE OCEAN FRONT

By July, George DeNardo, president of the Monmouth Shore Licensed Beverage Association, was calling on the city council to adopt mandatory penalties for drinking in public and littering. Mayor Kramer balked, saying there were already ordinances. DeNardo countered with the suggestion that higher fines be issued. By the time the summer of 1980 was over, the city council had not resolved the issue of public abuse of alcohol on city streets.

There was one small victory in North Asbury Park when residents successfully fought against the request to transfer the liquor license from the old Deck House on Lake Avenue just west of Grand to a vacant twenty-eight-room hotel on Sixth Avenue; the surrounding area had turned residential after World War II. Michael Bruno, a partner in Ginacal Resorts Inc., wanted to renovate the small hotel at 300 Sixth Avenue into a luxury boutique property with a kitchen, dining room, and, most importantly, a cocktail lounge, for which he needed the Deck House liquor license. Hammering away at the problems of noise and debris that they already endured from the existing late-night bars on the oceanfront entertainment circuit at the edge of their neighborhood, residents convinced the city council to not grant the transfer.

But their fight to keep additional liquor licenses out of North Asbury Park wasn't quite over. Two years earlier, Essex County businessman Frank D'Allessandro, who had bought the seventy-four-year-old Hye Hotel at 307 Sixth Avenue, renovated it and renamed it the Pier Six Hotel. D'Allessandro was negotiating for a liquor license for the small, dimly lit basement bar that locals had once called the Pit in his new Pier Six Hotel. He was eager to continue the image makeover of the old hotel, which included moving away from the property's old identity as yet another watering hole attractive only to city denizens.

Empty for three years, the hotel had reverted to owners Emanuel and Ara Kulhanjian, sons of John Kulhanjian, an Armenian immigrant who also ran a dry cleaners and tailor service in the Monterey Hotel. The Kulhanjians paid the $14,645 in back taxes before the city foreclosed on the property, and then sold it to D'Allessandro for $17,000. D'Allessandro reportedly spent $80,000 to upgrade the four-story building, including changing from oil to less costly gas heating, a new roof, security, and sprinklers, a new hot water heater, carpeting, and new electrical wiring and Sheetrock. In

ANTIPASTI — APPETIZERS		
Succo di Pomodoro	Tomato Juice	.50
Coppa di Frutta Fresca	Fresh Fruit Supreme	.95
Antipasti Variati	Cold Antipasto	1.75
	Hot Antipasto	2.25
Scampi	Shrimp Cocktail	1.50
Prosciutto e Melone	Italian Ham and Melon	1.75
Vongole Fresca	Clams — Half Shell	1.50
Vongole Reganate - Casino	Clams — Baked	2.00
Langostine Reganate	Langostine Baked	3.25

✣

ZUPPE — SOUPS		
Zuppa del Giorno	Soup of the Day	.75
Stracciatella	Chicken Broth — Egg Ribbons — Spinach	1.50
Tortellini in Brodo	Dumplings in Chicken Broth	1.50
Zuppa di "Posillipo"	Escarole — Tiny Meat Balls in Chicken Broth	1.50
Zuppa di Vongole	Clam Soup (in shells)	2.25
Zuppa di Vongole al Vino	Special — Clams in Tomato Broth and White Wine	2.25

FARINACCI — FARINACEOUS		
Fettucine "Posillipo"	Egg Noodles — Heavy Cream and Grated Cheese	3.00
Fettucine "Dominick"	Egg Noodles — Tomato Sauce, Ricotta, and Mushrooms	3.00
Fettucine Filetti Prosciutto	Egg Noodles — Tomato Sauce and Italian Ham	3.25
Linguine alle Vongole	Linguine — Red or White Clam Sauce	2.75
Linguine Con Pesto	Linguine — Basil and Cheese Sauce (in season)	2.50
Gnocchi di Semolina	Small Dumplings — Meat Sauce	3.50
Manicotti	Delicate Crepes — Ricotta Filling — Meat Sauce	3.00
Ravioli Bolognese	Cheese Filled Pasta — Meat Sauce	3.00
Tagliatelle Verde	Green Noodles — Any Sauce	3.00

At your request we will make any type pasta (macaroni) with your favorite sauce.

✣

ABOVE *Culturally more acceptable than the burlesque shows at the Savoy was the imported entertainment to accompany the tantalizing Armenian and Greek dishes at Asbury Park's leading Armenian hotel, advertised here in the city's 1975 guidebook. Many Armenian immigrants who fled the 1890 and 1917 holocausts worked in New York's garment industry and began vacationing in Asbury Park at the turn of the twentieth century. Pike Archives.*

LEFT Buon Appetito! *Frank Giordano's circa 1930 menu for Posillipo's was written in Italian and English. Pike Archives.*

1980 D'Allessandro was also negotiating to buy the old Madison House Hotel, the property directly to the north of Pier Six on Seventh Avenue, for hotel parking.

"The scarcity of oceanfront property suitable for tourists near North Jersey's urban areas, coupled with escalating gasoline prices, makes Asbury Park's resurrection as a resort town viable," said the Bloomfield resident in a March 23, 1980, interview in the *Asbury Park Press*. "The oceanfront has to be developed and cleaned up to draw a good class of people into the city," he continued. "And once they're here, they'll need hotels to say in, restaurants to eat in and stores to shop in. The entire downtown area will be able to flourish."

Counter Culture

IN 1970, WHEN I WAS NINETEEN, I WORKED FOR Henry and Estelle Teitjen, who owned The Press Box [with entrances on both Mattison and Cookman Avenues]. Henry worked in the kitchen with Willie the cook, whose lunch special was veal "armigian"; Estelle ran the front and did some of the baking. Estelle made cheesecake or had her sister do it for her. They were both good cooks.

The Press Box had a real soda fountain. They also served fresh-squeezed lemonade. During strawberry season we always had fresh berries for shortcake. There was always a lot of homemade food, which was why we were always so busy. Lunch went from 11:30 to about 3:00, Monday through Saturday, and we ran our feet off. Every day I would leave smelling like French fries and quite in need of a shower.

I worked the early shift and ran the front counter. I got coffee and lunch for most of the local shopkeepers on a regular basis. Betty [Tripodi] from the Country Fair got an English muffin and coffee to go. Marvin and Lorraine [Goldstein] from Le Plume had their coffee at the counter. Scottie [Eitman] from Reeds [Jewelers] would take his across the street. Richie Rediker [whose father's uncle Joe

Rediker launched Reeds Jewelers] would just come in to bust chops because it was a good way to start the day. Scottie would come back at lunch and order a sliced egg and tomato sandwich on white toast every day that he worked. The "Bob and Irving" gang [Army/Navy surplus on the southwest corner of Cookman and Main] would sit at a table in the back.

Staffing at The Press Box was interesting. Several girls I had gone to school with passed through. The regular waitress, Gerry, had been there for many years. Gerry's daughter, Debbie, came to work there as well as Marilyn, Gerry's sister. It was a revolving door. Leave and come back, over and over. . . . Estelle hired a guy named Jimmy and let him work the back end of the counter. Jimmy absolutely hated me with a passion because I had a better station than he did. It came with seniority—what can I say.

Many of these people have passed over. I hope they're having a good cup of coffee in the great reward.

– Francesca Garsh, owner
Evergreen Art Gallery, Spring Lake

CHAPTER SIX

Downtown

EIGHTEEN NINETY was a gilded year for Asbury Park businesses. Iron footbridges finally replaced the two hand-pulled ferries across Wesley Lake. While the eastern bridge at Heck Street brought throngs of happy pedestrians from Ocean Grove into the amusement and entertainment circuits at any time of the day or night, it was the opening of the western bridge, connecting the Grove to the Park at Emory Street, that unofficially blessed the resort's commercial epicenter where Cookman, Mattison, and Bangs Avenues converged.

Rising up the slight incline from residential Lake Avenue, the wide Emory Street approach to Cookman was landscaped with a center mall of grass and flowerbeds, bounded by a simple whitewashed iron fence. On the left was Samuel LeMaistre's Lace Shop, a prime location graced by a series of award-winning display windows along Emory and around the corner to Cookman. On the southeast corner of Emory and Cookman was a rustic two-story wood-frame produce stand, a holdover from the previous decade. Farther east along Cookman were stylish businesses that catered to the public's leisure tastes: artists' studios, a framer, a bird dealer, a gilder, and stores for finished shoes, cigars, and candy.

In contrast, nearly all the businesses west of Emory to Main Street were of a practical nature: a fish market, a large dry goods store, a dentist's office, a shoemaker, grocers, an optician, two drugstores, and a bicycle shop that performed sales and repairs. Owners lived on the second or third floors or rented them out. Across Cookman from LeMaistre's was a four-story wedge-shaped building, bounded on

Asbury Park has a Board of Trade. This Board is never quiet. When it is not fighting with the railroad company, with Congress, or with the State Legislature, it is fighting with itself.

. . . While Asbury Park is fighting over the best means of advertising the town that it may live and flourish, Long Branch is looking for a hole in which to crawl and die to escape funeral expenses.

–*Asbury Park Journal*,
March 15, 1890
[excerpted from the *Long Branch Record*]

the north by Mattison Avenue, which entered the intersection on an angle, creating a point at the building's eastern end. Over the years, the ground floor housed a series of useful enterprises in keeping with the commercial nature of its block.

The two-story offices of J. Lyle Kinmonth's *Asbury Park Daily Press* were across Mattison, in a modest frame structure that abutted the massive Byram building, whose three-story stone presence imposed itself on the rounded Emory corner. The building originally housed the offices of the Asbury Park National Bank; in 1895 the U.S. Post Office moved in. Across Emory was the Commercial Hotel, an apt name for the downtown accommodations. But, like the fruit stand it faced across Cookman, a German émigré and his sons were to change the businesses that went on there.

White House Summer Executive Offices,
Asbury Park Trust Co. Building.   Asbury Park, N. J.

Economic Tripod

In this last decade of the nineteenth century Asbury Park was poised to develop a robust three-part business model based on travel, retail, and industry. Success would guarantee a financially secure community, increase the city's tax base, provide jobs for residents, and make profits for business owners. Already board of trade members were looking for ways to promote the resort as a year-round destination. Businessmen eager to capitalize new entertainment supported the idea that leisure was as much a pastime in winter as it was in summer. Parallel to the railroad tracks, an industrial north-south neighborhood of lumber mills, harness and carriage shops, laundries, and a sewing factory had room for expansion.

The potential of a commercial east-west corridor along Asbury Avenue, linking the resort to industries in the county seat of Freehold and farther west to the state capital of Trenton, showed itself early, thanks to the Drummond family. Along the outer reaches of Deal Lake in Ocean Township, the Drummonds had commercial kilns. Daily they baked and delivered thousands of bricks down Asbury Avenue to business addresses on and off

Main Street. Bricks were used to rebuild Cook's Beehive at the corner of Main and Cookman into the resort's first fireproof department store; later they were used to rebuild LeMaistre's. They were also used decoratively. The three-story Pennypacker Press building on Main Street and Fifth Avenue, overlooking the western end of Sunset Lake Park and the North Asbury Park train station, was done in the Dutch pattern style of alternating red horizontal and black glazed ends.

Just beyond the Drummond kilns, in the pine forest framed by Asbury Avenue and the Neptune Highway, were the city's main refuse site and the location of the Flavell Company, a foul-smelling fat-rendering plant that processed livestock remains from the city's butchers. This site became an important economic crossroads when the state renamed the highway Route 35 in 1929. The future was bright with potential.

The Mammoth versus the Five-and-Dimes

John Steinbach already had a dry goods store and warehouses on Main Street when he began taking measure of his other retail operation in Long Branch, where he and his brothers had gotten their start. What he observed was a slow but steady decline in that city's popularity since the death there of President James Garfield

in 1881. Asbury Park, by contrast, was generating a lot of attention. Smaller than Long Branch, its intimacy gave it an aura of selectivity; it seemed younger, with an air of newness and open land still available for retail and residential expansion. As local rivalries went, Asbury Park had an active business community, as evidenced by its board of trade. More importantly, because of its location in the southern half of Monmouth County, Asbury Park didn't have any other regional competition. Steinbach curtailed his involvement in Long Branch, bought the Commercial Hotel, and tore it down.

For his retail gamble, Steinbach hired New York building designers Robert Cleverdon and Joseph Putzel to come up with a paean to merchandising. The 1890s were, after all, the era of John Wanamaker, the innovative merchant from Philadelphia who had came up with the idea of combining many specialty stores into one large department store. Louis Bamberger was following his lead in Newark. So was David May in the mining community of Leadville, Colorado, and Joseph L. Hudson in the flourishing industrial city of Detroit.

As they had for their Sheridan Square clients in lower Manhattan, Cleverdon and Putzel chose the brick and terra cotta Italianate style popular among merchants. On the sidewalk level were enormous plate-glass display windows. Traveling upward, the eye found more large windows lining the second floor. These sheets of glass were flanked by sash windows to let in the fresh sea air. The third-floor masonry mass was broken by a series of four sash windows to line up exactly with the large plate windows one floor below. Defining the sets of four were piers with flat capitals that connected the third and fourth floors. Similar piers defined the large display windows on the first and second floors. Capping the building's fourth-floor design were slender windows with Romanesque arches. Before too long, Steinbach would add a mansard roof as a fifth floor. Because it shared the block with other businesses, Steinbach's store was six-sided, with three distinct fronts on the rounded corner at Emory. The entire building was outfitted in beige brick, almost golden in color. Steinbach then hired decorative architect F. H. Dodge, of New York, to design the all-important ground-floor interior. Dodge chose delicate terra cotta molding for the ceilings and side walls and had the trim painted white. Intent on removing any trace of having started in the rough-and-tumble dry goods business, Steinbach saw to it that all the fixtures and showcases were built from mahogany.

While Steinbach was preparing to cater to the upper and aspiring middle classes at his location east of Emory Street, Frank W. Woolworth was looking out for the working class. From the moment he opened his first store in Trenton in 1885, Woolworth relentlessly scouted New Jersey locations. The growing travel market represented a retail opportunity all its own, and after visiting Asbury Park in 1889, Woolworth set about acquiring a location for the resort's first five-and-dime variety store. He picked a location on Cookman Avenue west of Emory Street, with only one other business separating it from Bond Street, a working-class side street. Woolworth's business model was simple: low margin, high volume. As he did elsewhere in the country, Woolworth looked for two factors to influence his choice of location: easy delivery from a train depot and heavily trafficked sidewalks. With his modest one-story location a mere three blocks from the train and trolley station—and on that western strip of Cookman devoted to more practical enterprises—Woolworth found both. But he also received competition, for everywhere in the country

The 1916 façade of the hand-some Asbury Park Press building was a multi-faceted one decorated by patterned brick, mullioned windows, and a row of concrete lions' heads placed above its fifth-floor windows. The paper's loading docks were located on the opposite side of the building that fronted Bangs Avenue. Pike Archives.

that Frank Woolworth opened a store, archrival J. G. McCrory soon followed, and he was followed in turn by J. J. Newberry. In the twentieth century, H. L. Green followed Newberry. There they were, all in a row, all on Cookman Avenue, all west of Emory Street. This pattern of similar competition in close proximity to one another would repeat itself throughout most of the new century.

True to John Steinbach's observation, Asbury Park thrived as a commercial hub even if the beach and hotel circuits remained largely closed to activity through the winter months. At the turn of the century, Monmouth County was growing in population and with a mix of businesses that spanned agriculture, manufacturing, and services. New residents not only had new homes to decorate but extra money to spend on leisure. They were also taking better care of themselves, and sought out the services of opticians, doctors, dentists, bankers, and lawyers. While they could patronize the steamboat towns of Victorian rivals Red Bank or Keyport or go to Broadway in Long Branch, shoppers came to Asbury Park because it was a destination that offered a wide range of merchandise, much of it imported. The city's growing émigré population who clerked its retail trade gave it an extra frisson of sophistication as the sounds of foreign accents could be overheard in shops all over the downtown.

John Steinbach's fully realized, full-service, five-story department store, circa 1940, was already in competitive trouble as retail stores in Asbury Park itself began to siphon off Steinbach's business by specializing in shoes, furniture, ladies' elegant dresses and evening wear, men and boys' clothing, and baby wear. Pike Archives.

No single business address was turning shopping into a destination more than Steinbach's Mammoth Department Store. Sons Walter and Arthur Steinbach annually went on buying expeditions to Europe and shipped back the latest designs in Bavarian china, Czechoslovakian crystal, Black Forest knickknacks, Irish linen, Parisian hats and lingerie, and soft Italian leather gloves for men and women. The pair didn't limit their buying power to just the family business; the brothers also shopped wholesale for other family-owned department stores in the

New York metropolitan area, notably Goerke's, which had stores in Elizabeth and Stamford, Connecticut.

Ten years into the twentieth century Asbury Park was poised to make the next revolution in the wheel of commerce, literally and figuratively. After years of agitation and litigation with Ocean Grove—and the fortuitous creation in 1910 of the state Public Utilities Commission—Sunday trains finally were allowed to stop in Asbury Park in March 1912. In another sign of the city's twentieth-century status, later that month, the U.S. Post Office opened an independent facility on Bangs Avenue, north of the train depot. Architect Kenneth Towner designed an Italian Renaissance Revival building complete with an arched loggia opening onto Bangs, creating a plaza approach to the post office. By this point, Asbury Park had twenty-three mail carriers and eight substations throughout the city.

More Mammoth

Widowed for most of his sons' lives, John Steinbach just couldn't retire. In 1921, at the age of seventy-one, he bought the rest of the Cookman Avenue

The more conservative Steinbach brother, Walter, was the department store's finance officer, acutely aware of the balancing act he was performing between the store's bottom line, which was diminishing as a result of outside competition and Arthur's constant requests for money to shore up the Berkeley-Carteret. Pike Archives.

Working for the Steinbachs

I BEGAN WORKING IN STEINBACH'S WHEN I WAS fifteen years old [in 1930]. They put me in the infant's department wrapping gifts. At that time we worked Wednesday and Friday nights. We had a coupon and it was for a full-course meal for a quarter in the restaurant. Back then they had what they called a red carpet. We had a doorman. All of our buyers had to be college graduates.

We had a party every year [at] Christmas. The girls got candy and the men got a bottle of liquor. Thanksgiving time, we also got a turkey.

Once a year we had the White Elephant Sale where we could buy the best coat, all wool, for $5. You could buy a dress for $2. We [were trying] to get rid of inventory.

We weren't allowed to wear slacks. You [had] to be properly dressed at all times. We could only wear gray, navy, brown, or black. No chewing gum. No leaning on the counter. We had to have inspection of our fingernails every morning.

Walter and Arthur Steinbach were very private. "Good morning," "Good afternoon." If something was wrong [they] would not say a word. [They] would go to the buyer and just say, "Fire that person for chewing gum."

– Geraldine Seyler Lavinthol
Long Branch, New Jersey

Joint promotions in the resort's off-season helped keep up the bottom line and employees on payroll. The J. N. Bearmore Company's best-known contract was for the Paramount and Convention Hall roof (really two roofs connected by a third one), which was made more memorable by the series of skylights the company installed over the connecting arcade to let light in. Pike Archives.

block; had dentist Llewellyn Hetrick's house and office at the point of Cookman and Bangs physically removed to land overlooking Deal Lake in Loch Arbor; tore down the rest of the retail buildings on the block; and proceeded to replicate the Cleverdon and Putzel design all the way to the point where Cookman and Mattison Avenues came together. With boosterism typical of the period and the newspaper, the *Asbury Park Morning Press* reported, "Asbury Park is to have the largest department store in any resort in the world." For emphasis it added, "The store will be one of the largest in the state, no city being excepted. . . . At present the largest store in Monmouth county and an attraction to visitors from all over the state, the 'Mammoth' will be even more mammoth and the 'City Store in the Country' more citified."

For a construction cost of $150,000, Steinbach consolidated his various warehouses and upholstery workrooms and installed three passenger elevators, two freight elevators, fifty telephones, a soda water counter, a section for automobile supplies, a hairdressing and manicuring salon, and a drugstore. Cold storage for furs was on the drawing boards for a later date. Power for the elevators came from the store's separate generating plant, built opposite the department store's Bangs Avenue doors. Before he died in 1931, Steinbach added a fifth floor and a water tower that later would be enclosed and adorned with a working clock.

But three years after his death, John Steinbach's more practical son, bespectacled Walter, brokered a corporate marriage with Woolworth rival S. S. Kresge, selling a half-interest in the Cookman Avenue enterprise with the ultimate hope of retiring from the competitive grind of the retail trade, which was on the rise as specialty clothing stores opened across Cookman Avenue. The goal was to have the Shore-based "mammoth" Steinbach absorbed into a larger, better-financed national operation. Already Kresge owned McCrory's, having bought out that chain in 1912. It also acquired the Palut family's department store in Newark in 1922. So why not a high-end merchandise store to give the bargain chain some cachet?

Chamber Trade

As part of a business trend sweeping the country, Asbury Park refashioned its old board of trade into a modern chamber of commerce in 1913, reflecting an increase in the downtown's retail and service sectors. The makeover included an effort to integrate various factions that had sprung up within the business community. The first group to be folded into the new chamber was the Asbury Park Boosters' Association. Soon the Asbury Park Business Men's Association relinquished its independence in

Clean Linen

IN THOSE DAYS [1930S] LINEN SERVICE WAS BIG business. The competition was on the prices. We started out at eight cents a towel. Finally it went to thirty-two cents a towel. But somebody could come in and say, "I'll give you the first delivery on the house." Now, for a big place, that was a nice piece of money.

I had Springwood and I'd stop at Swift's, the meat house right on the corner by the railroad, and at Altschuler's poultry house. The biggest account was Cuba's Spanish Tavern. That was a great account. I used to take a little time there and watch them rehearse the shows for the evening. Those were the days when race wasn't a problem.

Levin's. Hutter's Bakery. Joe Grossman's fish market. He always demanded 55-inch aprons. See, in those days they had sawdust on the floors. He always demanded a 55-inch

apron so it would hit his shoetops so he wouldn't get the sawdust on them. We also rented butcher coats and aprons, gray and tan. We used to supply gray jackets to a clerk at Knuckles Electric. You could rent a jacket for 42 cents a week. I'll bet you it's $2 now.

Down Cookman I'd do all the restaurants. The little luncheonette in Steinbach's. Harry's. The Summerfield Hotel. The Asbury Hudson Hotel. The coffee shop in the Empress. The Monterey and the Berkeley always had their own laundry. But every once in a while we'd supply special occasions at the Monterey.

– Albert Elker, ret., Consolidated Linen Supply
(Memorial Drive and Sixth Avenue, Asbury Park)
West Long Branch, New Jersey

order to unite its efforts with those of the chamber. The chamber procured new offices on the northeast corner of Main Street and Mattison Avenue in a stucco building with enormous glass windows through which display racks filled with brochures could be seen.

To further distance itself from the industrial-sounding trade board name, the chamber saw itself as a clearinghouse of commercial and hotel information instead of an agency to attract new industries. In a promotional book written in 1915, chamber president J. A. Waterbury, then district manager for the New York Telephone Company, stated that the mission of the Asbury Park chamber was different from that of other towns where the local economy was based largely on manufacturing. The Asbury Park Chamber of Commerce "must promote the interests of its merchants, its hotels and property owners, each of which plays an important part in the commercial welfare of the community. . . . Perusal of this book will leave no doubt in the minds of the readers that Asbury Park is not only the greatest summer resort in the country, but that it is an ideal place of recreation the year round, and an important business center." Just what those year-round recreational opportunities were, however, was never articulated.

The new chamber of commerce also had a director of publicity, Wilbur H. Pancoast, superintendent of the Consolidated Gas Company of New York. His express mission was to extol a carefree atmosphere in Asbury Park, where the city was "synonymous with rest and recreation" four seasons of the year. To do that, Pancoast coined the slogan "Town without a Frown" and had it stamped on postcards, brochures, buttons, tea towels, and every souvenir imaginable. He also commissioned a song to promote further a genial atmosphere in which to spend leisure time and disposable income.

Pancoast had just two years to market his publicity campaign before the United States entered World War I. Domestic travel plans were curtailed as Americans awaited the war's end and then, for some time afterward, as the federal government requested "gas-less" Mondays that curbed the use of automobiles. While the chamber had made a strategic decision to emphasize Asbury Park's resort and residential attributes over any manufacturing opportunities, another development would further diminish the city's chances of growing a diversified economic base. In the wake of World War I, advances in rugged, air-inflated tires for military use were appro-

A local debate raged over who baked better kosher rolls: Hutter's on Springwood or Kneip's on Prospect Avenue. In 1929, Kneip's received the contract to make dinner rolls for Steinbach's department store restaurant. In 1979 Aly Kahn, a Kneip grandson, made the last morning delivery to Steinbach's the day the department store closed. In 1985 the family recipes were sold to the Shore-based Freedman's Bakery. Pike Archives.

The HOME of the
FISCHER BAKING CO.
Railroad and Fifth Avenues
ASBURY PARK, N.J.

TOP *Dugan Brothers, Newark, set up a distribution warehouse on Munroe Avenue, just over the city line in the Whitesville section of Neptune, and launched the first serious head-to-head competition with local bakeries for home delivery of baked goods. Courtesy of Louis P. Booz III.*

BOTTOM *As part of an expansion move, the Fischer brothers came from Newark and opened a Shore branch of their commercial bakery on Railroad Avenue. By 1965 its doors were closed. Pike Archives.*

priated by the commercial sector, and the modern trucking industry was born. The long-term repercussion for locally owned businesses was the arrival of successful North Jersey firms eager to deliver goods and services to their customers who summered at the seashore. As the greater Asbury Park area's year-round population grew, so did its desirability as a consumer market for companies that made everything from linens to finished furniture, baked goods to soda pop.

In 1931, Joshua Lionel Cowan, who had been vacationing in Deal, used the Asbury Park station for Model No. 112 and subsequently Model Nos. 113 through 117 for his growing toy-train company. Pike Archives.

By this time, the resort's manufacturing zone along the railroad tracks was limping along. The *New Jersey Industrial Directory* of 1918 listed only a handful of factories in the Asbury Park area: Buchanon & Smock lumber mill; Croce Automobile Co., a trucking fleet for Croce's soda and candy distribution business; Flavell Co., the fat-rendering plant out west on Asbury Avenue; the Steiner and Valco factories where pajamas were made; and the American Box Co., carton manufacturers. As it had in past directories, the city made it a point to state that buildable land was available and "most favorably situated for industrial purposes south of Asbury Park and west of the railroad tracks"—veiled vocabulary for Morristown lawyer Frederick Burnham's West Side neighborhood. Other than industrial directories, there appeared little evidence the chamber of commerce was directly encouraging commercial growth along its railroad corridor, leaving West Side residents increasingly dependent on the East Side hotel circuit for what was, at best, seasonal employment. More to the point: promotional campaigns remained focused on the downtown retail district and the beachfront, and over the course of the twentieth century, private investment and public policy would create a more precarious economic ladder instead of a stable tripod.

The Post-Bradley Era

Within a year of James Bradley's death in 1921, the downtown took a major step in moving away from its early history as a Victorian resort with the demolition of the rustic wooden Queen Anne train depot it shared with Ocean Grove. The Central Railroad of New Jersey commissioned post office architect Kenneth Towner to design a building and parking plaza spanning the length of Main Street between Cookman and Bangs Avenues. Towner came up with a Beaux-Arts design with neoclassical detailing, which was gaining in popularity for civic buildings of that era and was complementary to the post office building. The new $200,000 station opened on November 2, 1922. In another blow to industry, the freight depot was eliminated.

The 1920s also signaled the first significant shift of second-generation residents away from manual labor to service jobs. One of the more notable and early examples occurred in the Clayton family. Rather than follow his father, Ira Clayton, into the East Side baking business he had established in 1896, Kenneth Clayton went into real estate sales. The young Clayton was doing so well that in 1924, when Freihoffer's Bakery, an eleven-year-old upstart from Philadelphia, wanted to expand its presence in Asbury Park, Ira Clayton agreed to sell it his 19,000-square-foot plant on Emory Street. Clayton didn't waste time in retirement, instead going to work

A Cookman Avenue Makeover

THE 550 BUILDING WAS COMPLETED AND A GRAND opening for the public occurred in early May 1938. The architect was Bernard H. Grad & Sons of Newark, New Jersey. The lobby was magnificent, built of imported Spanish marble, and red, white, and pink gladioli lined the corridor. The stair railings were constructed of stainless steel. I was eight years old at the time but never forgot the events of that day. Mother and Dad had already departed our small home in Upper Montclair. They wanted me to be present for the special occasion, and so they asked my first piano teacher and her husband, Lelah and George Nesbitt, to drive me down, and also attend the opening. It was a beautiful sunny day as I recall, and the grand opening occurred at a time when the economy had rallied in the fall of 1937 and then started down again, creating a black atmosphere of despair. The opening of 550 Cookman Avenue gave much inspiration to those citizens who witnessed this monument to faith for the future, and represented a tremendous risk on my parents' part since this building was erected with borrowed money at a time when offices, apartments, parking spaces, and stores could not be rented at all. It took World War II and the year 1940 to get the ball rolling into a successful venture and investment.

– Bruce Keator Fredericks
Colts Neck, New Jersey

with his son. In just one year the son-and-father team was boasting sales of $2 million from Asbury Park property alone. They soon acquired the Twin Cities Insurance Agency and moved their offices into the Asbury Park Trust Company building.

For its part, Freihoffer bought a sizable facility that spanned Sewall Avenue between Bond and Emory Streets. On one side of the avenue, shoppers could watch through windows as machines formed loaves, while across the street, the freshly baked bread was displayed for sale. But Freihoffer's wasn't impervious to outside competition. Other large-scale commercial bakers were moving in, creating a fierce competition among themselves as well as with Asbury Park's smaller family-owned bakeries. The race ultimately played itself out for dominance on the food aisles of the new self-service supermarket chain stores like the Atlantic & Pacific Tea Company (A & P), where the penultimate suppliers became regional and national corporations.

First Skyscraper

Nineteenth-century bank buildings, with their second and third floors available for rent to professionals such as doctors, dentists, and lawyers, were soon to find competition in the twentieth century, nowhere more dramatically than in the heart of downtown. The Byram building, which had sustained a fire in 1916, was remodeled in 1922 with the addition of two new floors, a marble foyer, and fire and burglar alarms. The new owner was the Asbury Park National Bank and Trust Company. Confectioner and Boardwalk restaurateur William J. Couse was president. By 1929 deposits totaled more than $3.5 million and trust funds totaled more than $1 million.

In direct design opposition to the nineteenth-century chiseled stone that was the Byram building, the new headquarters of the Seacoast Trust Company was designed under the direction of trust company president and department store buyer Arthur Steinbach as a Beaux-Arts structure in smooth yellow ochre Indiana limestone. Where the Byram building was marked by sheer granite mass, the Seacoast Trust was noteworthy for soaring neoclassical windows flanked by the flourish of Corinthian capitals. In fact, it was a streamlined version of architect Whitney Warren's design for the New York Yacht Club. A few years later the company added a $125,000 addition for a storage vault for furs and, on the second floor, a spectac-

The **Hindenburg** *airship as it sailed over Cookman Avenue; less than an hour later it burst into flames and crashed on landing at the Lakehurst air station. Courtesy of Catherine and Michael Barry.*

ularly ornate executive boardroom imported from seventeenth-century Italy, complete with a coffered ceiling and a white marble fireplace in which Arthur Steinbach had his initials carved.

The downtown's third signature bank building was designed by Theodore Brazer, who had designed the High Victorian Boardwalk "birdcage" and the Gothic-style Trinity Episcopal Church on Asbury and Grand Avenues. For his client, the First National Bank, Brazer chose a Dutch Colonial Revival style in brick with wood trim that evoked Greek Revival elements. The one-story building was erected on Mattison Avenue at the opposite end of the block from the Byram building. But it was a throwback to an earlier era in mercantile architecture. A new style was about to debut in Asbury Park.

One-time preacher turned railroad securities bookkeeper turned public utilities magnate Abram E. Fitkin, who summered in nearby Allenhurst, reorganized

Constructed of buff Indiana limestone above a base of black-gray granite, the electric company building, designed by Chicago architect Frank Chase, was crowned by decorative art deco spires. Eventually the deco elements at the roofline were modified. Pike Archives.

the Eastern New Jersey Power Company in 1923, and by 1926 he had sold it to the Utilities Power and Light Company of Chicago, owned by Samuel Insull. Locally, the company was known as the Jersey Central Power & Light Company. Its new owner was ready to make his presence known on the northern Jersey Shore, and Insull sent architect Frank B. Chase east with blueprints for an eleven-story art deco skyscraper.

Changing the residential nature of Bangs Avenue and Emory Street, the city's first skyscraper at 601 Bangs Avenue featured a street-level two-story interior atrium that was surrounded by a mezzanine-level balcony. In the center, the latest in electrical appliances that would magically make housework disappear were featured and were for sale. The upper floors were income-producing rentals from such varied services as dental laboratories and accountants' offices. At the festive gala opening on May 14, 1927, Mayor Clarence Hetrick—soon to be an electric company lobbyist—threw the switch to illuminate a brilliant display of red and green lights on the roof. An orchestra played throughout the evening. News reports cited the building as the tallest skyscraper between Newark and Atlantic City.

With his newly acquired seat on the New York Stock Exchange, Fitkin had not left the Asbury Park scene altogether. At the same time that 601 Bangs Avenue was under construction, Fitkin was investing in a more modest high-rise of six stories on the southwest corner of Grand and Summerfield Avenues. He temporarily leased the ground-floor showroom to Studebaker dealer Louis F. Lipsey while Lipsey waited for his own showroom to be completed at the western end of Summerfield next to the railroad tracks. Fitkin's office tenants were Asbury Park doctors affiliated with the Ann May Homeopathic Hospital in Spring Lake. Led by doctors James and Joseph Ackerman, in 1932 a new medical facility opened in Neptune with an initial donation from Fitkin, who wanted to memorialize his late ten-year-old son, Raleigh Fitkin, and Fitkin's own personal aide, Paul Morgan.

When Tastyeast, a subsidiary of the Charms Candy Company of Bloomfield, which made yeast-based snack bars, acquired 601 Bangs Avenue in 1944, the Jersey Central Power & Light Company moved some of its operation to Fitkin's all-electric building on Grand Avenue. The doctors moved to a new, smaller, plainer office building designed by Frank Cole two blocks away on Grand and Munroe Avenues.

The WJLK Genealogy

ON NOVEMBER 22, 1926, THE CALL LETTERS DWM were licensed to Donald W. May of Newark. In 1927 he moved his station to Asbury Park. By 1928, and under contract to the Asbury Park Chamber of Commerce, the call letters were changed to WCAP for "City of Asbury Park." The chamber's executive secretary, Thomas F. Burley Jr., was the station manager.

The chamber bought the station in 1931 and moved the studios from the JCP&L building on Bangs and Emory to Convention Hall. Ownership transfer occurred when Burley incorporated himself as Radio Industries Broadcasting Company. The station was briefly affiliated with CBS radio, which gave Asbury Park broadcasts national exposure.

In 1944, the Charms Candy Company and Walter Reade Organization Inc. bought a controlling interest in Burley's RIBC and moved the studios back to Bangs Avenue. Burley transferred the FM license to Charms on February 5, 1945. The transfer gave rise to the perception that the call letters stood for "We Charm Asbury Park."

On November 22, 1947, J. Lyle Kinmonth, *Asbury Park Press* publisher, began broadcasting an AM signal using his initials to launch WJLK. Three years later, for $75,000, he bought WCAP for its FM transmission strength, and the FM call letters were changed to WJLK. The studios were moved into the *Press* building at 605 Mattison Avenue. The 1 p.m. newscast was the station's most listened to program because it included a reading of the daily obituaries from the *Press*. Radio announcers

Bill Bransome, Lincoln Harner, John Wheeling, and Andy Parish all got their start here.

Radio pioneer and composer James L. "Jimmy" Shearer wrote a jaunty little ditty titled "Come to Asbury Park," which plugged the city. Dedicated to Mayor George A. Smock II, it was heard for the first time over WJLK on June 14, 1950. The lyrics include this line: "When you're feeling down and blue, Come to Asbury Park."

– With an assist from Chris Flynn
Ocean Grove, New Jersey

WCAP announcer Bob Longstreet (left), Doris Pilling, Paul Johnson, Phebia Thomas, Francis Jones, Katherine Bryan, and Betty Jackson prepare for an on-air reading of "The Sketch Book Players" in 1929. Pike Archives.

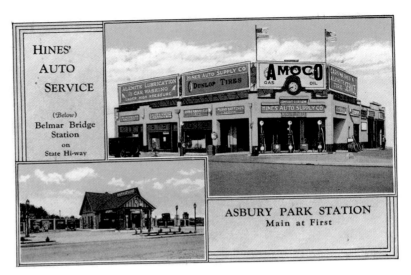

TOP *Asbury Park's Main Street was designated as state highway 4-N, a sign of its growing importance as a major Shore thoroughfare in the 1940s. Roland Hines, who would eventually be an Asbury Park mayor, had two successful gas and service stations, one in this resort and a second one about five miles to the south in Belmar on the Shark River. Pike Archives.*

BOTTOM *Car dealer Joseph Stein took over the local Studebaker franchise after the Indiana-based auto company filed for bankruptcy protection in the 1930s. In May 1946, Studebaker was one of the first car companies to launch its postwar models. This one was photographed in 1949 on Kingsley Avenue; the back of the Asbury Park Recreation Bowling Lanes, Fourth Avenue, can be seen in the background. Pike Archives.*

For a time, both 601 Bangs and the old Elks lodge on Heck Street were simultaneously referred to as the Charms Building. Walter W. Reid Jr. was listed as chairman of the Charms Company while his son, Walter W. Reid III, was listed as president of the wholesale confectioners located at the Heck Street facility. By 1988, when Tootsie Roll Industries of Chicago acquired the Charms Company, the company was long gone from Asbury Park.

In 1952 the County Gas Company of Atlantic Highlands leased the first three floors of 601 Bangs Avenue and acquired the gas customer base of Jersey Central

Power & Light Company for $16 million. Two years later, Tastyeast sold 601 Bangs to its tenant, which was about to change its name to the New Jersey Natural Gas Company, and Jersey Central Power & Light completely moved its operations to Grand Avenue.

Car Culture

Designated 4-N by the state until the great renumbering of the highway system in 1953 when it became Route 71, Main Street's nineteenth-century residential character was being displaced by assorted twentieth-century automotive businesses located north of the downtown's Bangs Avenue perimeter: neighborhood taverns, delicatessens and lunchrooms, tire stores, repair shops, and appliance stores. The latter competed with Sears Roebuck, which occupied the former Ford dealership on the northwest side of Main Street and Summerfield Avenue, and, later, a small, short-lived Montgomery Ward on Mattison Avenue.

At the start of the Jazz Age, the snappy little car that many wanted to drive was a Studebaker. Louis Lipsey was the local agent, with a territory that covered the northern Jersey Shore from Long Branch south to the Manasquan River. He built a 7,500-square-foot showroom and assembly plant by the railroad tracks on Summerfield Avenue for $175,000. The square building was all angular lines and soaring planes and was crowned by a decorative band of hieroglyphic-like designs just under the roofline.

For eight years Lipsey won second or third place in countrywide sales contests, selling more than 2,500 new Studebaker cars. His preowned business was doing well, too, with sales of more 4,000 secondhand cars, including rebuilt Studebakers. Lipsey had ten salesmen and fifteen mechanics on staff before the Wall Street crash of 1929 left him bankrupt.

In the 1930s, Joseph F. Stein, a Dodge dealer in Long Branch, relocated to Asbury Park, moving his garage to a stucco building on the northwest corner of Main

Designed by Newton Van Zandt, the short-lived Richelieu sports car was assembled in a small garage at 809 Railroad Avenue owned by Frederick Holznagle. Only an estimated fifty cars were made between 1922 and 1923. The venture was owned by a group that included local investors S. A. Reeves and R. G. Poole of the Merchants' National Bank of Asbury Park. Pike Archives.

OPPOSITE BOTTOM *Plaid stamps were given with purchases made at any A&P. An E. F. MacDonald Plaid Stamps Redemption Center opened on Main Street, between Summerfield and Munroe, across from Sears Roebuck. A redemption center for S&H Green Stamps, a competitor in the business of trading stamps for merchandise, was located at Cookman and Heck. Pike Archives*

The fleet of delivery trucks outside Le Parisien Cleaners & Dyers on Main Street is another testament to the economic thoroughfare 4-N was becoming circa 1930. Pike Archives.

Street and Fourth Avenue. Stein also acquired what was left of the Studebaker dealership and moved it from Summerfield Avenue onto the west side of Main Street between Munroe and Sewall Avenues. He set up a lot for secondhand cars across the street, just north of the YMCA.

He had three rivals close by. One was Harry Ingalls, who operated a high successful Buick dealership on the southeast corner of Main Street and Summerfield Avenue. George Van Wickle took over Park Chevrolet, started by his father-in-law, Malcolm Harris, on the northwest corner of Main Street and Second Avenue, while John Thomson's two-story show- and repair rooms for Ford were located on the southwest corner of Main Street and Summerfield Avenue. Stein eventually sold LaSalles and, most importantly, Cadillacs.

As mid-century approached, the dealers struggled with the tightly compacted addresses they had on Main Street. Peter S. Costanza, who had already relocated his repair garage from Springwood to the more trafficked Asbury Avenue near the railroad tracks, acquired the Ford dealership and moved it west on Asbury Avenue, past Ridge Avenue, just over the Neptune line to vacant land where he developed a more modern showroom. The Costanza family remained on Asbury Avenue until 1970, when Peter's son, looking at a still-growing business thanks to suburban homeowners, needed a larger lot and moved to Route 66, farther into Neptune and closer to the Garden State Parkway.

Many Springwood Avenue merchants achieved a certain level of success when they were able to secure a spot on Main Street. Seen here is the second generation of fruit and vegetable vendors from the Gubitosa family who moved to Main between Cookman and Springwood Avenues. After World War II the space was taken over when Bob and Irving's men's shop expanded. Courtesy of Gubitosa family.

Stein's son-in-law, former Associated Press photographer Martin Cohen, took over the burgeoning Cadillac business and moved onto the former Ford property on Asbury Avenue. As an indication of its share of the local luxury market, the dealership was renamed Gold Coast Cadillac.

More businesses opened on Asbury Avenue, making further inroads in what had become the resort's Little Italy neighborhood with the construction of Our Lady of Mount Carmel Roman Catholic Church in 1951. A linoleum outlet opened, as did more repair garages, barbershops, and convenience stores. The community's grocery and candy store was converted to Freddie's, a family pizzeria that became synonymous with good Italian home-cooked food served quickly and inexpensively. A couple of blocks to the east James Garrabrant opened Horner's Drive-In, a quintessential drive-in restaurant known for its barbecue sauce.

William C. Durant, the cigar salesman turned automobile titan who created, and then was twice ousted as president from, General Motors, turned up in Asbury Park in 1924. After he was fired from the company the first time he spent time at his summer home in Deal, north of Asbury Park; in 1921, he

THANK YOU FOR SHOPPING AT...

THE STORE THAT CARES...ABOUT YOU!

formed the Durant Motor Car Company. He opened an assembly plant in Elizabeth and three years later a pride-and-joy showroom on Railroad Avenue, directly opposite the North Asbury Park train station; the showroom occupied nearly the entire frontage between Fifth and Sunset Avenues. In 1932, a declining stock market and the Great Depression ended Durant's automotive career in New Jersey, but his showroom lived on as a supermarket and then as a sort of indoor mall with a collection of businesses that included Packard-Bamberger's of Hackensack, the neighborhood grocery store; a shoe repair stand; a luncheonette; and Potter's Beauty Parlor and Barbershop.

By 1946, Joe and Jack Hack were hosts of the Wagon Wheel, a lunchtime bar at 1114 Main Street between Third and Fourth Avenues. The triple entendre played itself out on a number of levels.

COLEMAN HOUSE BAR
206 MAIN ST. ASBURY PARK, N.J.
(OPP. R. R. STATION)

The Coleman House Bar, specifically its hand-carved, pirate-themed bar back, had been part of Phil Daly's notorious 1890s gambling club in West End, Long Branch. It was removed and retrofitted into the former Milan Ross real estate office sometime after 1934. Pike Archives.

Most closely it was a nod to Peter De Rose, the songwriter who wrote the melody for the 1934 standard "Wagon Wheels" and who had retired to Eighth Avenue in Asbury Park. The name also gave a historical nod to the vehicles that had traveled the roadway during founder Bradley's horse-and-carriage days. Given its proximity to Chevrolet and Dodge dealerships, it was a logical place for businessmen to close a deal over lunch and a beer or shot of whiskey. The Hacks also worked hard to develop a late-night shift for the tavern as a nightclub, promoting such local acts as the Three Kings "with Inkspot Arrangements," and serving snacks until 2 a.m.

New Promotional Prose

The mid-twentieth-century promotional heirs to the nineteenth-century *Torch* and *Seaside Life* were led by *Spotlight* magazine publisher and editor Conrad Lyons; *Like*, published in Allenhurst by Fred "Baron" Lehman; and another local picture sheet called *The Beachcomber*, which was based in Avon. All three publications carried large numbers of photos with captions chronicling who was dining, dancing, singing, partying, shopping, and, most importantly for advertising, where they were doing it. *Spotlight* was the most successful of this new group of advertorial publications, whose collective goal was to sell the concept of consumerism instead of tangible parcels of real estate.

Lyons was originally an advertising executive from the suburban Essex County. When he went out on his own after having worked for an advertising firm, he opened an office in Newark and initially concentrated on what were then the state's most influential counties: Essex and Hudson. Soon, though, Lyons followed the circuit of wealthy—and often politically well-connected—North Jersey residents who summered at the Shore. He opened a second office in Convention Hall in Asbury Park and hired various local photographers to supply him with pictures from Monmouth Park, the racetrack in Oceanport, and aspiring models in bathing suits from Steinbach's. Lyons and his wife, Connie, went so far as to rent an apartment at the Santander so they could be part of this influential circuit. Lyons's publishing reach grew to include Florida when he hired a field correspondent in Hollywood, a 1920s Florida resort that was attracting winter vacationers from Asbury Park as well as North Jersey.

Count Basie Live

IN THE EARLY 1940S, PHONOGRAPH RECORDS CAME only in one format, 78 r.p.m. A record sold for about thirty-five cents, and Tusting Music held a virtual monopoly on record sales in Asbury Park until later in that decade.

But tucked away on Munroe Avenue, just east of the railroad tracks, was the Casino Amusement Company, which placed jukeboxes in area bars and restaurants. Each record had two sides, and as one side was played over and over, the surface became worn by the needle and the sound deteriorated. Many times the other side was never played. Casino would empty their machines, [separate] any records that were not noticeably scratched, and put them up for sale on a table in their building. Depending on visual condition, each record was either five or ten cents each. It was at that table that I spend much of my youth.

Rummaging through those piles regularly, I found great jazz records by Duke Ellington, Count Basie, Louis Armstrong, Billie Holiday, and many others reclaimed from jukeboxes in Asbury Park. One day I picked up what seemed to be an unused Count Basie with "Broadway" on one side and "Jitters" on the other, both eventually to become classics. It cost me a nickel. It also started me on a path I've followed for sixty years, listening to the music of Count Basie.

There was a very small movie theater on Springwood Avenue, the State, which had gone out of business and was converted into a ballroom of the same name. And one night the attraction was Count Basie and his orchestra. Well, I couldn't miss this. The ballroom was packed. Count Basie noticed that I was the only white kid in the place, smiled at me, and waved me welcome. I've never forgotten that wonderful moment.

– Philip M. Rosenbloom
Monmouth Beach, New Jersey

In the February 11, 1961, edition, whose cover featured Dana Lee Aschettino, a Tom Lane model, to promote the Eighth Annual Jersey Coast Boat Show, an entire page was devoted to the "Monmouth Shore"; names were dropped there like so much bee pollen in preparation for warmer weather:

> Angelo and Evelyn Gatta of Finaldi's in Asbury Park, motoring in the Las Vegas area, hate to think of coming back to Asbury's snows. Joseph Locher, Asbury Park real estate and insurance broker, on crutches, negotiates nicely. Congratulations to model agent director and publicist Thomas Lane of Neptune who birthdayed [*sic*] January 28. . . . Louis and Mrs. Dohrman, he of the Waiters and Waitresses Union, Asbury Park, are off to Florida for short vacation. Asbury Park Boys Club Ladies Auxiliary held dinner last Saturday at the Kingsley Arms Roof, Asbury Park. Strolling the Boardwalk, handsome Bill Cassidy of Dolly Madison Ice Cream.

George Keator Fredericks, president of Keator Properties at 500 Cookman Avenue, hardly needed any kind of special prose to herald the winner of the five-and-ten-cent bargain wars on Cookman Avenue. It was J. J. Newberry. In 1954 Fredericks hired New York architect Ward W. Fenner to design a streamlined orange brick building to span the lots from 616 to 634 Cookman Avenue. Newberry's major discount competitor was W. T. Grant, located next door but with a fraction of the square footage. Woolworth, which never expanded beyond its original 1890 footprint, was no

Waiting for Santa on Main Street

THE DAY AFTER THANKSGIVING (OR MAYBE THE Saturday after), my cousins and I would be packed into the Studebaker with my parents. This was in the fifties. Dad would park at the North Asbury Station and we'd position ourselves on the east side of Main Street by Sunset Lake Park for the parade. Bands, balloons, vendors with twittering birds on slings—it was tremendously exciting—a mini-Macy's parade, but very grand to us. I recall that I was puzzled: there were balloons and balloon handlers, but they were much smaller than the ones I'd seen on Thanksgiving Day on our ten-inch TV. Why should that be? Asbury Park was, at best, as cosmopolitan as New York. We'd fidget, we'd gape, we'd complain that we were cold. But finally—there he was! Santa! And we knew that he'd be waiting to hear our most secret Christmas wishes at Steinbach's, in his very own frost village. And so, with Santa's arrival, and the fabulous lights stretched across Main and down part of Cookman, Asbury Park became a North Pole paradise.

– Mary Christian, Little Silver, New Jersey

longer a competitive threat. More importantly, at Newberry headquarters, the Asbury Park store was regarded as the sales leader of the company's Manhattan division. So important was its opening that family members involved in the business attended.

The new Newberry was labeled a variety department store, boasting thirty-seven different departments, a forty-seat fountain and snack bar with an option for take-out, an escalator linking the first and second floors, and a new entrance on Lake Avenue. Want a rug? Need dinnerware? Boys' pants? Costume jewelry? Nuts? Curtains and rods? Hosiery? Ice cream? Newberry's had it all, plus 300 employees to help you. Above the lunch counter, near life-size photographic images of Asbury Park's oceanfront from the Mayfair Theatre and Palace Merry Go Round all the way to the Monte Carlo Pool and Cabana Club lined the walls.

The new J. J. Newberry's opened on August 24, 1955. Thousands of orchids were given away to early customers and three Newberry family members still involved in the day-to-day operations of the family enterprise attended the opening. Courtesy of Milton Edelman.

Malled

Since the end of World War II, Monmouth County had been losing 3,000 acres of year to industry, housing, schools, and highways. Construction of the Garden State Parkway took 3,500 acres of county farmland. By 1960, just half of the county's 300,000 acres were devoted to agriculture, dairying, and the raising of flowers and nursery stock. On May 12, 1958, ground was broken on the old Succotash Farm in

Eatontown, ten miles north of Asbury Park on the pine-tree-lined Route 35 to Red Bank, and the northern Jersey Shore's retail history was about to undergo an irrevocable transformation.

Ten years in the planning, Monmouth Shopping Center was the third largest property in the state to be converted into a collection of retail stores connected by landscaped sidewalks. Built and owned by the Massachusetts Mutual Insurance Company, the 600,000-square-foot facil-

ity included a civic auditorium, and its perimeter was offset by acres of unlimited and unmetered parking.

Newark realtor Irving Feist was its manager, and he successfully lured one of his city's premier department stores, Bamberger's, as the anchor for the initial thirteen businesses, which included a restaurant and a post office substation. On the eve of the shopping center's opening in May 1960, Feist described the shift away from urban railroad-based designs to the new suburban roadway economy. "One day I took a helicopter ride. Over Eatontown I could see the outline of the Parkway and its approach to the Eatontown Circle. I could see a double axis developing between Red Bank and Asbury Park, Long Branch and Freehold," Feist said. "I saw that the area was served by highways and a tremendous amount of feeder roads. If it wasn't the geographical center of the county, it was the highway center."

It was also the death knell for Asbury Park. Already the city had sustained a number of body blows. Historically, its infrastructure had been based on the classic railroad model, using trains to move masses of people into the resort and trolleys to move them within its confines. Its wide boulevards were now little more than wide thoroughfares for funneling more and more vehicular traffic through town. Drivers were frequently stymied by lack of public parking. Businessmen and women who had themselves been raised in the city, worshipped in its religious houses, sent their children to its schools, and voted in its elections, no longer lived in Asbury Park. Many in the next generation became absentee landlords. In an echo from 1913, the chamber of commerce found itself divided into separate self-interest groups: beachfront, retail, and service and trade. And despite a listing of 600 members, the chamber was operating in the red. In 1968 it was disbanded.

Closer to Asbury Park than Eatontown, Middlebrook Shopping Plaza opened in 1970 on a former dairy farm at Route 35 and Deal Road in suburban Ocean Township. One of the first stores to move into this commercial strip was Fisch's department store from Springwood Avenue.

Fueled as much by economic as civil unrest, the West Side erupted with violence on July 4, 1970. Police from Asbury Park and neighboring towns, state troopers, and national guardsmen set themselves up on Main Street to ensure the street fighting wouldn't cross the tracks and spread through the historic downtown and to the beachfront. The civil unrest lingered. On August 1, 1970, a mysterious fire ripped through two buildings on Main Street just north of Springwood Avenue: Banker's Furniture and Monmouth Awning & Casual Furniture. Started on the West Side in 1939 by Frank Fritz and Edward Damon, Monmouth Awning began "with a capital of $10 and a sewing machine" and had been at its Main Street location for about seven years. But the Bankers went even further back, to 1896 when patriarch Harry Banker first opened his doors at 143 Main Street. Eventually the furniture business expanded into the 1890 Githens mattress company. Banker's Furniture was notable for another reason. It was one of the first in Asbury Park to offer deferred payment plans, or credit, for furniture purchases. Bob and Irving's, a men's and boy's

OPPOSITE *Walter W. Reid Jr., president of the Charms Candy Company, Bloomfield, opened a second packaging and clerical facility in the former Elks lodge during the early 1940s: it was an easier commute from his nearby home in Allenhurst. In addition to the fruit-flavored square candies, the company also had contracts to make medicines for such pharmaceutical companies as Playtex. In 1944 Charms, along with Walter Reade, bought a part interest in WCAP. Charms was eventually bought by Tootsie Roll of Chicago. Courtesy of T. Frank Appleby.*

That Seventies Shopping

I REMEMBER ASBURY WHERE MOM TOOK US FOR NEW school shoes and we went to Levin's (the original T. J. Maxx) to get inexpensive but nice pillowcases. When [we were] college age we went to a great grungy secondhand-book store [White's Gallery, Lake Avenue] and found a place [Victor's Factory Outlet, Cookman Avenue] that sold priced-wholesale Saint Laurent satin nightgowns just when we needed them. . . . Won't even mention the cafe where you bought tickets for the Port Authority bus. It smelled like old soup and old uncles. It's only recently that we expect everything to be appetizing.

– Lizzie Schippert, artist
Island Heights, New Jersy

clothing store, would later try this for clothes. Besides homes, Banker furnished the new YMCA and the American Legion clubhouse. Sam Banker, son of the founder, estimated his loss at $100,000 worth of inventory.

In 1971, after a private meeting with state and federal officials at the Jersey Central Power & Light headquarters on Grand Avenue, Robert Richter, who owned a shoe store, and Marvin Goldstein, owner of a stationery store, walked door-to-door signing up members to restart the chamber of commerce in order to qualify Asbury Park for government aid. In 1973, in a separate strategy that looked like more a cosmetic public relations move than a defined plan for urban renewal, Springwood Avenue was renamed Lake Avenue and Railroad Avenue became Memorial Drive, providing a new address for the local Social Security Administration offices.

The glory days of retail were past, and the 1970s were painful. In 1979, the city paid $42,000 to the Princeton architectural firm of Raymond, Parrish, Pine and Weiner, who designed a turn-of-the-century theme and twelve separate improvement projects that the city could undertake in stages. It carried out only one: a $56,000 sidewalk improvement for Press Plaza, the one-time gilded epicenter where Emory Street and Cookman and Mattison Avenues had first seen the glory era of downtown shopping in 1890.

Merchants criticized the plan for lacking ambition, prompting Gary Anderson of the city's Department of Community Affairs to counter in the *Asbury Park Press* with, "It must be realized by all concerned that there are no quick and easy solu-

BELOW *In the 1940s, customers shopping for furniture had quite a choice on Main Street: Banker's, White's, and the Main Street Furniture Exchange. Courtesy T. Frank Appleby.*

OPPOSITE *By 1970, Banker's had emerged as the most successful of the city's furniture stores and had moved to Main and Springwood. It was the target of a fire bomb in August 1970, one of the lingering effects of the West Side's July disturbances. Pike Archives.*

tions. . . . The downtown areas have experience a steady deterioration year by year for the past ten years. During this period, no real effort has been made by either the public or private sector to halt the negative trends." Anderson also pointed to "negative image problems and political controversy" as also having a detrimental impact on public confidence.

The economic tripod of the 1890s that had held so much promise was about to sustain another blow. In 1978 Seaview Square Mall, nearing completion on the site of the old city dump and Flavell's fat-rendering plant on Asbury Avenue and Route 35 in Ocean Township, was about to open its doors. Borrowing a page from the shopping center strategy in Eatontown, there was to be an anchor department store. But it wasn't from Newark. It was right out of Asbury Park and it was the beloved Steinbach's.

Unbeknownst to the public, S. S. Kresge had failed to absorb Steinbach's mammoth department store during the Great Depression. In 1943, Kresge sold the controlling interest in Asbury Park's flagship retail enterprise to Irving Goerke, owner of Goerke's department store in Elizabeth, the only other store for

Waiting for Customers to Return

ON JULY 4, 1970, IT SEEMED TO RAIN ASH FOR THE longest time. That horrible acrid smell was everywhere. The air was so still, much like that of 9/11 when you're just waiting for something else to happen. Businesses in town were closed for several days. There was absolutely no one around. It was scary. Police patrol was beefed up considerably, and I remember that my parents were afraid to let me go to work but I went anyway. We lived in Wanamassa [Ocean Township's bungalow community across Deal Lake's western end] and we could hear police and fire sirens and smell the city burning.

It took quite a while for things to get back to "normal." Normal wasn't like before. We had been robbed of our innocence. That idyllic existence we had was gone right along with the tourist traffic that had been Asbury Park's big ticket for so long. It seemed like everything we knew was gone in a blink of an eye.

– Francesa Garsh,
onetime waitress at the Press Box

Asbury Park's Downtown

People have to forget what downtown Asbury Park once was because it can never be like that again. Instead, the merchants have to give the downtown a new, younger, fresher look.

Asbury Park's business decline has paralleled the movement of large retail businesses to highway shopping centers. It was accelerated by social conditions and a depressed economy. But it became obvious in the 1960s that the city could no longer support a business community of the kind that prospered in the 1950s.

It has been difficult to effect change in Asbury Park. Some merchants were unwilling to accept reality and clung to the business means of the past. Today, however, the climate has changed and some talented young people have taken advantage of the city's positive aspects and begun a new and different business community that stands a good chance of making the downtown a desirable shopping area again.

– Asbury Park Press, editorial, June 21, 1980

which Arthur Steinbach continued to buy European merchandise. Michael Slovak, a Goerke executive, became Steinbach president. When the Goerke patriarch died from a fall down the stairs in his South Orange home, the pending merger was left in the hands of the Goerke estate, where it remained until the doors were closed for good on Cookman Avenue.

For two years Slovak had tried to keep both department store locations in operation under an agreement with the Goerke family trust. But the closing of the Cookman Avenue property was inevitable when the company was sold to an outside corporation. At 8 a.m. on Saturday, July 14, 1979, Aly Kahn of Kneip's Bakery delivered the last dinner rolls to the Garden Grill. At 5:30 p.m. Lynne Eitelberg of Long Branch and her nine-year-old daughter, Dana, were the last shoppers. Padlocks were placed on the doors leading into the store from Bangs and Cookman Avenues, and workmen nailed plywood over the plate-glass windows. The era of high-fashion shopping in Asbury Park was over.

A Return to Rail?

In 1977 the federal government passed the Surface Transportation Act, which opened the door to the possibility of creating a regional transportation hub in Asbury Park. After a three-year lapse, the mayor and council began discussing the possibility. The vision was large: create much-needed parking for shoppers and commuters alike, and on both the east and west sides of Memorial Drive; combine all the bus, taxi, and car services onto one central plaza around the train station; encourage new construction of apartments and condominiums to attract North Jersey and New York commuters.

But the visionary discussions came amidst demands by the Monmouth County Tax Board for the city to overhaul and update its property valuations. According to the board's records, the last citywide assessment had taken place twenty years earlier, in 1960. In the wake of the tax board's demands, city homeowners, who had paid 34.5 percent of the city's taxes while business properties contributed 65.5 percent, discovered the tax balance shifted as city hall asked them to assume a greater share, or 45 percent, of the municipal tax burden. The rationale was to raise taxes only a little on commercial properties in order to make them more attractive to prospective entrepreneurs.

At the same time, where founder Bradley had controlled Asbury Park's appearance with deed restrictions and by relying on a standard steeped largely in the Protestant ethic, the mayor and council of 1980 had to rely on more and more ordinances to offset rundown conditions. One new ordinance empowered code officers to fine both commercial and residential property owners until they brought their lots and buildings into modern compliance as part of the overall plan to attract new investors to Asbury Park. Once the hallmark of sidewalk advertising, plate-glass windows had

OPPOSITE *On May 1, 1960, New Jersey Congressman Harrison Williams used Steinbach's as a backdrop to promote patriotism and combat communism as part of Loyalty Day. Sitting in a stroller in the sparsely attended event was Dan Jacobson, who would become a journalist, lawyer, and state assemblyman from the Asbury Park area, and, as publisher of the downtown-based* triCity News, *a sort of spiritual heir to theater mogul Walter Reade Sr., who had once run for office in Asbury Park and had published a newspaper on the corner of Mattison and Bond. Courtesy of Milton Edelman.*

From Train Station to Transportation Center

CONGRESSMAN JIM HOWARD WAS A PROPONENT OF intermodal transportation. Asbury Park was depressed economically at that time and the thinking was that construction of such a center [combining rail, bus, and taxi service] would not only be a boon to transportation, but it would be an economic boon to Asbury Park, much like Journal Square in Jersey City, with a newspaper stand, luncheonette, flower shop, dry cleaners, a candy store, and Western Union.

The transportation department was saying, if we don't have to make all these little stops down the line, we could decrease the travel time between the Shore and the metro-politan area. My way of thinking was to make Asbury Park the main transportation center for the area [because we] had a lot of space for parking.

Well, turned out everybody wanted to have their own station. [Then] when the center was finally constructed, it outlawed the businesses that would be a natural adjunct to a major transportation [hub]. So, in a sense, we were back to square one.

– Dr. Lorenzo Harris,
Asbury Park councilman, 1973–1985

been boarded over, enabling prostitution to take place in the abandoned retail space. With the hope of preventing illegal activity from taking place, the mayor and council passed an ordinance to ban the boarding up of front windows.

All this did nothing to stop the march of Asbury Park's leading businesses out of the city to more spacious country campuses. In January 1980 the *Asbury Park Press* opened a 70,000-square-foot printing plant on the outskirts of Neptune, with close access to the state's highway system. In three years, the newsroom, radio station WJLK, circulation and advertising departments, and the offices of the editor and publisher were gone from Mattison Avenue. Also in 1980, New Jersey Natural Gas broke ground for a new regional headquarters in the onetime farming community of Wall Township on a section of state highway designated by the state as suitable for commercial and office development. While Jersey Central Power & Light promised publicly it was not moving, in a few years it consolidated its front office operations off Grand Avenue and back to Allenhurst where the utility had begun eighty years earlier.

CHAPTER SEVEN

The Society

TWENTY YEARS AFTER Asbury Park's founding, a number of issues began emerging to that would mark its civic character: founder James Bradley's paternalism; the year-round community's growing inability to achieve consensus; city hall's difficulty in determining a stable tax base; and persistent challenges at establishing a quality education for the resort's children.

Part of the problem was rooted in the state's then-nascent legislation for local governing bodies. Throughout the second half of the nineteenth century and into the twentieth much of New Jersey's real estate was undergoing extensive development and new municipalities were being created. In 1879, a full ten years after the Methodists had created the self-governing Ocean Grove Camp Meeting Association within the township of Neptune and nine years after Bradley began privately laying out Asbury Park, Neptune Township established its independence from Ocean Township. Both Ocean Grove and Asbury Park were located at the eastern end of Neptune Township. In 1890 Asbury Park already had a board of commissioners to oversee the resort's daily business; Bradley was a member. In 1891 Trenton passed a law that formally allowed for the creation of independent boroughs within a township, and by 1894 Neptune officials were publicly questioning how, without being able to receive taxes from either borough, the township would pay for roads that went through it to Ocean Grove and Asbury Park.

Neptune's government seat was in the thriving village of Hamilton, several miles inland. To the farmers who were the township's elected officials, the sea-sprayed

---

For a Public Hall, the Law Relative to Its Construction

BUSINESS MEN IN ASBURY PARK GIVE THEIR VIEW OF THE MATTER.

It is probable that a borough hall will soon be built. . . . The law . . . passed last May . . . [says] boroughs of over 8,000 inhabitants can erect borough halls at a cost not to exceed $25,000.

Commissioner Tenbroeck favored the site at the corner of Bond street and Mattison avenue. . . . "Mr. Bradley has offered to donate this ground . . . ," he said, "provided we can put up a building free and clear of all indebtedness."

Water Commissioner John A. Githens [said], "I favor having a large school house with a large hall which can be used both by the school and the town. I am not in favor of a borough going into the real estate business."

(continues next page)

(continued from previous page)

J. H. Winans wants the hall to be built on Railroad square, where it can be seen by people passing in the railroad trains. The hall would enhance the value of property in the Park.

Dr. H. S. Kinmonth was of the opinion that . . . the borough could do without a public hall. "The borough is now bonded for the water works," he said, "and I think that should answer for a while yet. . . . It is easy enough to get in debt, but it is a hard matter to get out of it."

– The Shore Press,
September 26, 1890

———

beaches and scrub pine along the Shore were worthless for agriculture. But for big-city real estate entrepreneurs such as Bradley, their value was nearly beyond measure. Eventually, Neptune Township would let the developments of Neptune City on the Shark River, Avon, and Bradley Beach go their own way. In 1897 Asbury Park, east of the railroad tracks, declared its independence from Neptune, continuing with its commission form of government, with Bradley on board. Various businessmen took turns at being chosen mayor from among the ranks of elected board members. Each commissioner was in charge of a municipal department and its budget. There were five departments: public affairs, revenue and finance, public safety, public works, and parks and public property. But in Asbury Park, Bradley's sense of civic duty affected how these departments were budgeted.

As the city's largest real estate owner and developer, the president of New York–based Bradley & Smith brush makers affected the resort's inner workings more than was immediately apparent. Out of his own pocket he paid for the first fifteen miles of sewer mains and pipe installation so that that each new homeowner would have no excuse for not paying the small sum they still owed to hook up to the main line in the northern Jersey Shore's most modern, sanitary resort. As owner of the Boardwalk, Bradley paid for its regular repairs, as well as salaries for lifeguards and the borough's

The Ariel Club spent one year as a cycling club for women, affiliated with the League of American Wheelman, before becoming a social organization whose members today are descendants of Asbury Park's original families. Courtesy of the Ariel Club.

policemen. He provided classrooms to educate the small but steadily growing number of youngsters, first two rooms in Park Hall, the resort's cottage-sized first municipal building on Main Street, and then later in Educational Hall, a building he bought at the Philadelphia Centennial Exposition of 1876 and had relocated to Grand Avenue. In those early days, he also paid the teachers' salaries.

But Bradley also withheld some of his largest landholdings, notably the blocks immediately north and south of the Monterey Hotel as well as nearly all the land along the southern bank of Deal Lake, from development that could have improved the city's tax base. In addition, Bradley alternately donated or sold, as suited his sense of noblesse oblige, various parcels, chief among them the prime corner lots along Grand Avenue, which went to Protestant denominations and were taken off the tax rolls. The effect was to hobble the borough finance department's efforts to come up with a reliable forecast of tax income. Summer residents exacerbated the situation by balking at paying for any

James Bradley supported the Asbury Park Fishing Club by building the members a clubhouse at the northernmost end of the Boardwalk, overlooking both Deal Lake and the Atlantic Ocean. Eventually, the city took ownership of the building and turned it into a rental income property when it allowed James Plasteras to convert it to a restaurant. Pike Archives.

extras such as sewer hookups, sidewalk and curb installation, and macadam roadways in front of cottages they lived in only three months of the year. Bradley also continued to hold fiercely to his singular vision of a conservatively moral temperance resort despite the commercial constraints it placed on the city's merchants, who paid higher property taxes than residential owners did, as well as mercantile taxes.

In 1894 Bradley was both a state senator and an Asbury Park city commissioner. After his fellow commissioners complained in the newspapers about his lack of attendance, Bradley showed up for a meeting in 1895.

"I think I do something for Asbury Park," Bradley said. "I supply your cells and a night watchman. I pay all the policemen on the beach and study the welfare of the people in my own way. I have lost $40,000 at the foot of Sixth Avenue last year. I pay to defend your seafront from the inroads of the sea. I have built a house where contagious patients may be taken, and supply all the paraphernalia. I think I am entitled to be—what do you call it?—an ex-officer. I am getting to be an old man. I want to live in peace and harmony with you all. I don't want discord."

Bradley was sixty-five years old. Eight years later, when he was seventy-three, Bradley finally bowed to relentless public and private pressure to sell both his Boardwalk and sewer system. The Boardwalk went for $100,000 and the sewers for $50,000, with a stipulation that Bradley receive the yearly fees for the next thirty years. A few months later, when Bradley criticized the $183 invoice for painting the city's septic tank, city engineer Rufus Savage fired back that the sewer system Bradley had sold the city had only been worth $5,000. And so went the level of civility over municipal matters: for every gesture interpreted as authoritarian there was sure to be a public backlash.

The Certainty of Tax Uncertainty

By November 1913, Bradley's old corporation yard at Lake Avenue and Bond Street was being used, at his indulgence, as a playground by Asbury Park children. When the commissioners decided to acquire the land for an armory for National Guard Company H, New Jersey Infantry, public debate raged over the possible loss of property taxes and what really was the best use for the downtown parcel. Businessmen in the immediate area wanted to see the corner lot developed as either a warehouse or a garage—enterprises complementary to the bustling retail district. But with the looming probability that the United States would go to war in Europe, patriotic sentiment won out. Real estate valuations for the property swung wildly from an estimated $40,000 to a modest $4,000. In the end, Bradley was paid $18,750 for the lot, and the property was taken off the tax rolls.

Later that same month, taxes were at issue again when fifty residents protested their tax assessments to a Monmouth County commissioner in charge of tax equalization. George Pittenger's automobile was twice assessed for $300. The Sunset Hall theater was fully assessed despite evidence that construction had just started. Over on the annexed West Side, Mamie McKell was taxed for a nonexistent building on her

Wesley Place property. Some assessments were overturned, others reserved for a decision at a later date. But amid the reassessments it was revealed that the city tax collector was working from his own personal maps of Asbury Park while the city tax assessor worked from a separate set of maps entirely, their origins and source of data unclear. Both men complained that city hall had never supplied either one of them with accurate, up-to-date property maps. How the disparity was finally resolved amid the finger-pointing was unclear, but by the end of the next decade, improper municipal procedures and a lack of standard codes would start to catch up with city hall.

A New Patriarch

Clarence Eugene Francis Hetrick, son of an Asbury Park realtor, was honing his political skills at this time, and he was elected mayor in 1915. Bradley was eighty-five and increasingly absent from Asbury Park, spending longer periods in New York than at the Shore. In 1921 Bradley died, and the city of Asbury Park, under its new civic patriarch, Mayor Hetrick, undertook the most ambitious expansion program the resort would see in the twentieth century. Heeding the political lessons learned from the 1906 annexation, which had delivered votes, Hetrick paid attention to the West Side, particularly Burnham's original development in the southwest quadrant.

TOP *In 1915 the Benevolent Protective Order of the Elks (BPOE) built a handsome neoclassical clubhouse on the northwest corner of Munroe Avenue and Heck Street in one of the city's entertainment districts. The clubhouse soon doubled in size with nearly half a million dollars in construction and furnishings, including a double-height social hall on its second floor that served as a small convention site. The fourth floor featured a fully equipped children's clinic, and at street level the lodge collected rental income from a seafood restaurant. The expansion led to the lodge losing its clubhouse during the Depression, when it went broke. It would later get another one in a private house in North Asbury Park. Pike Archives.*

BOTTOM *The once-glorious lodge rooms were used as back office space for the Charms Candy Company, social security and draft board offices, and some municipal departments that could no longer fit into the crowded city hall. The city jail was briefly located next door in a parking garage. In the late seventies, the Elks' social hall was a gay disco bar known as the M&K. Pike Archives.*

In an early form of urban renewal, he encouraged real estate investment that saw the replacement of rundown shacks with attractive homes and businesses and made sure all the roads were paved. He offered municipal civil service jobs to residents of this neighborhood, many of them African and Italian Americans, women, and Jews who might have difficulty finding year-round employment in the biased city. He supported the construction of a new high school on Sunset Avenue. Hetrick also undertook the resort's most public display of civic pride with construction of the exuberantly designed Paramount Theatre and Convention Hall, boasting that it didn't have to make money for the city; its very existence would be enough to attract the traveling public to Asbury Park.

As happened elsewhere in the country, the 1920s expansion boom turned to bust when the New York Stock Exchange crashed in October 1929. Asbury Park found itself saddled with an enormous debt of construction-cost overruns of $4 million for the Boardwalk plus payment on the $2 million bond for the new high school. By 1932, 46 percent of Asbury Park's property owners could not pay their taxes. In another two years, the city had to issue scrip to pay its employees.

By 1933, after seventeen years as mayor, Hetrick had amassed an intimidating amount of influence. By now a lobbyist for the electric utilities, he was dividing his time between the nation's capital, a vacation home on the Hudson River in New York State, and his West Side residence on Fourth Avenue in Asbury Park. His political cronies with no formal training in finance or municipal management were running the city in paying positions. Stories surfaced about bagmen who were paid for coveted Boardwalk concessions, and there were other suspicions of money not making its proper way into the municipal coffers. The current government structure had to go.

In October 1934 a special referendum called for a new municipal government that would rely on a professional manager to run the city and a nonpartisan council that would be elected every four years. The referendum passed, and Sherman Dennis, the Monterey Hotel manager, was elected as mayor from the slate of winning

Just as the resort was gearing up to celebrate its fiftieth anniversary, its ninety-three-year-old founder was found to be gravely ill. At 10 p.m. on June 6, 1921, Bradley died at the Hotel St. Denis in Manhattan from bladder cancer. He was laid to rest in the Gillespie family mausoleum in Woodlawn Cemetery in the Bronx where his wife, who had died on Valentine's Day, 1905, was also interred. Eight days later, on June 29, 1921, a $17,000 statue of Bradley, carved by Pittsburgh sculptor Giuseppe Morretti, was unveiled in Atlantic Square. The park's floral landscape included cannas, which could withstand ocean breezes. Pike Archives.

An outgrowth of the Ariel Club was the Saturday Club, which became the Asbury Park Woman's Club in 1900. Among the members shown in this undated photo is Barbara Samaha, second from right, a Lebanese émigré who became the most successful woman business owner on Cookman Avenue when she opened her upscale dress shop, Dainty Apparel, one block from Steinbach's. Courtesy of the Board of Trustees of the Woman's Club of Asbury Park.

candidates. Hetrick was out, and he was not pleased. He launched a recall election the following year, setting a precedent for recall elections that would mark Asbury Park politics throughout the rest of the twentieth century. During the recall campaign, Dennis died, apparently as a result of stress. Grocer John Palmateer was appointed to fill the remainder of Dennis's term, which lasted until the recall election, when Hetrick was voted back into office. However, by this time, he had a new opponent, C. Oliver Armstrong.

As the Depression ground on and Asbury Park fell deeper behind in taxes owed Trenton, an auditor for the New Jersey Department of Local Government was put in charge. That auditor was Armstrong. He was made overseer of the city's fiscal affairs while the city was placed under state control. In 1938, when an $11 million refunding program was finally launched, Asbury Park was freed from state control but not from state supervision. The debt load still had to be managed. Armstrong remained in place to guide city officials through the complicated financial channels, and he was made city manager.

A World-Class Education

Instead of a perfect seaside resort fashioned in the image and likeness of its founder, residents found themselves living in a community whose utopian ideal didn't work too well after Labor Day. The single most persistent civic issue to cause long-lasting strife was parents' desire to create a first-rate educational and athletic program for their children.

Helen and James Bradley's lack of children, coupled with Bradley's own brief education, which had ended at the eighth grade, limited the founder's vision when it came to education. In 1894, mothers—many of them seasoned temperance crusaders—led the charge for a modern high school, and voters agreed to pay for its construction. For his part, Bradley donated six small lots that he already had surveyed on Bond Street for residential construction. Lined with tidy, modest homes,

LEFT *At St. George Orthodox Greek Orthodox Church, the immigrant Greek community established a comprehensive after-school program of language, culture, and religion on Grand and Summerfield Avenues. Pike Archives.*

BELOW *Although it was a service club during World War II, the Asbury Park Kiwanis was also noted for its collective theatrical talent and alternated regular fund-raising performances between the Lyric and, shown here, the St. James. Pike Archives.*

SIXTH ANNUAL "KIWANIS KAPERS"—ST. JAMES THEATRE
Asbury Park, N. J., November 18th & 19th, 1930

Bond and its parallel north-south twin, Emory Street, represented the downtown's working-class neighborhoods south of Asbury Avenue and just a couple blocks off Main Street. Two years later and at a building cost of $65,000, a new high school opened with enough extra classrooms to accommodate elementary school–age pupils living on the East Side. Meanwhile, the previous high school building, the aging wooden Education Hall originally featured in the 1876 Centennial Exposition in Philadelphia, was recycled one last time in 1906, when it was relocated from Grand Avenue to Railroad Avenue, where ended its days as a garage.

In 1907, as construction was finishing on the new red-brick elementary school on Third Avenue, named for Bradley, Frederick Burnham's original community was agitating for a new facility to ease the overcrowding in its two elementary schools.

It took nine more years before the cement was finally poured to build Bangs Street School. When the doors opened in 1918, the pattern of racial segregation that already existed was carried into the new school: children from the Free Colored School on Springwood Avenue went through the doors into Bangs South, and the next generation of immigrant children from Prospect Avenue School went to Bangs North. The wood-frame Springwood facility was torn down while the brick Prospect School was converted into an apartment house. Intentionally or not, the blocks taken by eminent domain to build Bangs Avenue School effectively cut down traffic flow between Springwood and Bangs Avenues.

By 1918 the nearly all white population at Bond Street School was bursting at the seams. Asbury Park's status as a receiving district contributed to the overcrowding. From as far south as Bradley Beach and Avon and north to Deal and Ocean Township, students poured into the city's school district, creating the greatest population impact at the high school level. Asbury Park's high school was the only public school serving the area's population.

As the bungalow community of Wanamassa across Deal Lake grew into a year-round community, its children attended the nearby Bradley School instead of the Oakhurst School administered by Ocean Township some three miles away. But with overcrowding there leading to a school that operated in shifts, Wanamassa parents

The Asbury Park Auditorium, circa 1910. Pike Archives.

persuaded Ocean to build a new school for the southern end of the township in 1928. Families from surrounding towns such as Interlaken and Deal opted to pay tuition to send their children to Wanamassa instead of the Bradley or Bond Street schools.

Faith-based education eased some of the overcrowding for a while. Catholics established two elementary schools: on the East Side the Irish built the Holy Spirit Lyceum and staffed it with the cultured Dominican Sisters; on the West Side, the Italians of Our Lady of Mount Carmel had an elementary school run by the strict Filippini Sisters by the time they had built their second parish church on Prospect and Bangs Avenues. For high school, there were a number of regional parochial schools that graduates attended instead of going to Asbury Park. In the mid-1960s, Russell G. Ranney expanded his secular private day school, which he had started in Rumson by renting the Sunday school classrooms and multipurpose gym, lunchroom, and stage at Trinity Episcopal Church on Grand and Asbury Avenues. The two-story red-brick building would turn out to be an ideal academic incubator for later private programs after the Ranney School left for a country campus. Later in the twentieth century, Asbury Park High School graduates sent their children to this college preparatory school, believing that their own alma mater no longer provided the superior level of education they had received there.

The postwar suburbs were expanding, and so was the demand for modern educational facilities. Public housing was also on the upswing in Asbury Park, replac-

A Kreizman or a Reiseman?

FROM 1945 UNTIL HIS RETIREMENT IN 1985 AS Hebrew school principal for Temple Beth El, my father, Sam Kreizman, prepared close to one thousand boys for their bar mitzvah and about half as many girls for their bat mitzvah and confirmations. In those days, the synagogue was located on First Avenue and Emory Street and the Hebrew school and social hall were around the corner on Asbury Avenue. They came from all over the greater Asbury Park area: the Ansells from Allenhurst; the Redikers and Conners from Deal; the Cinnamons and Breners from Interlaken; the Friedmans of Loch Arbor; the Greenspans and VanGlishs of Ocean Township; and, of course, the Ru-

bins and Frankels of Asbury Park. Some smart, some not so smart, some accomplished singers, some tone-deaf, and some with voices changing.

The Hebrew teacher at the only other synagogue in Asbury Park, Sons of Israel on Asbury Avenue [east of Grand], was Solomon Reiseman. Both teachers were such institutions that local Jewish kids, instead of asking what temple someone belonged to, would simply ask, "Are you a Kreizman or a Reiseman?"

– Judge Ira Kreizman,
Monmouth County Superior Court
Freehold, New Jersey

ing single-family homes on the West Side and adding still more children to the district. It was becoming obvious the board of education could not keep up with the effects of real estate development. Overcrowding and a deteriorating facility at Bond Street led to another academic secession in 1953, when Deal built an elementary school for its growing population of year-round children. The third and most dramatic secession occurred in 1965, when Ocean Township High School opened.

The Glory Days of High School

Planning a first-rate academic and athletic program for children was not a high priority in the resort. The task was left to a handful of dedicated and largely unsung teachers who influenced individual students. Other than recording the periodic demands for a new school building, the periodic requests for increases in teachers' salaries, and the annual spring graduations, the newspapers reported little else about the resort's education program.

Before Bradley died in 1921, Bond Street School was straining to accommodate all the students under its roof. With the gymnasium converted to academic use, physical culture classes were relocated to the old Presbyterian Tabernacle Bradley had bought and moved to Sunset and Ocean Avenues back in 1889. He had renamed the building the Asbury Park Auditorium and winterized it for such use as indoor tennis and basketball. In the fall and spring, high school students traveled in the opposite direction on Sunset Avenue to the athletic grounds on Deal Lake, where Bradley had installed the bicycle racing track for the League of American Wheelman in 1894. This pattern continued until Bradley's death, when all his undeveloped parcels—including the athletic grounds—came on the real estate market.

Murray Gordon, owner of Murray's Army/Navy Store on Main Street, dressed for a meeting of the International Order of the Redman, a fraternal organization that attracted a number of members with German heritage. Courtesy of Andrew Bartlett, president of Murray's Army & Navy, Bradley Beach, New Jersey

It wasn't just mothers who wanted a better school system. The resort's professional class, educated themselves and married with children, came to realize the gravity of the situation. Together with likeminded businessmen who placed a premium on education, they waged a public campaign for a new high school facility. Their goal? Bradley's athletic grounds, especially as the forty-three-year-old auditorium had by now been replaced by the Berkeley-Carteret Hotel. But the education campaign was competing with Mayor Hetrick's long-running convention-center campaign, and a special referendum had to be held for the $2 million bond to build the high school. Mary Vaccaro Martin, who was ten years old at the time, recalled, "A lot of us children were given placards that supported the referendum, and we paraded around town to urge the public to vote for our future." The measure passed.

The new high school facility, with a neoclassical front on the three-story building, a Roman amphitheater design for a football and track stadium, and clay tennis courts, opened its doors in 1927. Even as the Depression set in, there was much to brag about. "The [high] school offers five full four-year courses to provide for the various needs of the different courses. Two of these courses prepare pupils for admission into college," stated *The Story of Asbury Park: The Record of Progress and Achievement, 1916–1931*, a publication compiled by the Asbury Park Woman's Club. Of course, the school report couldn't omit property value. "Present real estate values would indicate the high school to be worth $1,100,000 while the stadium is worth $400,000."

More athletic coaches were hired, various sports teams won titles, and eventually Asbury Park High School fielded an Olympic hopeful by the name of Frank Budd, a gifted athlete and an African American who had been denied the opportunity to play on the junior varsity baseball team. Budd turned to track instead and made it to the qualifying rounds for the Rome Olympics in 1960. Two years later he would set a world record for the 100-yard dash with a time of 9.2 seconds.

During World War II the stadium briefly served as the winter training camp for the New York Yankees, who played one exhibition game, noteworthy because it was racially integrated, recalled Nicholas Baldino. The other team was the Brooklyn Dodgers, who had recently signed Jackie Robinson.

Graduates of Ivy League schools were hired for many of the teaching positions at the high school. Foreign language classes had their own after-school clubs, as did radio, theater, the school newspaper, and a host of other enrichment programs. Bandleader Arthur Pryor's successor, Frank Bryan, became the music teacher. For the next thirty years, high school students received a classical education, whether they were headed for college or for the business world. It was not unusual for graduates to go to elite institutions such as the Massachusetts Institute of Technology, Dartmouth College, or Johns Hopkins University.

What I Learned in Elementary School

BOND STREET ELEMENTARY SCHOOL IN THE 1940S was a smorgasbord of cultures east of Main Street. The rooms, with their high, ornate tin ceilings, huge windows letting in the light and city noises, and wide halls with gleaming wood floors, was the setting for a no-frills education delivered by veteran teachers and supervised by principal Lester Edinger. Part of the Bond Street experience for sixth, seventh, and eighth graders was the weekly walk along busy city streets to the Bangs Avenue School for sewing, cooking, and shop with "Pop" Shannon. Another [experience] was gained on the small fenced-in asphalt playgrounds where kids organized their own games, learned to get along with each other, while young girls played quietly beneath the metal fire escapes eavesdropping on the "big girls" as they sat sharing secrets. That's how we learned that student Walter Costello [fortuneteller Madame Marie's son], known as "King of the Gypsies," was not returning to school because he was getting married!

– Marjorie Douglas Edelson,
Bond Street School, class of 1950
Ocean Township, New Jersey

The Postwar Years

In the aftermath of World War II, Asbury Park found itself struggling to stabilize its tax base once again. In August 1946, the city realized $67,075 from the sale of twenty-four delinquent properties with the hope they would go back on the tax rolls. It also looked for ways to create new tax ratables. Sunset Lake Park, Bradley's vision of an uninterrupted expanse of green from the North Asbury Park train station to the sea, was subdivided in the mid-1950s, with the land closest to the depot split into two parcels. The city sold one lot to a bank and the other to an insurance company, thus creating two tax-producing properties while leaving along Main Street a sliver of green that was renamed Firemen's Park. It also entertained an apartment house proposal from a New York City developer for the eastern end of Sunset Park; public outcry forced the plan's withdrawal. As car ownership grew, the city looked for ways to accommodate shoppers

The Salvation Army's presence in Asbury Park began during the temperance crusades of the nineteenth century and in the twentieth century expanded into social welfare programs. The Salvation Army built a high-rise on Fifth Avenue as a retirement home for its workers; the building is slated for private conversion at the time of this writing. Pike Archives.

and so converted the green lawns along Wesley Lake into parking spaces; it even considered paving Overlook Park on Lake and Grand Avenues before public opinion put a stop to those discussions.

City Manager Oliver Armstrong retired in 1955. By 1960, according to the Monmouth County Board of Taxation, Asbury Park stopped assessing most of its commercial and residential properties. Instead, it found ways to meet its municipal obligations by applying for newly created state and federal government programs. Now, instead of whispers about Hetrick's bagmen, the speculation about lining private pockets with public money centered on the 10 percent rule that were becoming the modus operandi in government bid specifications all over New Jersey, with an automatic 10 percent added to public bids or contracts. This money would be skimmed off the top to pay the politicians.

As the 1960s unfolded, school overcrowding returned as an issue in Asbury Park. The eighth grade at Bradley School was moved into the high school, where all the students were put on split sessions. Sophomores, juniors, and seniors went to morning classes; the eighth grade and freshmen went to school in the afternoon. By this point, all the buildable land in Asbury Park had disappeared except for the vacant Monterey Hotel site, sitting on prime real estate on the oceanfront. The Ocean Township Board of Education approached Asbury Park and asked about the possibility of forming a regional high school district and erecting a modern facility on an open tract of abandoned farmland. But the Asbury Park Board of Education, with the backing of the mayor and council, refused to consider a site not in the city. In what appeared to be record time, less than twelve months, a new high school opened in Ocean Township.

The flight of upwardly mobile whites as well as blacks out of Asbury Park was picking up. For African Americans, the main suburb became Neptune, which had built a new high school in 1960. Many of Asbury Park's Italian and Jewish residents moved to Ocean Township, where Temple Beth-El relocated, as did the Jewish Community Center, which had been on Comstock Street. The aftermath of the civil disturbances

Remembering Alma Mater

THOSE LATE FIFTIES AND EARLY SIXTIES WERE THE best of times for Asbury Park High School. The engraving over the east doorway, under which we walked every day, proclaimed in one word the school's challenge to us: Strive.

How can we measure the impact of the demanding Beatrice Van Campen who taught us English; Esther Royster and Dorothy Lieberman [history]; Evelyn Ross [math]; Frank Bryan [music]; Rachel Vecchione [Latin]; the affable athletic director Gus Villapiano and the driven Bill Bruno, the Bishops' football coach.

Inspired by them, my goal was to be like them and influence young lives in the ways they influenced me. I remember Nick Merli, the legendary track coach who was my English teacher. He taught me that a sense of humor goes a long way in reaching students. My senior English teacher,

Ruth Jones, convinced me that maybe I had a talent for writing and encouraged me to pursue and develop that skill.

Thanks in large part to their encouragement and guidance, and from the vantage point of forty years, I remember those days in APHS with fondness and pride for they helped make me who I am.

Soon our school days will be ended,
Swift they're passing by,
But we always will remember
Dear old Asbury High.

– Ronald S. Danielson, APHS Class of 1962
Principal, Memorial Junior High School,
Eatontown, New Jersey

of July 4, 1970, only accelerated a process than had begun ten years earlier. Many who remained in Asbury Park became the urban poor, and the quality of leadership began to disintegrate. Retired city clerk Mary V. Martin, who worked in city hall from 1933 to 1979, observed that competency among the mayor and council declined in the mid-1960s. In an interview that appeared in the *Asbury Park Press* of February 17, 1980, Martin also described the city as "living to today and not planning for tomorrow."

By 1980, sixty-two years after it was built, Bangs Avenue School was starting to fall apart. It still had its original plumbing fixtures, and toilets frequently backed up. The student population was bulging at 700, and textbooks were outdated. The board of education estimated repair costs at $3.1 million. As if that weren't enough of an expenditure, it was looking at building an annex to the Bradley School and making repairs to Bond Street. The referendum put before the city's beleaguered voters was a whopping $6.9 million. In a city of under 15,000 people, fewer than 1,000 voters showed up at the polls, and they rejected the bond issue 611 to 307. The board returned with a second referendum for just the $3.1 million for Bangs Avenue. That passed, its costs lessened by a one-time grant of half a million dollars from Trenton and 70 percent of the remainder to be paid by the city's annual aid from the state.

That same year, Holy Spirit Lyceum closed. According to the Reverend John H. Meehan, the problems had started ten years earlier when the inner-city parish of

From King "Dream" to Hope for Education

I WAS IN ELEMENTARY SCHOOL WHEN DR. KING CAME to speak at the high school on October 7, 1960 [when he was attending the General Baptist Convention of New Jersey, which was held in Asbury Park that year]. My mom sang in one of the choirs and I sat in the front row of the balcony, leaning up against the rail to listen to him. I was so impressed with his speaking. I remember wanting to be like him, fighting for civil rights.

My father had a barbershop on Springwood [between] Fisch's and a cab company. My mother was a seamstress. We were living on Union Avenue. [Asbury Park] was very segregated at that time. The only Caucasians we saw were the Italians who owned markets on Springwood. When eminent domain was used to take our homes for urban revitalization we moved to Neptune.

Years later when I visited Atlanta and went to see some of the historic sites dedicated to Dr. King I vowed that when I became an adult I would do something to serve my community.

– Alexis Harris, principal and founding member of Hope Charter Academy, Asbury Park, New Jersey

TOP *Thomas Smith was sworn in as the city's first African American police chief in 1968; he later became the city's first black mayor and then a district assemblyman. Clerk Mary V. Martin did the swearing in as City Manager Paul Herman looked on. Tax Collector Helen Pride held the Bible. Courtesy of Mrs. Thomas S. Smith Sr.*

BOTTOM *Black Americans had a civic presence on Main Street in the early part of the twentieth century when Bethel A.M.E. had this handsome church on the Fourth Avenue corner before it relocated in the late 1940s into Burnham's West Side neighborhood. In the background is Park Chevrolet. Pike Archives.*

Holy Spirit began to change. The Lyceum's student body was 40 percent African American Baptist. Only twenty-three parish families, most of whom were white, were sending their children to Holy Spirit. In February 1980, the Lyceum was sending students home because their parents had failed to pay the tuition.

Asbury Park's financial troubles deepened. Federal and state urban aid was slowing. In 1979 the city's tax rate was the highest in Monmouth County at $9.42

per $100 of valuation. The city's municipal budget was about $9.3 million, but it was running at a deficit. There was $1.18 million in uncollected taxes. The city had lost $2 million in ratables that same year. By April 1980 the county board of taxation demanded that Asbury Park start a revaluation of all its properties—the first in twenty years. The process was tumultuous. One estimate showed that all properties in Asbury Park had been assessed at less than two-thirds of their market value. According to city tax assessor Sam Befarah, the goal was to have all properties assessed for roughly the amount for which they might be sold in the current market. Businessmen had complained bitterly for years that their properties were overvalued while residential property was underassessed. By trying to create parity between commercial and residential properties, officials hoped they could make the city more attractive to investors. The next blow came when census figures revealed that Asbury Park was losing population. It fell to Sam Addeo, the newly appointed city manager, who had grown up in the city, to break the news

Over the years, the Asbury Park Boys Club, now the Boys and Girls Club of Monmouth County, enjoyed the support of area business and civic leaders. Seen here the day the new swimming pool was dedicated are architect Floyd Scott, left; Aberdeen attorney Philip N. Gumbs, who was a board member and the first African American to be elected to the Monmouth County Board of Chosen Freeholders; and Springwood Avenue electrician William Knuckles. Courtesy of Hortense Knuckles Reed.

that Asbury Park might not qualify for additional federal aid because its population had dipped below 15,000. According to Addeo, middle-class flight compounded the city's problems. Since the beginning of the steady exodus, homes and seasonal residences had been subdivided into multiple-dwelling units for low-income residents and rent-subsidized welfare residents; this type of housing is commonly called Section 8 after the federal program that funds it.

A political group calling itself the Forward Five demanded a recall election. Leaving aside the bond issue for Bangs Avenue School, the group charged the mayor and council with putting the city in debt by constructing a new city hall. It faulted the council for trying to close the municipal budget gap with the sale of such city assets as the city-owned golf course in Neptune as well as by putting the public library up for sale. The Forward Five also criticized the council for supporting the sale of the Bond Street School property.

In a recall effort that reached a new level for confusing the political process, Mayor Ray Kramer was removed from office by 17 votes: 1,111 to oust him and 1,094 to keep him in office. Improbable though it may seem, he was voted into office on the same ballot with a higher number of residents—1,163—voting to keep him in office. That came about because there were designated columns for both incumbents and candidates, and the incumbents were listed a second time as candidates. Dr. Lorenzo Harris experienced a similar voting disparity and was reelected to office from the candidates' column despite being recalled as an incumbent. Henrietta Zachary, on the other hand, the first woman and second African American to serve on the city council, was voted out. In the aftermath of the election, charges of voting irregularity focused not on the ballot itself but instead on the mental patients living in city hotels and boardinghouses who were sent to the polls with sample ballots listing specific candidates for whom to vote. Meanwhile,

From Fathers to Sons

WHEN MY FATHER [BASKETBALL AND TRACK COACH Gus Villapiano] was in school, Asbury had been state champions in football. He played on the same team with Butch Bruno [football coach]. In our home we lived and died this stuff. I remember as a kid sitting in the house listening to my father and guys who would stop in and they'd talk basketball or football [plays] all night.

My first year of varsity football was my sophomore year in Asbury, 1965. Asbury was big, almost like a college in those days. [The local schools] played in the Shore Conference. Asbury Park played Trenton, Perth Amboy, Union, Elizabeth, the big [city] schools. We were Group IV state champions. But locally, the two rivals were Long Branch [football] and Neptune [basketball]. Asbury was always at the next level. And we all thought that, too. We went to Asbury, we all thought we were the cream of the crop.

Four thousand people would be standing around our football field for the Thanksgiving Day game against Neptune. The basketball games had to be held at Convention Hall because neither [school's] gym could hold the people. The rivalries were so big [because] everyone wanted to beat Asbury Park because of who we thought we were.

One of the critical moments in the fall of Asbury Park was when Ocean Township went to Asbury and talked about building a regional high school in Ocean to ease the overcrowding. Asbury turned them down: "You're just a sending district." [So] Ocean went and built a new high school. We were living in Oakhurst by then [and] my father said I had to go to this new school.

"Dad I can't do that. I can't go over there. I can't play a junior high school schedule."

"You have to go."

"I'll live with Grandma [or] my aunt."

"No, you have to go help the school."

[By my] senior year we got to play a varsity schedule. Our very first game was against Rumson and they beat us seven to six.

Looking back, my father was right. It was selfish that I wanted to be in Asbury. I sucked it up and did what I had to do. It was a character builder. I helped Ocean get started.

– Phil Villapiano, outside linebacker,
Oakland Raiders, Buffalo Bills

The federal Citizenship and Naturalization Law was enacted in January 1941, and classes were held to help alien residents become U.S. citizens. In some cases names were modified: Shebelli to Shebell, Braglia to Brown, Michaelapolis to Michals, Scotti to Scott, Silverstein to Stevens, Traverso to Travers, and Anschelwitz to Ansell. Seen here are graduates of an Asbury Park Americanization class. Courtesy of Howard Zegas.

resident and city realtor Floyd R., Scott Jr., an African American designer working with the architectural firm of Kellenyi Associates in Red Bank, was the lead man on the city hall project. Scott's vision called for a four-story building with a basement garage and 80,000 square feet of municipal office space. Regrettably, with the 1980 recession, Scott's plan had to be scaled down. Eliminated were the underground garage, two floors equaling 42,000 square feet, and new furniture for city hall employees. In the end, the new city hall was built with $1.6 million from the federal Economic Development Administration (EDA) under the Public Works Employment Act while the council chamber was built with a separate EDA grant of $250,000. The rest was raised through city bonds. The words of caution expressed by druggist-turned-real-estate entrepreneur Hugh Kinmonth ninety years earlier were still going unheeded: it was easy enough to get into debt, but harder to get out.

Epilogue, 2002

THE POSSIBILITY OF A NEW glory days for Asbury Park began hopefully enough in 2000, when Cuban-born Jersey City restaurateur and dynamic events promoter Domenic Santana and a group of North Jersey investors bought the Stone Pony. The sagging building received the kind of slick nostalgic makeover that baby-boomer vacationers could easily associate with Jimmy Buffet's Margaritaville in Key West or B. B. King's nightclub in Memphis, without the food. The Memorial Day weekend of 2000 was a spectacular musical reunion festival of legendary Shore bands and up-and-coming newcomers eager to add the Pony to their résumés.

In 2001, a new municipal election was held in which voters chose from several slates. Afterward a recount uncovered significant voting irregularities. In the end, the result was a historic city council that was sweepingly diverse even by New Jersey standards. The new mayor, Kevin Sanders, who managed a downtown employment firm and was a musician, represented the fifth generation of his African American family living in Asbury Park; his wife, Adrienne,

was president of the board of education. The deputy mayor, James Bruno, a retired city fire inspector, was a third-generation Asbury Park resident of Italian descent and son of state championship–winning football coach Butch Bruno. Confined to a wheelchair by multiple sclerosis, he ran the most politically savvy campaign, with the only ticket to have three winning candidates. College-educated house painter-turned-realtor John Loffredo became conservative Monmouth County's first openly gay elected official, a testament to the growing influence of gay and lesbian home and business owners in Asbury Park. The only holdover from the previous administration was the former deputy mayor, a retired electrician, John Hamilton, a relative newcomer to Asbury Park who had been a rare voice of reason on the previous council. After the recount, the last member added to the council was Kate Mellina, a Philadelphia native and former AT&T manager who had tried her hand as the owner of a fiber art gallery on Cookman Avenue. (Mellina bumped Dr. Arnetha Lofton, an arts education teacher in Asbury Park public schools, who had been the lowest vote getter in the original election.) For the first time in recent memory, Asbury Park voters had elected officials with an ability to build consensus. Many residents hoped they would finally steer the city toward a positive future, and before too long that started to happen.

Before the year was over, M. D. Sass, a Wall Street investment firm, paid off the tax liens against failed oceanfront developer Joseph Carabetta; received the development rights for the fifty-six fallow acres; inked a joint development deal with brothers Larry and Glenn Fishman, principals in First New Jersey Real Property Management of Lakewood; and tapped Cushman Wakefield, one the nation's largest real estate brokers, to find the right retail mix for the project. In 2002, Governor James McGreevey pledged $4 million in state funds plus fast-track approval for the plans.

To engage the community in the new development deal, an unprecedented two-day marathon *charrette*, an intense design effort that revealed a new urban plan for Asbury Park, was open to the public and held in the Berkeley-Carteret's largest ballroom. It was led by Miami-based architect Andreas Duany, the country's leading proponent of a school of municipal planning called New Urbanism. The philosophy was rooted in the centuries-old model of vest-pocket parks, neighborhoods mixed by income, retail, and entertainment, and plentiful sidewalks to decrease the reliance on automobiles. More than six thousand people attended these meetings.

The urban plan drafted for Asbury Park's waterfront called for a townhouse neighborhood where Walter Reade's theaters had once stood overlooking Wesley Lake. An entertainment district centered on the Palace block and Casino included the proposal of a new hundred-room hotel. A combination of retail and office units would line both sides of Ocean Avenue north to the Paramount, and the Boardwalk would be retrofitted with multistory mini-malls that would leave each avenue vista open. Lastly, high-rise residential development was slated for the various blocks that had once held the hotels of the nineteenth century. The Sass-Fishman team also promised to upgrade the city's sewer plant.

Thomas Appleby was the leading real estate agent for James Bradley, getting started in 1885 on the corner of Main Street and Mattison Avenue. The building photographed here in the 1930s is now a restaurant, Bistro Olé. Courtesy of T. Frank Appleby.

With 30 percent of Asbury Park's properties held by nonprofit organizations and city hall still facing a budget shortfall from insufficient property tax income, the mayor and council made a hard decision to allow the deteriorating Boardwalk, Paramount, and Convention Hall and the even worse Casino to go back into the kind of private ownership that had last existed when founder James Bradley was the city's leading developer. After nearly one hundred years, what once had been income-rental assets for the city would now be tax-generating properties from the millennium's new developers, Sass-Fishman. In a 2002 edition of Wall Street's *Daily Deal*, Martin D. Sass said he envisioned spending $30 million in infrastructure repair in addition to the $21 million that had launched the project. Sass said he was prepared to have the project take ten years.

The rest of the business investment climate in the city of Asbury Park continued to improve, bolstered by the U.S. attorney for New Jersey, Christopher Christie, and the Monmouth County prosecutor's office. Working in tandem, they won fraud convictions against out-of-town realtors who were found guilty of using straw owners to inflate the prices of barely habitable homes to unsuspecting buyers. Another investigation, this one into extortion charges, led to the voluntary resignation of City Manager Terrance Weldon, the city's one-time fire chief and mayor of Ocean Township. At least one elected official from the previous administration and a former housing authority director were indicted on charges of influence peddling.

The city council hired a municipal manager who not only had formal training but also had previously served as Montclair's municipal manager. The council also hired a new public safety director who had gained national recognition for his work on gang violence and bias crimes while working for the Monmouth County prosecutor. In the private sector, the mismanaged Boys and Girls Club of Monmouth County, where thousands of dollars of computers donated by Bruce Springsteen had been stolen, gained a new director when the national organization stepped in and appointed a professional manager with a record of running successful clubs in the Midwest.

In another positive development, the state department of education redoubled its efforts to monitor the city's troubled school district, beset by poor test scores and accusations of mismanaging a budget that was larger than city hall's. Meanwhile, the always-generous Springsteen donated band instruments to support the fledgling efforts of Asbury Park students, whose instruments had been stolen in 2003. And on the gridiron, a well-coached Pop Warner team reached the 2003 national playoffs, raising hopes that football at Asbury Park High School might once again experience glory in the not-too-distant-future.

The beleaguered Palace Amusements attracted a band of supporters known as Save Tillie, devoted Springsteen fans from around the world that were trying to block the Palace from demolition. Springsteen had featured the building—physically and symbolically—in lyrics and music videos and had even used the smiling Tilyou icon on tour T-shirts. Inspired by the success of cultural historians and travel officials in the Beatles' native Liverpool, Save Tillie envisioned part of the new Asbury Park as a musical heritage destination. Save Tillie put the Palace on eBay to find a buyer who could meet Sass-Fishman's $2.5 million asking price. There were no takers, and in 2004 it was torn down. It remains to be seen if the city and its business community will articulate a strategy to preserve its history and promote it.

No one denies Asbury Park has a long way to go. If a reminder were needed, the film *City by the Sea*, starring Robert DeNiro, was shot in Asbury Park, which served as a stand-in for a South Shore town on Long Island on the skids. Cable television's *The Sopranos* also offered scenes of desolation featuring the deserted Boardwalk, rundown Convention Hall, and the shabby triple-X movie house that once was once Walter Reade's Lyric Theatre.

Springwood Avenue is still waiting for a renaissance. A suggestion of the difficulties that lay ahead for the city's poor surfaced in a student essay that won a contest held by the Stephen Crane House on the East Side. The young man wrote eloquently about moving to a tough public housing project from a single-family home on the West Side that had been sold to real estate speculators.

But for one glorious moment in July 2002, it seemed nothing could hold Asbury Park back. In a promotional bonanza, the NBC's *Today Show* was aired live from the Boardwalk on the release date of Springsteen's CD *The Rising*. Viewers saw freshly planted palm trees on the beach, crowds spilling out of Convention Hall and onto the beach and Boardwalk, and the ocean shimmering under blue skies. Springsteen did the city another favor by showing *Today Show* co-host Matt Lauer around town past evidence of the city's comeback. And he donated ticket sales from his preshow rehearsals to some of his favorite local causes. More than ten thousand people crowded into Asbury Park that week. Nostalgic memories of the days that once were and dreams of what they might be once again were everywhere.

Bibliography

Adams, Judith A. *The American Amusement Park Industry: A History of Technology and Thrills.* Boston: Twayne Publishers, 1991.

Aron, Cindy S. *Working at Play: A History of Vacations in the United States.* New York: Oxford University Press, 1999.

Baker, Fred, with Ross Firestone, eds. *Movie People: At Work in the Business of Film.* New York: Douglas Book Corporation, 1972.

Barrett, Richmond. *Good Old Summer Days.* New York: D. Appleton-Century, 1941.

Boeschenstein, Warren. *Historic American Towns along the Atlantic Coast.* Baltimore: John Hopkins University Press, 1999.

Burton, Hal. *The Morro Castle: Tragedy at Sea.* New York: Viking Press, 1973.

Eid, Joseph. *Trolleys in the Coast Cities.* Brick, N.J., 1979.

Feifer, Maxine. *Tourism in History: From Imperial Rome to the Present.* Briarcliff Manor, N.Y.: Stein and Day, 1985.

Gallagher, Thomas. *Fire at Sea: The Story of the Morro Castle.* New York: Rinehart and Company, 1959.

Gargiulo, Vince. *Palisades Amusement Park: A Century of Fond Memories.* New Brunswick, N.J.: Rutgers University Press, 1995.

Goldstein, Stan, and Jean Mikle. *Rock and Roll Tour of the Jersey Shore.* Ocean Grove, N.J., 2002.

Grover, Kathryn, ed. *Hard at Play: Leisure in America, 1840–1940.* Amherst, Mass.: The Strong Museum/University of Massachusetts Press, 1992.

———. *Teenage New Jersey, 1941–1975.* Newark: New Jersey Historical Society, 1997.

Guinness, Alec. *Blessings in Disguise.* New York: Warner Books under arrangement with Alfred A. Knopf, 1987.

A Half Century of Dedicated Service: The Story of New Jersey Natural Gas Company. Wall, N.J., 2002.

Jackson, Kenneth T. *Crabgrass Frontier: The Suburbanization of the United States.* New York: Oxford University Press, 1985.

Johnson, Nelson. *Boardwalk Empire: The Birth, High Times, and Corruption of Atlantic City.* Medford, N.J.: Plexus Publishing, 2002.

Karcher, Alan. *New Jersey's Multiple Municipal Madness.* New Brunswick, N.J.: Rutgers University Press, 1998.

Kunstler, James Howard. *Home from Nowhere.* New York: Simon and Schuster, 1996.

Lofgren, Orvar. *On Holiday: A History of Vacationing.* Berkeley: University of California Press, 1999.

McGilligan, Patrick. *Jack's Life: A Biography of Jack Nicholson.* New York: W. W. Norton, 1994.

McKay, Lenore Walker. *The Blacks of Monmouth County: A Bicentennial Tribute.* N.p., 1976.

Papa, Carrie. *The Carousel Keepers: An Oral History of American Carousels.* Granville, Ohio: McDonald and Woodward, 1998.

Plunkett-Powell, Karen. *Remembering Woolworth's: A Nostalgic History of the World's Most Famous Five-and-Dime.* New York: St. Martin's Press, 1999.

Romanowski, William D. *Pop Culture Wars: Religion and the Role of Entertainment in American Life.* Madison, Wis.: Intervarsity Press, 1996.

Thomas, Gordon, and Max Morgan Witts. *Shipwreck.* New York: Stein and Day, 1972.

Tomlinson, Gerald. *Murdered in Jersey.* New Brunswick, N.J.: Rutgers University Press, 1994.

Wein, Gary. *Beyond the Palace.* Victoria, B.C., Canada: Trafford Publishing, 2003.

Works Progress Administration. *Entertaining a Nation: The Career of Long Branch.* N.p., 1940.

Wright, Giles R. *Afro-Americans in New Jersey: A Short History.* Trenton: New Jersey Historical Commission, 1988.

Index

LIKE MANY, MY MEMORIES OF ASBURY PARK ARE TIED to various rites of passage. The first significant one came thanks to Greg Sariotis, former YMCA swim coach, who bought the Oakhurst Country Day Camp in Ocean Township. An Asbury Park High School athlete coached by the legendary Gus Villapiano, Greg made sure his country campers had a seashore experience. Each August we went to Asbury Park; we were given tickets for rides on the Boardwalk, in the Casino, and in the "big kids" Palace, which had the best dark rides a ten-year-old could imagine in the 1960s. Greg also gave us a chance to canoe at Sunset Landing, navigating the water lilies and learning how to roll out in Deal Lake. (When I was a senior in high school, my prom date took me there for one last canoe ride before we went away to college.)

The author at the miniature golf course at Sixth Avenue in 1961, with the Monterey Hotel in the background. Pike Archives.

I can also vividly recall sitting with my immigrant French mother in the Mayfair Theater balcony so she could hear *Gone With the Wind* in English for the first time. I was surprised by the tears streaming down her face just as Scarlett swore she would never be hungry again. Afterward, she talked with me for the first—and only—time about what it had been like living in Nazi-occupied Paris, reduced to eating rabbits for protein.

The next rite of passage was getting my driver's license and proving my ability to "do the circuit"—that metaphorical strip on the way to adulthood that went past the bars on Kingsley, 'round by the Casino, and back up Ocean, past the bikers hanging at Mrs. Jay's and flirting with the boys driving cars for the first time, too.

My working life also began with Asbury Park connections. The summer of '74, I waited tables at Mac's Embers in Long Branch where the hostess was the henna-red Etta whose previous post had been at the Monterey's Miamian Grill. The tall, white-haired, and mustachioed baker, Karl, also came from that hotel, bringing with him the cake recipes that had been the Monterey's allure for countless little girls' birthday parties.

The following summer I upgraded my tips waitressing at Howard Johnson's, parking my car every night by the Salvation Army retirement home on Fifth Avenue and never worrying for my safety. And in the bicentennial summer I clerked in the downtown newsroom of the *Asbury Park Press* for college credit and a $100 check. My mentor was business editor Herb Nebel and his taciturn sidekick and real estate editor who wore a nightshade and sleeve garters.

After I graduated, the paper offered me a full-time job and I met Ellen Carroll, who eventually became the editor of her family's own weekly newspaper in the city and a lifelong friend, offering me a job after my father died from complications of Alzheimer's.

In fact, even most of those who helped me care for my dad in his final years had an Asbury Park connection: Kathy Hurst Parratt, a third-generation Asbury Parker who was president of the Ocean Township Historical Museum; LaShonda Stark whose son was baptized at True Vine Baptist on DeWitt and her aunt Beverly Smith, who told me stories about the Cotillions in Convention Hall; and finally Ruby Strickland, a God-fearing caregiver who worshipped at the Good Hope Baptist on Washington because it had rhythm and who told me the best burgers in Asbury Park were at the notorious Tap Room. She was right. ↝